Apocalyptic Paul Theology

Bloomsbury Political Theologies

Series edited by Ward Blanton (University of Kent), Arthur Bradley (Lancaster University), Michael Dillon (Lancaster University) and Yvonne Sherwood (University of Kent)

This book series explores the past, present and future of political theology. Taking its cue from the groundbreaking work of such figures as Derrida, Agamben, Badiou and Žižek, it seeks to provide a forum for new research on the theologicopolitical nexus including cutting-edge monographs, edited collections and translations of classic works. By privileging creative, interdisciplinary and experimental work that resists easy categorization, this series not only re-assets the timeliness of political theology in our epoch but also seeks to extend political theological reflection into new territory: law, economics, finance, technology, media, film and art. In *Bloomsbury Political Theologies*, we seek to re-invent the ancient problem of political theology for the twenty-first century.

International Advisory Board
Agata Bielik-Robson (University of Nottingham)
Howard Caygill (Kingston University)
Simon Critchley (New School of Social Research)
Roberto Esposito (Scuola Normale Superiore)
Elettra Stimilli (University of Rome La Sapienza)
Miguel Vatter (University of New South Wales)

Titles in the series
The Withholding Power: An Essay on Political Theology, Massimo Cacciari
Unnatural Theology: Religion, Art and Media after the Death of God, Charlie Gere
Modernity and the Political Fix, Andrew Gibson
Debt and Guilt: A Political Philosophy, Elettra Stimilli
Apocalyptic Political Theology, Thomas Lynch

Apocalyptic Political Theology

Hegel, Taubes and Malabou

Thomas Lynch

BLOOMSBURY ACADEMIC
LONDON • NEW YORK • OXFORD • NEW DELHI • SYDNEY

BLOOMSBURY ACADEMIC
Bloomsbury Publishing Plc
50 Bedford Square, London, WC1B 3DP, UK
1385 Broadway, New York, NY 10018, USA

BLOOMSBURY, BLOOMSBURY ACADEMIC and the Diana logo are trademarks of
Bloomsbury Publishing Plc

First published in Great Britain 2019
Paperback edition published 2020

Copyright © Thomas Lynch, 2019

Thomas Lynch has asserted his right under the Copyright, Designs and Patents Act, 1988,
to be identified as Author of this work.

For legal purposes the Acknowledgements on p. ix constitute an
extension of this copyright page.

Cover image: *The Garden of Earthly Delights*, 1490–1500 (oil on panel), Hieronymus Bosch,
(c. 1450–1516) © Prado, Madrid, Spain / Bridgeman Images

All rights reserved. No part of this publication may be reproduced or
transmitted in any form or by any means, electronic or mechanical,
including photocopying, recording, or any information storage or retrieval
system, without prior permission in writing from the publishers.

Bloomsbury Publishing Plc does not have any control over, or responsibility for, any
third-party websites referred to or in this book. All internet addresses given in this
book were correct at the time of going to press. The author and publisher regret any
inconvenience caused if addresses have changed or sites have ceased to exist, but can
accept no responsibility for any such changes.

A catalogue record for this book is available from the British Library.

A catalog record for this book is available from the Library of Congress.

ISBN: HB: 978-1-3500-6474-4
PB: 978-1-3501-7718-5
ePDF: 978-1-3500-6473-7
eBook: 978-1-3500-6475-1

Series: Political Theologies

Typeset by Newgen KnowledgeWorks Pvt. Ltd., Chennai, India

To find out more about our authors and books visit www.bloomsbury.com
and sign up for our newsletters.

For Hannah

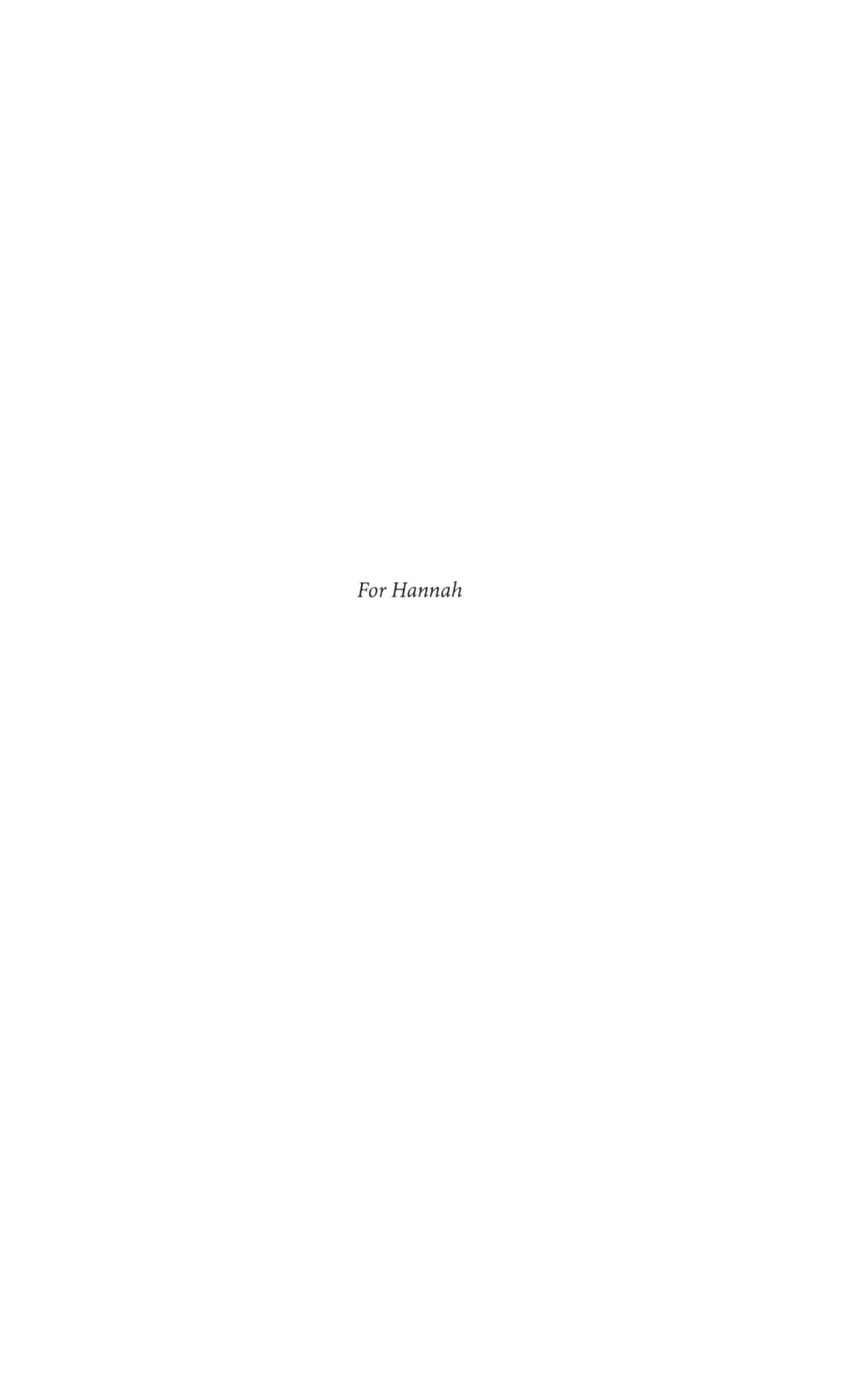

Contents

Acknowledgements	ix
Abbreviations and Notes on Translation	xi
Introduction	1

1 Philosophy, Political Theology and the End of the World 7
   What is political theology? 7
   What is this world that ends? 13
   Conflicts and antagonisms 27
   Imagining the end 32
   Questioning the apocalypse 35

2 Implicit Political Theology: Reading Hegel's Philosophy of Religion 37
   Joachim, Hegel and the end of the world 38
   Representational thought: An outline of Hegel's philosophy of religion 49
   Hegel's implicit political theology 53
   Philosophy and the return to representation 59
   Conclusion 62

3 Spiritual Disinvestment: Taubes, Hegel and Apocalypticism 65
   An introduction to Taubes 66
   Taubes and Hegel 71
   Apocalypticism and the question of history 78
   Taubes and Bloch 82
   Anti-liberal tendencies in Hegel, Taubes and Schmitt 86
   Transcendental materialist readings of Hegel: From Taubes to Malabou 91

4 Plastic Apocalypticism 97
   Malabou, Hegel and plasticity 98
   Plastic apocalypticism: Taubes and Malabou 101

	The problem of novelty and the rejection of the transcendent	103
	A Blochian supplement	111
	Contingency and plastic apocalypticism	113
	Conclusion	122
5	Pessimism and Hope in Apocalyptic Living	127
	Living with the absence of alternatives	127
	Pessimism and surrender	131
	Living towards the end of the world	137
	The end	141

Notes 143
Bibliography 181
Index 197

Acknowledgements

I am grateful to Paul Murray, Marcus Pound, Gerard Loughlin and the Centre for Catholic Studies at Durham University for their support and guidance and to Christopher Insole and Graham Ward for their feedback on early versions of this work. During this time I was exceedingly fortunate to have a supportive academic community that challenged me to think about this project from a variety of perspectives, including Roberto Alejandro, Tina Beattie, Andrew Brower Latz, Josh Furnal, Marika Rose and Susan Royal. I benefited from an opportunity to present my apocalyptic reading of Malabou at an interdisciplinary workshop at the University of Edinburgh. I am thankful to Michael O'Rourke for this opportunity and to Catherine Malabou for her remarks.

Liza Thompson was kind enough to listen to my ideas and encourage me to submit a proposal to Bloomsbury, and Frankie Mace patiently answered my endless questions. The conversations at the annual meetings of the International Network for Experimental Philosophy and Theology have been vital to further developing this project. I am particularly thankful for Jayne Svenungsson's willingness to engage in lengthy discussions of the nature of political theology and apocalypticism. At key moments in the development of the first and last chapters, Amaryah Armstrong, Daniel Colucciello Barber and Alex Dubilet were generous enough to engage in conversation, provide feedback or share their own work.

The last stage of preparing this book coincided with taking up a position at the University of Chichester. The many discussions I have had with colleagues there have provided great opportunities to think about the connections between religion, politics and philosophy. I am especially grateful to Ruth Mantin, Benjamin Noys, Stephen Roberts and Graeme Smith. I also benefited from a University of Chichester Research Development Award that provided the time to finish writing.

Though academia can sometimes feel like a solitary pursuit, one of its great joys is forging relationships with people who push you in profound ways and shape the way you think. Though they do not always share my conclusions, whatever is of value in the following work has been shaped by Michael O'Neill Burns, Mark Mason, Ulrich Schmiedel, Anthony Paul Smith and Hannah Strømmen. Words cannot express how much their friendship and support has meant over the years of trying to figure out what it means to think the end of the world.

Finally, I am grateful to my parents, who have always encouraged my desire to pursue my love of philosophy, and to my wife, Hannah, who has been my partner in this research, as in everything.

Abbreviations and Notes on Translation

Hegel

All citations give the page number of the English edition first, followed by the German.

E1–3   *Encyclopedia of the Philosophical Sciences*, 3 Volumes

The Encyclopaedia Logic: Part I of the Encyclopaedia of Philosophical Sciences with the Zusätze. Translated by T. F. Geraets, W. A. Suchting, and H. S. Harris. Indianapolis, IN: Hackett, 1991.

Hegel's Philosophy of Nature: Part Two of the Encyclopaedia of the Philosophical Sciences (1830): with Zusätze, translated by A. V. Miller. Oxford: Clarendon Press, 1970.

Hegel's Philosophy of Mind: Part Three of the Encyclopaedia of Philosophical Science (1830) with Zusätze, translated by A. V. Miller. Oxford: Clarendon Press, 1990.

Enzyklopädie der Philosophischen Wissenschaften im Grundrisse (1830). Werke, 8–10.

ETW   *Early Theological Writings*, translated by T. M. Knox. Philadelphia: University of Pennsylvania Press, 1996.

Frühe Schriften. Werke 1.

LPR   *Lectures on the Philosophy of Religion*, translated by R. F. Brown, P. C. Hodgson and J. M. Stewart, edited by Peter C. Hodgson. 3 vols. Oxford: Oxford University Press, 2007.

Vorlesungsmanuskripte I (1816–1831). Gesammelte Werke, Band 17, edited by Walter Jaeschke. Hamburg: Felix Meiner Verlag, 1987.

PR	*Outlines of the Philosophy of Right*, translated by T. M. Knox, edited by Stephen Houlgate. Oxford: Oxford University Press, 2008.
	Grundlinien der Philosophie des Rechts oder Naturrecht und Staatswissenschaft im Grundrisse, Mit Hegels eigenhändigen Notizen und den mündichen Zusätzen. Werke 7.
PS	*Phenomenology of Spirit*, translated by A. V. Miller. Oxford: Oxford University Press, 1977.
	Phänomenologie des Geistes. Werke, 3.
RG1–2	'Review of C.F. Göschel's "Aphorisms: Part One and Two"', translated by Clark Butler. *Clio* 17, no. 4 (1988): 369–93.
	'Review of C.F. Göschel's "Aphorisms: Three"', translated by Clark Butler. *Clio* 18, no. 4 (1989): 379–85.
	Berliner Schriften, 1818–1831. Werke 11.
SL	*Science of Logic*, translated by A. V. Miller. London; New York: George Allen & Unwin; Humanities Press, 1969.
	Wissenschaft der Logik I. Werke 5.
	Wissenschaft der Logik II. Werke 6.
W1–20	*Werke*, edited by Eva Moldenhauer and Karl Markus Michel. 20 vols. Frankfurt: Suhrkamp, 1969–1971.

I have modified standard English translations in two key ways. First, the translator or translators of several texts have chosen to capitalize certain nouns, particularly Spirit, Knowledge, Subject and the Absolute. This decision imbues these terms with a potentially metaphysical significance that I want to resist. Throughout, I have altered these translations accordingly. Second, *Vorstellung* has sometimes been translated as 'picture thinking'. For reasons that I explain in Chapter 2, I find this translation limiting and have used 'representation' throughout.

Taubes

CS   *To Carl Schmitt: Letters and Reflections*, translated by Keith Tribe. New York: Columbia University Press, 2013.

OE   *Occidental Eschatology*, translated by David Ratmoko. Stanford: Stanford University Press, 2009.

PT   *The Political Theology of Paul*, translated by Dana Hollander. Stanford: Stanford University Press, 2004.

I also drawn on the essays collected in *From Cult to Culture*. These writings span 1949–1984 and, though they are arranged thematically in a single volume, each of the chapters is a stand-alone work and thus cited individually.

Bloch

AC   *Atheism in Christianity: The Religion of the Exodus and the Kingdom*, translated by J. T. Swann. 2nd edn. London: Verso, 2009.

HT   *Heritage of Our Times*, translated by Neville Plaice and Stephen Plaice. Cambridge: Polity Press, 1991.

PH   *The Principle of Hope*, translated by Neville Plaice, Stephen Plaice and Paul Knight. 3 vols. Cambridge: MIT Press, 1995.

Malabou

FH   *Future of Hegel: Plasticity, Temporality and Dialectic*, translated by Lisabeth During. London: Routledge, 2005.

OA   *The Ontology of the Accident: An Essay on Destructive Plasticity*, translated by Carolyn Shread. Cambridge: Polity Press, 2012.

PD   *Plasticity at the Dusk of Writing: Dialectic, Destruction, Deconstruction*, translated by Carolyn Shread. New York: Columbia University Press, 2010.

Introduction

It seems like a good time to write a book about the end of the world. Since beginning research for this book in 2009, there has been no shortage of events that seem to herald the end: the rise of the Islamic State of Iraq and Syria (ISIS), the election of Donald Trump, escalating fears about climate change and various other crises seem to keep the spectre of the end perpetually in the news. Some of these events may indeed turn out to represent endings, though the nature of those endings remains to be seen, but what is remarkable is that the abundance of looming catastrophes has provoked a renewed investment in the standard responses: ISIS will be crushed by 'Western' military force, political crises will be overcome if we trust the democratic process and new forms of technology will help us address climate change. Put another way, almost no one faces these supposed apocalypses apocalyptically. Many forget that endings take work. The world may yet surprise humanity with its persistence.

The following chapters are my attempt to explore what it means to think apocalyptically. They are motivated by the conviction that it is only with a peculiar admixture of pessimism and hope, a blend in which the two become virtually indistinguishable, that we will be able to confront the realities before us. This account of an apocalyptic political theology is assembled through engagements with the work of Hegel, Taubes and Malabou, with the assistance of Schmitt and Bloch. It entails careful engagements with the writings of each: reading Hegel's philosophy of religion, engaging Taubes's work and drawing out the apocalyptic implications of Malabou's concept of plasticity. These tasks are not taken up for their own sake but in the service of developing a notion of plastic apocalypticism. In this sense, this is a book focused on thinking *with* Hegel, Taubes and Malabou rather than thinking *about* each of their ideas.

The first chapter offers an outline of apocalyptic political theology, providing initial answers to a set of key questions: What is political theology? What is the world? and Why must it end? Political theology is a term that is now used to describe a wide variety of perspectives, including theologically determined political analysis, political religion and approaches to thinking the nature of the law and the political. I define political theology in a narrow methodological sense indebted to Schmitt, Benjamin, Taubes and Agamben, among others. This political theology engages in what Schmitt calls the 'sociology of concepts' and then uses these concepts to critique the world. Apocalypticism, as one such concept, is as debated a term as political theology. While acknowledging its Jewish and Christian origins, I argue that these origins are beginnings rather than final definitions. Apocalypticism is a conceptual tool for critiquing the world, and that tool has mutated through repeated usage.

In developing this apocalyptic thought, I address recent critiques of both apocalyptic thinking and political theology. Some of these concerns are animated by too narrow a conception of apocalypticism, such as the notion that it relies upon the intervention of a transcendent divine figure. Others focus on the real issue of anti-liberal tendencies of apocalypticism and political theology. This anti-liberalism is taken up in later chapters, too, as I argue that it cannot be reduced to the authoritarian or totalitarian forms often invoked to dismiss critiques of the world.

Defining this world and desiring its end are intimately related tasks. I begin with Schmitt's discussion of the imposition and emergence of a legal and political order that transforms the earth into a world. While this provides a useful starting point, I argue that it is an inadequate account of this order. Underneath his description of the division of land, sea, air and space, there is another set of divisions: nature, capital, gender and race. Put another way, Schmitt has an insufficient ontology of the world. Drawing on feminist materialism and aspects of social constructivism, I offer an account of the world that attends to the interaction of social and material relations such that this distinction between social and material begins to lose its usefulness. Through this blurring, it becomes clear that the divisions of nature, capital, gender and race are not merely conflicts in the world. They are irresolvable antagonisms that constitute the world. The chapter concludes by considering the implications of this view of the world and the difficulty of thinking its end.

The second chapter begins to develop a political theology capable of thinking the end of the world. I outline a genealogy that connects Joachim of Fiore to Hegel and onwards. This genealogy is either a story of perpetual struggle and the hope for something different or a dangerous indulgence of theology's worst political implications. Either way, this genealogy is significant for my argument in two key ways. First, it establishes Hegel as a key figure for both political theology and apocalypticism. Second, this genealogy is central to Taubes's account of political theology.

In this genealogy, Hegel does *something* to the relationship between theology and philosophy. The nature of this something is often left undefined. To clarify Hegel's contribution to political theology, I engage in a close reading of Hegel's philosophy of religion in order to specify his understanding of the relationship between religion, philosophy and politics. Hegel argues that religion and philosophy share a truth but think this truth differently. Philosophy thinks abstractly while religion engages this truth in the form of representations. Both modes of thinking are essential, as religious thought generates a philosophy that then returns to religious representations to creatively re-engage them. Hegel's more direct engagements with the political role of religion have received attention, but I argue that this notion of religion as representations presents an implicit political theology. His method of thinking philosophically with theological concepts opens up new ways of using apocalypticism to critique the world. The Hegelian concepts introduced in this chapter form the basis of the engagement with Taubes and Malabou. They each provide new ways of engaging Hegel's philosophy, reformulating and transforming his ideas in the course of a 'plastic' reading.

While Hegel's overt political theology can be conservative, his implicit political theology is more disruptive. As Schmitt himself argues, it preserves 'revolutionary sparks'.[1] In the third chapter, I argue that Taubes fans these sparks into a flame. Taubes's work has emerged from relative obscurity due to the recent philosophical interest in Paul, but this attention is usually limited to passing footnotes. This chapter offers a more substantial engagement, showing how Taubes offers distinct accounts of both political theology and apocalypticism. These accounts, respectively, can be summarized as experimenting with theological materials and disinvestment from the world. His development of these ideas and his reading of Hegel are key to arguing for an immanent version of apocalypticism that avoids critiques of its reliance upon transcendent intervention.

While Taubes's understanding of apocalypticism is helpful in developing an immanent apocalyptic political theology, there is a hesitation when it comes to confronting the end. On the one hand, he is spiritually disinvested from the world, but on the other, he cautions against the nihilistic tendencies of the apocalyptic. The fourth chapter explores this hesitation with the assistance of Catherine Malabou's work on plasticity. Malabou offers a reading of Hegel that focuses on the nature of the future and opposes messianic tendencies, again reinforcing the argument for an immanent, disruptive change. Drawing together explorations of immanence, contingency, negation and trauma, she provides a philosophical framework that, with Hegel and Taubes, is capable of articulating what it means to look forward to the end.

Finally, the book concludes by circling back to the specific world described in the first chapter. What does it mean to think the end of the world today? I argue that it should take the form of an active pessimism. This form of pessimism may refuse the hope of this world, but it has not surrendered. Living negatively in the world requires a constant investigation of what it means to engage in this refusing, of cultivating habits of refusal and of developing the capacity to sustain this refusal as a mode of negatively being in the world. This refusal entails a strange hope rooted in the end rather than an investment in what would come after.

It is possible that it has always been a good time to write about the end of the world. It is conceivable that in every age every society has its pessimists, its doomsayers and those that cloak their misanthropy or nihilism with a layer of intellectualism. This depiction of apocalyptists recalls Kierkegaard's knight of infinite resignation. The book concludes by taking up Kierkegaard's discussion of this knight and the contrast he draws with the knight of faith. In opposition to both of these figures, I propose a knight of apocalyptic pessimism as a model of what it might mean to live apocalyptically.

Hegel is a key figure throughout these chapters, but it is important to note that this book does not end with Hegel. There has been a great deal of work, most notably by Slavoj Žižek, that turns to Hegel in an effort to rethink religion, theology and politics. Indeed, whether he is cast as hero or villain, he inevitably appears in recent work in political theology. He is important for both Taubes and Malabou, but they are not primarily Hegel scholars. Rather, they think with Hegel, even when that entails thinking against Hegel. Hegel is a resource, not an authority. He helps articulate a problem well, because he is part of the history of that problem.

Viewing Hegel as a resource rather than an authority, to think with rather than about Hegel's work, is in keeping with the spirit of Taubes, as well as other twentieth-century apocalyptic thinkers. Deleuze and Guattari, describing the French novel, write, 'It can only conceive of organised voyages . . . It spends its time plotting points instead of drawing lines, active lines of flight or of positive deterritorialisation.'[2] The following chapters are an attempt to determine new lines of flight rather than merely plotting the points of Hegelian philosophy and political theology. This apocalyptic political theology is not an attempt at recovering what has been lost. It is not a return. It is an attempt to experiment, to make use of a concept in order to think anew the world and its end. Such efforts always entail risks, not least trying to draw together disparate and sometimes contradictory voices. Perhaps this cacophony can anticipate the chaos that the *katechon* tries to restrain.

1

Philosophy, political theology and the end of the world

Calls for the end of the world inevitably provoke a series of questions: What is this world? Why should it end? What would it mean to think of such an ending? A more developed response to these questions will require passing through Hegel, Taubes and Malabou, but an initial exploration of political theology, the world and apocalypticism will serve to orient the following discussion.

What is political theology?

For the purposes of this book, political theology is a methodology focused on the relationship between political and theological concepts. It seeks to understand the political history and significance of theological ideas, the theological history and significance of political ideas and to use theological ideas to explore the nature of the political.

This approach is clearly indebted to Carl Schmitt while also complicating his famous, if now clichéd, description of political theology. While it is true that Schmitt writes '[a]ll significant concepts of the modern theory of the state are secularised theological concepts', his work is often reduced to this genealogical approach.[1] However, this genealogy is only a part of his wider work in the sociology of concepts.[2] 'This sociology of concepts transcends juridical conceptualisation oriented to immediate practical interest. It aims to discover the basic, radically systematic structure and to compare this conceptual structure with the conceptually represented social structure of a certain epoch.'[3] At times this takes the form of identifying structural analogies, such as that between the exception and the miracle.[4] At other points, he investigates the limits of specific political situations and the emergence of novel social structures that initiate new historical epochs.[5] Schmitt's point is that politics operates within a political framework that it cannot justify. The structural analogy between the political and theology is found in beginnings, ends, the dynamics of change and modes of control.

Even though his approach is more multifaceted than its contemporary invocations sometimes indicate, it is certainly not without issue. Aside from the obvious problem of his National Socialism, there are other, more methodological problems.[6] For the purposes of developing a concept of political theology, the most important is his privileging of the theological. In critically receiving his work, it is thus particularly important to question the simplicity of his notion that the theological is converted into the political.[7] Such a framing too readily accepts an easy division between the theological and the political – a division which is itself both theological and political. The political and theological are two modes of expressing power. These modes are interconnected and mutually informing. There is no neat, linear process of secularization. Theological ideas appear in the political, not as the result of transformation or importation, but because those ideas were always already caught up in power relationships and their concomitant forms of knowledge. The more philosophically inclined political theology developed here maintains that there is no theological thought isolated from the political, nor thinking the political in isolation from the theological. There are, however, discourses that emphasize one or the other.

This form of political theology is thus not concerned with 'political religion'. Rather, it focuses on the theological illumination of the political (and vice versa) as well as the processes by which religion and politics are divided such that they can be recombined to name a problem. The political is a discourse of beginnings and endings, transformations and collapses. In this sense, the political is outside the bounds of politics. It is a zone of teleological suspensions, exceptions and miracles.[8] There is an exercise of power at the origin of any order that lies beyond that rules of that order. The preservation of that order legitimates its suspension. Though the day to day of politics displays symptoms of the political, political theology is concerned with those symptoms only to gain access to the underlining condition. It is concerned with the political itself.

Moving beyond Schmitt's genealogical and analogical forms of political theology, Taubes offers a more constructive approach. Taubes summarizes this approach as a 'working with theological materials' (*PT*, 69). He goes on to describe his method in terms of intellectual history, but his texts show experimentation as well as historical investigation. Combining Schmitt and Taubes, political theology is an investigation of the intertwined history of theological and political concepts in order to utilize those concepts to critique the world.

Of course, there are other understandings of political theology. Vincent Lloyd identifies three approaches: broad (the general intersection of religion and politics), narrow (associated with Schmitt and the legacy of his work) and sectarian.[9] The above definition is most amenable to a narrow, particularly philosophical form of political theology, but that in no way discounts these other views. Indeed, there are important overlaps between this vision of political theology and more sectarian versions of political theology. For instance, Michael Kirwan offers a political theology concerned with religion understood as 'complexes of belief, worship and action which are deeply embedded in practices and traditions, and which are felt to be crucial to both individual and communal self-understanding'.[10] This understanding of religion, and the political significance of practices and traditions, is essential to the implicit political theology I will later identify in Hegel. However, Kirwan goes on to ask questions such as: 'Can a *polis* exist, be sustained, without God? ... But how, then, does such a polity and its leaders avoid placing themselves on the Messiah's throne.'[11] These questions begin to raise issues of political religion, straying into more sectarian territory.

Similarly, emphasizing the theological aspect, Andrew Shanks takes political theology's essential task to be understanding

> the gospel as a practical basis for the belonging-together of a community. Not just at the level of all speaking the same religious language, or all operating within a common framework of symbolism and ritual; but at a much deeper, and broader, level than that. This deeper level is constituted, partly, by a body of shared *experience*, underlying and coming to expression in the symbolism and ritual. And partly it is constituted by a set of shared *ethical standards*, a general consensus to what is to be admired and what condemned, or how disagreements are to be managed and resolved.[12]

Shanks is doing political *theology*. It is a different conversation.[13]

Differentiating a narrower, more methodical understanding of political theology is a clarification, not a dismissal. Emphasizing political theology as a methodology merely distances this notion of political theology from analysis of political religion or religious politics. Recent discussions of political theology are often positioned in relation to the return of religion, whether that return is greeted as a crack emerging in the facade of Western liberal order or decried for the same reason.[14] While political theology in a narrower sense can be part of those conversations, it can also operate without concern for the political views or roles of specific religious communities.

This differentiation of forms of political theology is particularly important in the light of recent critiques of political theology. These arguments often blur any distinction between political theology as a methodology, as religiously motivated political movements and as theocracy. The broad question of religion and politics quickly shifts to a critique of sectarian examples. Mark Lilla's *The Stillborn God*, for instance, is an explicit critique of political theology.[15] He understands this term to indicate 'a primordial form of human thought' many thought had been superseded by Western liberal democracy.[16] The main concern of his argument is to analyse the enduring appeal of political theology, particularly messianic ideas, and the challenges they pose for contemporary politics.[17] In Lilla's condemnation, however, one struggles to identify anything resembling the narrow form of political theology defined above. There is no mention of any of the central figures traditionally associated with political theology, such as Schmitt, Benjamin or Agamben (though he has addressed Schmitt elsewhere).[18]

If Lilla takes aim at political theology in the broader sense, John Gray strikes closer to the narrower form.[19] He frames his critique in terms of utopianism, millenarianism and apocalypticism rather than political theology, but the focus of much of his analysis is a familiar historical account tracing dangerous theological ideas from Joachim of Fiore through the secularizing influence of Hegel to Marx, National Socialism and other forms of extremism or totalitarianism. For Gray, these later seemingly non-religious ideas remain tainted by an original theological sin. Their theological origins may have been forgotten, mutated by secularization, but they continue to shape the political imaginary of the West.[20]

If Shanks is doing political *theology*, Lilla and Gray are critiquing the same. Shanks emphasizes the political implications of theology, while Lilla and Gray argue against the theology's political implications. Leaving aside the question of whether Lilla, Gray or Shanks is correct, they all share a similar configuration of religion or theology and politics. Though Gray's analysis is sometimes a kind of political theology in the narrow sense, this analysis remains focused on the problematic relationship between religion and politics. For Gray, the concept of a world transforming revolution is itself religious and hence problematic.[21]

Lilla's and Gray's critiques can thus be split into two veins. First, they are focused on critiquing political theology in the sense of political religion. In this respect, there is often insufficient awareness of political theology beyond political religion, with Lilla in particular reducing the former to the latter. These critiques are ultimately affirmations of secularism. While it is true that political religion, theology and political theology all offer examples of the celebration of the failure of secularism and the announcement of the post-secular, these categories themselves are subject to political theological dismantling. Triumphalist, theological forms of post-secularism risk repeating the flaws of secularization theory in arguing that religion was waning but has now returned to address the limitations of Western liberalism.[22] By contrast, the political theology I am developing here is asecular or desecularizing.[23] It is not interested in celebrating or denigrating the relationship between the political and the theological. It thinks with an indifference to these distinctions. Political theology is not about offering theological solutions to political problems but maintaining that the political as such is inseparably mixed with the theological.

Second, Lilla and Gray are concerned with the continuing political legacy of theological ideas. More specifically, they react to a political theological critique of liberalism. Both reject the optimism that accompanies revolutionary ideas and are worried by visions of fundamentally different social and political orders. Here, their critiques are more pertinent to a narrow conception of political theology. This tradition has indeed been marked by a deep ambivalence with regard to liberal politics. From Schmitt onwards, political theology has accused the liberal narrative of denying the violence that marks its origins and continuation. For example, both Schmitt and Benjamin argue, in different ways, that this violence is not a misapplication of liberal principles but endemic to the political. Lilla's and Gray's rejection of political theology is thus rooted in real concerns, even if that rejection is muddled by a mixing of terms and traditions.

These concerns are shared by those who focus more exclusively on political theology in the narrow sense. For instance, Jayne Svenungsson has recently argued for a theopolitics defined in opposition to political theology. Yet, there is still an ambiguity regarding the concept of political theology that complicates her survey of prophetic practice, messianism, apocalypticism and political theology. Svenungsson is arguing in favour of a ' "theopolitical" interpretation of the prophetic motif, invoking a form of justice that does not allow itself to be reduced to any existing political order, in contrast to has come to be known as "political theology" – the tendency to use theological claims to support a specific political agenda'.[24] Though she returns to this definition of political theology as 'theologically sanctioned politics', her focus is on politics in the most general sense, rather than particular states, parties or other organizations.[25] In this sense, she remains less concerned with political religion or religious politics, and more on the political as such.

As with Lilla and Gray, Svenungsson offers a critique rooted in a definition of political theology that misses key aspects of Schmitt, Taubes, Benjamin and other central figures that have come to define this narrower political theology. Their work is not a theologically legitimated politics but an analysis of the political as such that reveals its structural analogy to theology. Yet, again paralleling Lilla and Gray, at the heart of this critique is a rejection of political theology's suspicion of liberalism. Svenungsson wants to defend a concept of divine justice, but one that is part of an intrahistorical process of redemption rather than an external apocalyptic intervention.[26] Theopolitics offers an unachievable, transcendent and divine justice that endlessly interrogates any and all concrete political arrangements. It has faith in this process of interrogation as a means of achieving justice. Contra Taubes, Benjamin, and other apocalyptic political theologians, law and order are the preconditions of emancipation rather than obstacles to be overcome.[27] Where Svenungsson departs from Lilla and Gray is her integration of theological perspectives into this vision of a legal and political progress oriented at a justice it can never ultimately realize.

Considering Schmitt, Taubes, Benjamin, Agamben as well as Derrida, Badiou and Žižek, it becomes clear that there is something happening in a body of literature that escapes these critiques of political theology – an element irreducible to the various forms of theologically legitimated politics. Thinking about political theology in terms of method, rather than focusing on the relationship between religion and politics, helps clarify this ambiguous issue. This methodological political theology can then be used to analyse the ways that politicized theologies are rooted in political theological perspectives but without reducing political theology to this concern. This form of political theology concentrates on the historical and contemporary significance of the analogy between theology and the political.[28] It is interested in the political limitations of any politics and the way those limitations are negotiated, repressed or confronted.

This approach, in its focus on these limitations, must still respond to critiques that identify an ambivalence, suspicion or hostility to liberalism. For even the more methodological forms of political theology, liberalism often stands for a politics that denies the political. Political theology's fascination with the problems of origins, limitations and exceptions means that it is often focused on disruption, revolution, messianism and, occasionally, apocalypticism. From this perspective, it offers thoughts on how to think about the pervasive forms of injustice that persist in an era defined by at least nominal commitments to liberal ideas.

Whether or not Lilla's, Gray's and Svenungsson's critiques of political theology's suspicion of liberalism are fair depends on how one views this era. If gradual and intrahistorical progress within the existing order is capable of rendering the world more just, then Svenungsson is right to emphasize slow change and the importance of continuity.[29] If something more intrinsic is wrong with the world, then it is necessary to investigate the resources of apocalypticism.

What is this world that ends?

Evaluating political theology's critique of liberalism thus requires an account of the world. The possibility of change within the world depends on the nature of both the change and the world. What is it that makes the world a world rather than a political economy, ideology or social reality?[30] And what kinds of change are possible within that world? This section lays out an initial account of this world, for understanding the peculiar hope of its end requires addressing the nature of the world itself.[31] Such a clarification is especially necessary given recent critiques of the notion of world.[32]

Schmitt's analysis of the transformation of the earth[33] into a global legal order provides a political theological starting point. His notion of the *nomos* shows the constitution of the world through the organization of land, people and things. Expanding on Schmitt, I argue that this organization occurs through a set of divisions that can be summarized by the terms nature, capital, gender and race. These divisions do not operate independently but are shaped through a series of complex intersections. These intersections are the difference between an arbitrary set of relations and the enduring configuration worthy of the name 'world'. These divisions are not divisions within the world – they are the world. It is this inescapable configuration that presents the question of the end.

Schmitt: From earth to world by way of law

Schmitt is fundamentally concerned with the imposition, maintenance and protection of order. One of his key names for this order is *nomos*: the 'Greek word for the first measure of all subsequent measures, for the first land-appropriation understood as the first partition and classification of space, for the primeval division and distribution'.[34] As Schmitt explains, the *nomos* is an order governing 'appropriation, distribution and production' instituted by power.[35] It is 'a matter of the fundamental process of apportioning space that is essential to every historical epoch – a matter of the structure-determining convergence of order and orientation in the cohabitation of peoples on this new scientifically surveyed planet'.[36] This apportioning begins with an appropriation of land that institutes a complex social, economic and political order. The concrete division of the earth and the organization of people that is the origin of the very law that now perpetuates that order. *Nomos* takes the earth and makes it a world through a process of divisions and distributions that are just as fundamental as the physical world in which we live.[37]

Schmitt's *nomos* is defined first in terms of land, then sea and finally air (with brief nods to the possibilities of space). This *nomos* is thus a question of the governing of terrain or space. He is particularly concerned with a spatial, political and legal order that exceeds the state but is still Eurocentric.[38] The sea, for example, is initially an anarchic space that gradually becomes subject to a law that is not simply imposed unilaterally but emerges in the course of developing relations among empires.[39]

Schmitt's account of *nomos* helps develop a concept of the world in two ways. First, *nomos* captures the connection between earth and the world. Sovereignty requires territory; power is rooted in material appropriation.[40] However, this connection is not fully developed by Schmitt as he is concerned with the way that *nomos* divides the earth. This focus ignores the way that *nomos* becomes *part of the earth*. It is not enough to describe *nomos* as it acts on material reality – *nomos* and material reality shape one another.[41] Analysing the relationship between *nomos* and material reality from only one direction, as will be clear later in this section, makes the *nomos* seem more fragile than it is.

Second, Schmitt's discussion of *nomos* reflects his anxiety about the possibility of its collapse and the shape of the *nomoi* to come. *Nomos of the Earth*, as well as Schmitt's later work on the partisan, are fundamentally works reflecting an anxiety about the contingency of this *nomos*. He is conscious of the fact that the emergence of new ages entails new *nomos*.[42] Yet, even more terrifying is the prospect that the *nomos* will be overwhelmed – order will give way to the chaos that it struggles to contain.

This anxiety is most clear in his discussion of the *katechon*. Schmitt argues that the historical Christian empire was always aware of its end. It was shaped by the promise of eschatological fulfilment and the desire to delay its arrival. For although the end ushers in the Kingdom of God, it equally heralds a time of judgement and destruction. It is this delay, the preservation of the continuity of the imperial world, that is its defining task. 'The decisive historical concept of this continuity was that of the restrainer: *katechon*. "Empire" in this sense meant the historical power to *restrain* the appearance of the Antichrist and the end of the present eon; it was a power that withholds.'[43] The end will come, but the empire fights to delay that end.[44]

Schmitt raises this concern about the possibility of the end in relationship to utopian ideas as well. In the midst of a discussion of England and changes within maritime law, he offers a passing remark on Thomas More's *Utopia*. Again, the passage reflects Schmitt's awareness of the contingency of the *nomos*, 'manifest in this book, and in the profound and productive formulation of the word *Utopia*, was the possibility of an enormous destruction of all orientations based on the old *nomos* of the earth'.[45] Though this notion of utopia is never connected to *katechon* or the chaos it entails, Schmitt clearly associates destruction and utopia. For Schmitt, all order is haunted by the possibility of collapse. As Julia Hell argues, such anxiety about the endings of empires is not uncommon. Yet Schmitt's work is marked by a particular 'apocalyptic urgency'.[46]

This katechonic anxiety is flawed in two ways. First, his identification of threats to the *nomos* is predictably problematic. For Schmitt, the naming of the enemy of the *nomos* is foundational to the possibility of international law.[47] He uses the *katechon* to explore an imperial fear, so the locus of that anxiety is the real or perceived enemies of empire.[48] Schmitt understands the enemy as the collective other or stranger. The war against the enemy is a war between peoples.[49] His declaration that '[w]ar is the existential negation of the enemy' is chilling when viewed in the light of his Nazism.[50] *Nomos* and *katechon* can still be used to think both the world and its end, but it must be done in the shadow of Schmitt's own use of those concepts. Second, he underestimates the ability of the world to persist. Underlying Schmitt's dynamic account of *nomos* is a fundamental continuity. Empires rise and fall, but there is always an empire. True, the transition of power from one empire to the next is often a violent and destructive process, but nonetheless it is the preservation of a distinct form of power. Even as the division between land and sea changes, it is not a radically new relationship, but a reconfiguration and expansion of recognizable modes of rule. He is right to recognize the possibility of the end of the world, but too quick to declare its advent. 'The world survives.'[51]

Schmitt himself seems to recognize this point to a degree, cautioning those who see the end on the horizon.

> The new *nomos* of our planet is growing irresistibly. Many see therein only death and destruction. Some believe that they are experiencing the end

of the world. In reality, we are experiencing only the end of the former relations of the land and sea. To be sure, the old *nomos* has collapsed, and with it a whole system of accepted measure, concepts, and customs. But what is coming is not therefore boundlessness or a nothingness hostile to *nomos*.[52]

And yet, *Nomos of the Earth* concludes with Schmitt's concern about the antipolitical tendencies of globalization and liberalism. He is torn between the assertion that what appears as the possibility of utter annihilation and chaos is really just another coming *nomos* and the fear that, perhaps this time, the destruction will be real.

It is this second flaw that necessitates a deeper exploration of the world. While Schmitt helpfully describes the way that *nomos* converts the earth to a world, his account of this process must be deepened. The earth has been divided (land, sea and air), but imperial conquest and the friend/enemy distinction are insufficient explanations for the shape that the world has taken. The *nomos* that divides the world is also itself a feature of that same world. The appropriation, distribution and production of land, sea and air (as well as the human and other-than-human bodies that live on and in these territories) are not merely surface alterations but fundamental transformations of the world they made and are making. What Schmitt fails to recognize is the materiality of *nomos*. Understanding the materiality of these processes and the manner in which they constitute a world will require naming a new set of divisions. Thinking through these new divisions, it becomes apparent that the world will not end as easily as Schmitt fears.

To move beyond the divisions of land, air and sea, I argue that the contemporary order is divided according to nature, capital, gender and race. With the exception of gender, these divisions are already present in Schmitt, but only occasionally. There is passing acknowledgement that land appropriation is a question of capital and the taming of nature. This process of land appropriation is racialized; whose land can be appropriated by what means depends in part on one's position in the racial hierarchy.[53] Like Schmitt's land, air and sea, these divisions are fundamentally about appropriation, distribution and production, but it expands Schmitt's focus on land to include bodies. It is these relations between land and bodies that constitutes a world.

Discussing how these divisions make a world is difficult and contentious. For one, why should these divisions be taken as constitutive rather than a wider or completely different set of relations? Sexuality and religion, for example, would seem to be key to understanding the world. The divisions of nature, capital, gender and race are particularly significant in three ways. First, as will be explained below, they take a particularly oppositional form. These are antagonistic divisions, leading towards a 'Manichean worldview'.[54] Second, they incorporate many other divisions. While sexuality is not reducible to questions of gender, nor religion to race, understanding these four divisions provides resources essential to analysing those divisions. Finally, nature, capital, gender and race are deeply related such that it is impossible to tell the story of one without incorporating the others. This interrelatedness is not reductive. Race cannot be reduced to the division of capital, but a full account of race requires an account of capital. In addressing each of these divisions, the others are slowly pulled in. As such, this process of gradual mixing will be the model for the following outline of the world. In discussing nature, the consequences for gender emerge. Then the parallels (and differences) between gender and race reveal something of the nature of capital, all of which returns the conversation to the topic of nature. In the course of this discussion, an ontology capable of describing the relationship between *nomos* and materiality will gradually take shape.

Nature and capital

Nature is the natural starting point. The divide between humanity and nature is often essential to the definition of the human. The gender and racial hierarchies that come to define the world draw on this essential division. To be less than human is to be more of nature.

In recent years, the designation of the present geological epoch as the 'Anthropocene' has taken on a significant role in shaping humanity's conceptions of its relationship with the rest of nature. The term designates the epochal shift from the Holocene to an age in which humanity has taken on a geologically significant role.[55] Dating this transition is understandably difficult, but Paul Crutzen, who first proposed the term, has suggested that the shift occurred between 1800 and the 1950s.[56] By the mid-twentieth century, humanity had created its own geological epoch.

The term and debates about dating immediately generate questions that extend beyond nature itself to questions of capital and intrahuman differences. Clearly a long series of developments, from the discovery of fire to the burning of fossil fuels to the Industrial Revolution, led to this shift. Conceiving of these changes in terms of the Anthropocene risks eliding that the series of events affected different groups of people differently. The intensified consumption of fossil fuels during the Industrial Revolution was an uneven process inaugurated by an incredibly small group of people. 'Capitalists in a small corner of the Western world invested in steam, laying the foundation stone for the fossil economy; at no moment did the species vote for it with feet or ballots, or march in mechanical unison, or exercise any sort of shared authority over its own destiny and that of the Earth System.'[57] The Anthropocene, in describing humanity's impact on the Earth, artificially unites humanity. Culpability is distributed much more equally than the wealth generated by the processes primarily responsible for climate change.

In other words, considering 'humanity's' relationship to nature requires investigating the way that the Industrial Revolution and capitalism divided some humans from other humans and nature. As Jason Moore argues, the capitalist economy was and is reliant upon 'cheap nature'.[58] Cheap food, cheap energy and raw materials are all taken from an uncompensated nature.[59] The basic human relationship to nature is one of expropriation. For Moore, the Anthropocene can thus be more accurately described as the 'Capitalocene'. Humanity's impact on the environment is due to its reliance on fossil fuels and that reliance is inextricably caught up with capitalism. Without the energy provided by fossil fuels there is no capitalism and the spread of capitalism accelerates their usage.

Not everyone agrees with this assessment. Dipesh Chakrabarty, in particular, has argued that there are two flaws with this critique of the Anthropocene. First, he argues that 'leaving aside the question of intergenerational ethics that concerns the future, anthropogenic climate change is not inherently – or logically – a problem of past or accumulated intra-human injustice.'[60] Chakrabarty readily admits that there is an inequality of consumption and waste, but argues that it is reductive to explain all aspects of climate change by an appeal to capitalism.[61] While it may indeed be reductive to reduce *all* aspects of climate change to capital, Moore, Andreas Malm and Alf Hornborg convincingly argue that the climate change being experienced today is inextricably linked to the form of the global economy. As Malm argues, that form and its reliance upon fossil fuel was imposed on a large percentage of the world's population.[62] Responding to Charkrabarty's objection requires taking into consideration the way that capital is related to nature, both now and historically, as well as the way that capital shapes other key forms of social relations (or non-relation). In other words, it requires an account of the world.

The relationship between nature and capital is particularly important for providing such an account. First, it is nature, more than any other division that reveals the inescapability of the world. As will become clear in the following sections, the world names a set of intersecting material and social relations.[63] Second, as the terms Anthropocene and Capitalocene indicate, human actions are both part of nature and capable of changing that nature. As Moore, Malm and Hornborg demonstrate, this vision of nature is essential to the relations named by 'capital'. The emergence of an economy rooted in fossil fuel was from its inception connected to uneven development and the exploitation of labour. The antagonism is not between humanity and nature, but between some humans, other humans and nature. The damages of climate change will be unevenly distributed.[64]

Gender

To expand this account of the world beyond nature and capital, it is useful to view Moore's discussion of cheap nature and Malm and Hornborg's critique of the Anthropocene narrative within the context of Silvia Federici's analysis of capitalism, gender and race. Federici argues that the human–nature relationship directly shapes European (and eventually North American) views of women and informs the shifting notions of race that accompany colonial expansion. For Federici, the process of primitive accumulation is central to the transformation of these relationships. The rapid privatization of land, through both the enclosure of public land and colonialism, not only intensified existing relations and enabled new means of extracting value from the natural world, it also transformed social relations.[65] While this is obviously true in terms of labour, it may be less obvious how these changes shifted ideas about gender and race.

With regard to enclosures, Federici tracks numerous ways that land expropriation impacted the lives of women in Europe.[66] Most crucially, women were deprived of the commons, a space of at least limited social autonomy, which made it increasingly difficult to find ways to support themselves outside of reproductive labour.[67] As the market became the determiner of value, this reproductive work, the literal production of the worker, became increasingly devalued.[68] By the time this process culminated in the emergence of the full-time housewife in the nineteenth century, the implications of this devaluing become clear: 'the separation of production from reproduction created a class of proletarian women who were as dispossessed as men but, unlike their male relatives in a society that was becoming increasingly monetarized, had almost no access to wages, thus being forced into a condition of chronic poverty, economic dependence, and invisibility as workers.'[69] The willing transformation of some humans' relationship to nature disrupts other humans' relationships to each other and nature.

The shift in humanity's relationship to the rest of nature brought about by the move from production for use to the money economy (capital) also introduced new and intensified forms of sexually differentiated labour (gender).[70] 'Proletarian women became for male workers the substitute for the land lost to the enclosures, their most basic means of reproduction, and a communal good.'[71] As work became increasingly defined in terms of the wage, women's labour was defined as non-work, 'a natural resource, available to all, no less than the air we breathe or the water we drink.'[72] For Federici, this change marks the key difference between gender dynamics under capital and the unequal relations of earlier periods. Though such inequality is undeniable, 'women's subordination to men had been tempered by the fact that they had access to the commons and other communal assets, while in the new capitalist regime *women themselves became the commons*, as their work was defined as a natural resource, laying outside the sphere of market relations.'[73] As Federici's language reflects, it is not only nature that provides the cheap labour necessary for the functioning of capital. The transitions during the period of primitive accumulation simultaneously mark the emergence of the world of the Capitalocene and effect 'a unique process of social degradation that was fundamental to the accumulation of capital and has remained so ever since.'[74]

As women's labour became as economically vital as it was uncompensated, it became ever more important for the state or church to regulate women's bodies. In particular, the European population crisis of the sixteenth and seventeenth centuries lead to increasingly brutal punishments for women who do not reproduce or who in any way challenge the stability of the patriarchally ordered home.[75] The primary means of recognizing the indispensable role of women was the severity of the persecution that accompanied any deviation from that role. Federici finds this same anxiety around women's shifting roles and the regulation of the body at the heart of European and North American witch-hunts. 'The witch-hunt condemned female sexuality as the source of every evil, but it was also the main vehicle for a broad restructuring of sexual life, that conforming with the new capitalist work-discipline, criminalised any sexual activity that threatened procreation, the transmission of property within the family, or took time and energies away from work.'[76]

Federici notes that these gender issues are often viewed in isolation from other concurrent developments. She draws connections between the expropriation of communal lands and the way that witch-hunts 'expropriated women from their bodies'.[77] The relationship between these changes in conceptions of nature, capital, gender and race too often go unnoticed.

> It should . . . have seemed significant that the witch-hunt occurred simultaneously with the colonization and extermination of the populations of the New World, the English enclosures, the beginning of the slave trade, the enactments of 'bloody laws' against vagabonds and beggars, and it climaxed in that interregnum between the end of feudalism and the capitalist 'take off' when the peasantry in Europe reached the peak of its power but, in time, also consummated its historic defeat.[78]

To overlook the connections between these changes is to miss the emergence and sedimentation of the world.

This parallel between nature and gender has of course long been a central thesis of ecofeminist critique.[79] Federici's contribution is to position the connection between gender and nature within the development of capitalism. There are certainly forms of pre-capitalist patriarchy, but the world she describes is one of the mutual reinforcing divisions of nature, gender and capital.

Race

As indicated by Federici's references to colonialism and slavery, these divisions intersect with race as well. The founding of European capitalism and colonial expansion were dependent upon 'the subordination and exploitation of their own women, on the exploitation and killing of Nature, on the exploitation and subordination of other peoples and their lands'.[80] The concept of nature as beneath humanity and ripe for exploitation informs understanding of both gender and race and that exploitation is essential to the flourishing of the form of capitalism that eventually assumes global dominance. Federici draws attention to the parallels between attitudes towards women and 'Indian savages'. In both instances, degradation and terrorization are part of a sustained project of expropriating labour (in the case of women) and land (in the case of indigenous people).[81] The parallels are clear – these categories are considered inferior due to being more ruled by nature, not yet having been liberated by Enlightened rationality (or not being capable of such liberation).[82] There are similar connections between gender and other racial classifications. 'For the definition of Blackness and femaleness as marks of bestiality and irrationality conformed with the exclusion of women in Europe and women and men in the colonies from the social contract implicit in the wage, and the consequent naturalization of their exploitation.'[83] Both groups are considered untrustworthy or fickle and the sexual powers of both groups are to be feared. Women, for example, were judged more prone to witchcraft due to their inability to control their sexual urges.[84] In the seventeenth century, the devil became Black and his race became associated with 'an abnormal lust and sexual potency'.[85]

Federici touches on the figure of the slave, but recent work in the theory of race and Blackness goes much further in examining anti-Blackness as constitutive of the world. Perhaps the strongest version of this argument comes from Frank B. Wilderson III who argues the exclusion of Blackness from the sphere of the human is essential to the structure of the world – 'No slave, no world.'[86] This exclusion is what Wilderson and others, following the work of Orlando Patterson, call social death:[87]

> *Blackness*, refers to an individual who is by definition always already devoid of relationality. Thus modernity marks the mergence of a new ontology

because it is an era in which an entire race appears, people who, that is prior to the contingency of the 'transgressive act' (such as losing a war or being convicted of a crime), stand as socially dead in relation to the rest of the world.[88]

Blackness is not like other racial categories. For Wilderson, it does not hold the hope of other racial positions or the focus of other forms of oppression. The liberation of the slave is not analogous to the liberation of women, the indigenous or the worker.[89] In fact, 'the so-called great emancipatory discourse of modernity – Marxism, feminism, postcolonialism, sexual liberation, and the ecology movement' rely on 'grammars of suffering' derivative of but separated from the position of the slave.[90] Nancy Fraser makes a similar argument, showing that the Marxist emphasis on the exploited worker does not sufficiently consider the expropriation of racialized subjects that is constitutive of capitalism. By tracing 'historical regimes of racialized accumulation', Fraser moves her analysis beyond the figure of the worker.[91]

Yet, Wilderson's Afro-pessimism goes even further than Fraser's argument that racialization is a precondition for capitalist exploitation, arguing that 'the structure of the entire world's semantic field . . . is sutured by anti-Black solidarity. Unlike the solution-oriented, interest-based, or hybridity-dependent scholarship so fashionable today, Afro-pessimism explores the meaning of Blackness not . . . as a variously and unconsciously interpellated identity or as a conscious social actor, but as a structural position of noncommunicability.'[92] Here Wilderson echoes Fanon's analysis of the Holocaust. For Fanon, 'the Jew can be unknown in his Jewishness. He is not wholly what he is.'[93] While the exclusion of Blackness from the world is constitutive of the world, other divisions (what I will discuss as conflicts in the following section), no matter how violent or prolonged, remain 'little family quarrels'.[94] Both Fanon and Wilderson see these fights as taking place within humanity, while Blackness remains excluded.

While the logic of capital can explain some elements of race as a constitutive division within the world, Wilderson's analysis of anti-Blackness reveals a libidinal element that exceeds the economic.[95] He describes this excess as the gratuitous violence of slavery. While in earlier periods of history most people were susceptible to gratuitous violence, Wilderson argues that in the late

Middle Ages this violence begins to 'mark the Black ontologically'.[96] In light of this marking, this constitutive exclusion, Wilderson, citing Fanon citing Aimé Césaire, reaches an apocalyptic conclusion: the only thing worth starting is the end of the world.[97]

Wilderson's analysis of race shows that the divisions of nature, capital, gender and race are connected in their constitution of the world, but they are neither analogous nor reducible to one another. The racial division of the world brought about by slavery cannot be reduced to capital, but, along with the racial divisions of colonialism and settler colonialism, it is coeval with capital.[98] Capital without these divisions is inconceivable, but aspects of patriarchy, racism and ecological destruction precede and escape the logic of capital. Yet it is also true that capital shapes the function of each of these divisions today. Even if capitalism cannot explain slavery, it is still the case that slavery and the colonial system it enabled was essential to the industrialized capitalism that has come to define the world.[99]

The ontology of the world

Much more could be said about each of these divisions, both individually and as they overlap and intersect with one another. There are debates within the attempts to theorize each division, questions of logical and historical priority and different conceptions of the relationship between divisions. The purpose of this chapter is not to provide an exhaustive account nor to adjudicate between perspectives but to indicate the general shape of the world. Combining Schmitt and this account of nature, capital, gender and race provides this overview. Schmitt provides the history of the legal and political transformation of the earth into a world through processes of appropriation, distribution and production. That history leaves out or insufficiently develops how territory and bodies are selected as appropriable, the way that identities determine distribution and the different forms of productive labour: slave, housewife and worker. There are two levels of analysis: territory versus culture; the political, legal and economic versus the libidinal.

The effort of combining these two levels results in an ontology of the world. The material division of territory, bodies, libidinal fears and vulnerability to gratuitous violence interweave to create a whole. Nancy Tuana formulates this kind of ontology in terms of the 'viscous porosity of the categories "natural," "human-made," "social," "biological"' that are materially related in an 'interactionist ontology'.[100] As the above account of the world argues, the interpenetration of these categories does not collapse into an undifferentiated unity. Rather than abandoning these categories, they can be reframed within a wider unity – not the static unity of the Western metaphysical tradition, but a dynamic, interactionist unity.[101] The result is an 'ontology that *rematerializes the social and takes seriously the agency of the natural*'.[102] This materialization of the social is the key to the combination of the two modes of analysis.

Take the earlier discussion of nature as an example. Malm and Hornborg argue that climate change 'has arisen as a result of temporally fluid social relations as they materialise through the rest of nature'.[103] Thinking about climate change within the framework of the Capitalocene requires not only considering how human actions impact the rest of nature, but the way that those actions actually *change nature*.[104] This material mixture of nature and the social, cultural and political does not mean that these distinctions cannot still serve an analytical purpose.[105] Understanding that human actions are themselves part of nature and that there are other actors responding to climate change is the first step in taking the agency of the natural seriously. It is to grasp the material nature of what Anna Tsing calls 'multispecies world making'.[106] Likewise, race may not be a biological category, but the consequences of historical racial formation is not just ideological, but material.[107] The world was and continues to be constituted by the 'emergent interplay' of these categories.[108]

Looking forward to the next chapter, Tuana's ontology can also be expressed in Hegelian terms. World spirit, for all the vitriol its various deployments have rightly attracted, is about nature becoming self-conscious. Human subjectivity is the world thinking itself.[109] While nature and spirit are often read as opposed in Hegel, this is too simplistic. As Angelica Nuzzo argues, 'spirit's liberation *from* nature is more precisely its liberation *within* (and *with*) nature.'[110] While Hegel himself would not go as far as Tuana's viscous porosity, his notion of spirit is one that is necessarily in an ongoing entanglement with nature.[111] Though he preserves a hierarchy between spirit and nature, taking this ongoing entanglement as a dependency on nature allows for a more porous interpretation of Hegel.[112]

This rejection of hierarchy is also the key difference between this account of the world and Heidegger's.[113] His understanding of world is similar in emphasizing 'the worldhood' of *Dasein*'s environment and the way that a series of relations come to form a whole that provides the often-invisible background against which humans live.[114] Yet in claiming that 'the stone is worldless, the animal is poor in world, man is world-forming', he fails to think through the deeper form of interaction described by Tuana.[115] Though his inclusion of the stone and animal in his account of the world challenges the denigration of the 'natural world' in much of Western philosophy, he still upholds what Philip Tonner describes as 'transcendental anthropocentrism' in which the wider world is reduced to its significance for *Dasein*.[116]

Tuana's ontology is also helpful in highlighting the contingency of these material and social relations without denying their reality. Nature, capital, gender and race are similar in that they all mark constructed but naturalized distinctions. Nature is conceived in opposition to 'the human' or culture, but both the human and cultural are natural. Nature simply is what is. Or as Sally Haslanger puts it, 'If we endorse a broad naturalism that takes the world to be a natural world that includes as part of it social and psychological events, processes, relations and such, then it would seem that to be non-natural (at least within the empirical domain) is to be nonexistent.'[117] Capital divides the world into worker and owner. Race splits the world into Black and white. Gender poses woman against man. These binaries may be socially constructed and culturally determined, but they are not individually chosen. Masculine and feminine are assigned. Rejection of these labels does not undo the initial assigning or remove their social implications. Racial classifications can be discarded, but that does not change the fact that the world racializes people.

Conflicts and antagonisms

Nature, capital, gender and race summarize the set of relations that constitute the world. In considering the materiality of these relations, it becomes clear that the world is not something chosen but something individuals are positioned by. Humans and the rest of the nature are subject to the world and this world is both violent and inescapable. Establishing this violence and inescapability is key to understanding the need for apocalyptic thinking. Objections to apocalypticism often focus on its violence and destruction. Yet these objections often speak of the world as if it is not already violent, not only in the sense of arbitrary interpersonal violence but also in the sense of the violence inherent to the divisions that are the world. To return to Schmitt's language, the *katechon* is neither passive nor pacific. Even if this violence is acknowledged, however, one could hold out hope for an alternative rather than call for the end of the world. There could be different arrangements of material and social relations. Societies can gradually change. Communities can conceive of alternative ways of living together, becoming examples of ecologically responsible, egalitarian, non-gendered and deracialized forms of life. Apocalypticism should have good reasons for rejecting these hopes. Considering the nature of violence and the inescapability of the world will result in a more precise understanding of the divisions – nature, capital, gender and race. These are not merely conflicts within the world but antagonisms that define it.

As the discussion of gender and race shows, the divisions constitutive of the world entail violence that is often gruesome and interpersonal. Yet the world is violent in another sense – the world *itself* is violent. Slavoj Žižek differentiates these modes of violence by referring to the first as subjective and the second as objective. Subjective violence can be policed. Charges can be filed and punishments handed out. Objective violence, on the other hand, is more difficult to address. Objective violence can itself take the form of the law and police.[118] It is this second that is the violence of the world: 'the more subtle forms of coercion that sustain relations of dominance and exploitation, including the threat of violence'.[119] It is a habitual violence that accompanies being in the world. Rob Nixon describes this mode of violence as 'slow violence': 'a violence that occurs gradually and out of sight, a violence of delayed destruction that is dispersed across time and space, an attritional violence that is typically not viewed as violence at all . . . a violence that is neither spectacular nor instantaneous, but rather incremental and accretive, its calamitous repercussions playing out across a range of temporal scales'.[120] It is this often imperceptible, dispersed, 'normal' violence that is the violence of the world.

The reason that nature, capital, gender and race are so important for thinking the world is that these are spheres of objective or slow violence. There are clearly forms of interpersonal racism or gender-based violence, but these divisions are also violent in ways that remain invisible (to many people) in the process of constituting the world.[121] In moving from thinking of these divisions individually to considering the ways they overlap and intersect, the world becomes an intractable problem. How does one address climate change without reinforcing racial or economic inequalities? How can economic issues be addressed without re-entrenching racial tensions? Attempts to redress oppression or inequality may not only result in unintended consequences but the mutually reinforcing nature of these divisions also reveals the difficulty of addressing any one. 'Solving' gender inequality would involve rethinking the functioning of capitalism as a whole, because the uncompensated domestic labour of women is essential to sustaining monetarily recognized labour of workers.[122] The same is true for nature – capitalism predicated on cheap nature is unsustainable. Rethinking humanity's relationship to the rest of nature requires rethinking the fundamentals of economic life.

In positing that these divisions are forms of objective or slow violence that constitute the world, I am arguing that they are not merely unresolved tensions and conflicts. They are what Wilderson calls antagonisms: 'an irreconcilable struggle between entities, or positions, the resolution of which is not dialectical but entails the obliteration of one of the positions'.[123] Humanity cannot be reconciled with nature, for it is the opposition to nature which is definitive of humanity. It is human rationality and volition in contrast to instinctual animality and the cold determinism of nature, that defines the enlightened and Enlightened (hu)man. To change humanity's relationship to nature is not a matter of recycling, driving hybrid cars and walking to the farmer's market. It is the obliteration of a humanity that is anything more than natural. Similarly, the relationships between worker/owner, Black/white and masculine/feminine are not dialectical.[124] There is no possibility of resolution. These terms are defined in opposition to one another. To anticipate the discussion of Malabou, the world is plastic. It is plastic in the sense of malleable, for the world has clearly seen changes. Yet, plasticity also has an explosive sense and there are limits to the malleability of the world.

These limitations mark the world as inescapable. It takes the form of a totality with no beyond or outside. Daniel Colucciello Barber makes this point, arguing that the world 'presents itself in two moments – as *the given* and the as *the possible* . . . it serves as the name of the already existent, or of that which may be subjected to critique, but it likewise serves as the name of the alternative that is imagined or invoked (even if only implicitly) by such a critique'.[125] As Malabou will show, that is not the same as claiming that there is no hope or no possibility of something new. Rather, it is to claim that such hopes and possibilities must be hopes and possibilities that are not of this world. Or, as Benjamin says through Kafka, 'there is an infinite amount of hope, but not for us'.[126]

Apocalypticism is rooted in this conviction that it is not just aspects of this world, but this world itself that is unethical.[127] There is no world underneath these antagonisms. It is not the world, on top of which is laid capitalism, sexism, racism and other ideological formations. Those formations, in their complex intersection, are the world. There is a saying, often attributed to Frederic Jameson, that it is easier to imagine the end of the world than the end of capitalism.[128] This sentiment is redundant – the end of capitalism would be the end of the world. There is no remainder not positioned in relation to capital. There are pre-capitalist, 'pericapitalist' and post-capitalist forms of life and exchange that are not yet capitalism or resist capitalism, yet these are all still positioned in relation to capital.[129]

This world is hegemonic, but not homogenous. All people do not all exist in the same relation to the world. There are different versions of racial logics, but there is no world outside of racial logic. That logic is tied to a conception of nature, human and other-than-human, that is employed to differentiate people according to a hierarchical system. That hierarchy legitimates practices of appropriation, distribution and production. Different people have different conceptions of nature, but those conceptions exist in a world structured by capital's configuration of nature. The ecological consequences of this configuration are not equally distributed, but follow established patterns of inequality: capital, gender and race. Put another way, there may be 'many worlds in the World',[130] but they all exist in relation to the discipline of the world. The globalized nature of capitalism combined with the material manifestations of the social, political and economic relations required by and shaped by capital – the Capitalocene – means that there is nothing left untouched.

Even those positions that seem to exist outside of the relations of capital live in capitalism's world. Take, for example, Eduardo Viveiros de Castro's perspectivism.[131] As he explains, in certain Amerindian cosmologies, the nature–human relationship is reversed. Rather than a universal nature experienced by different species (human, jaguar, macaque, etc.), there is a universal humanity differentiated by its experience of a multitude of natures. Yet even this perspectivism cannot escape the hegemony of the world. The jaguar may be a human, but the jaguar is a human in a world where the ice caps are still melting.

As Malm, describing the connection between nature and capital, explains,

> [t]he fossil economy has the character of a totality, a distinguishable entity: a socio-ecological structure, in which a certain economic process and a certain form of energy are welded together. It has some identity over time ... A person born today in Britain or China enters a preexisting fossil economy, which has long since assumed an existence of its own and confronts the newborn as an objective fact. It possesses real causal powers – most notably the power to alter the climatic conditions on planet Earth.[132]

The world is a dynamic whole, to return to Tuana's language, that is both a set of constitutive antagonisms and the conditions of possibility for conceiving responses to those antagonisms. And as both Tuana and Haslanger show, these antagonisms are material. There is objectivity to the world. It imposes itself on all living and non-living things. To be real, material and objective does not mean necessary in any ontological sense. These antagonisms are necessary, but only necessary for the world. If one is willing to abandon the world, new, if indefinable, possibilities become possible. The world can be rejected, but this rejection requires more than updating ideas or shifting social attitudes. It is a real and material change.

The possibility of this change is the focus of apocalyptic political theology. As Bruno Latour argues, there is a form of apocalypticism that historicizes the world, revealing its contingency.[133] It is a reminder that humanity has not, in fact, reached the end of history. Apocalypticism is thus not concerned with meteors destroying the Earth. It is not necessarily interested in climate change, strictly speaking. Rather, apocalyptic political theology explores the essentially traumatic process of addressing the antagonisms that constitute the world. These material and social relations cannot be resolved within the world, because they *are* the world. This impasse requires imaging the end of the world – a traumatic end that exceeds the legitimizing discourses of ethics and politics (understood in opposition to the political). Such an end is the possibility of other possibilities.

Imagining the end

There are a number of ways of living in a violent and inescapable world. One is to accept this situation and develop social and political projects within its constraints. Or, one can hold out hope for the redemption of the world. Such hope can take a variety of utopian forms, including messianism. Finally, one can apocalyptically reject the world. Recent political theology has focused on the eschatological or messianic, often defined against apocalypticism. Much as the term political theology has come to be used to cover a diverse set of concerns, eschatology, messianism and apocalypticism have become increasingly ambiguous. In philosophical writing, the distinctions between these terms can become obscured, but as Svenungsson's critique of political theology demonstrates, whether one adopts messianic or apocalyptic has significant political consequences. Indeed, Roland Boer critiques Taubes for this lack of precision.[134] While Boer may be right that the distinction between these terms is at times elided in *Occidental Eschatology*, Taubes nonetheless develops a distinctive and philosophically rich apocalyptic political theology. I will return to an exploration of Taubes's idiosyncratic version of apocalypticism in later chapters, but a more general definition of apocalypticism in contrast to these other concepts will provide context for that discussion.

Roland Boer, in his work on political myth, differentiates between these eschatology, messianism and apocalyptic perspectives. He defines eschatology as concerned 'with the transition from the present, somewhat undesirable age to another that is qualitatively better by means of an external agent, who usually turns out to be God.'[135] Messianism is a subcategory of eschatology, one in which 'a particular individual, divinely appointed and directed, effects the transition from old to new.'[136] Finally, the 'apocalyptic refers to both a means of interpretation and a body of revealed knowledge, acquired by divine message or on a journey to the heavens.'[137] Boer notes that apocalypticism is characterized by dualisms and 'is usually a sign and an expression of intense political and social oppression'.[138] The need for deliverance coupled with dualisms results in a dependence on an external, divine intervention, replicating messianism's problematic reliance on transcendent intervention.[139]

While Boer's initial differentiation of these concepts is a useful starting point, he is primarily concerned with narrow theological definitions that stem from the biblical tradition rather than tracing how the concept has developed over time. As John J. Collins points out in his *Apocalyptic Imagination*, frequent, vague use of 'apocalypse' across a number of fields has resulted in a wider meaning.[140] Collins, more open to this expanded range of meanings, argues that a 'movement might reasonably be called apocalyptic if it shared the conceptual framework of the genre, endorsing a worldview in which supernatural revelation, the heavenly world, and eschatological judgment played essential parts'.[141] Similarly, Malcolm Bull embraces this more diffuse meaning, comparing 'apocalyptic' to 'epic'.[142] It is commonplace to refer to an 'epic' event without this usage entailing all the nuances of that literary genre. In the same way, the term apocalypse has expanded beyond its biblical and theological origins, no longer referring only to the Jewish and Christian traditions. Bull thus agrees with Collins that 'apocalypse' denotes a diverse group of related literary forms and comes to refer to a group of related but distinguishable historical movements.[143]

Bull goes further than Collins, however, and argues that apocalypse is a universal feature of human societies. To make this argument, he shifts from considering apocalypse theologically to considering the term's philosophical, psychoanalytic and theoretical meanings. He understands this universal apocalypticism as the reinclusion of excluded elements of society. Drawing on Kristeva's notion of the abject, he argues,

> The reversal of customary taboos embodied in apocalyptic may extend beyond the disregard for taboos in millenarian cults, and the identification of eschatological confusion with the dissolution of the taboo. There is much to suggest that the genre is not just a revelation of the dissolution of taboos, but itself a taboo revelation. What is seen in apocalyptic vision is more often than not a series of symbols embodying what is otherwise prohibited.[144]

Apocalyptic (and other messianic and eschatological) movements are often antinomian. The approaching end dissolves social and political norms. Chaos erupts in anticipation of the coming end of order. Bull argues that the work of Mary Douglas and others establishes that this order is rooted in binary classifications.[145]

> If apocalyptic is a revelation of the contradiction and indeterminacy excluded at the foundation of the world, then what is revealed may require a particular form of revelation. In societies where bivalence is assumed to be natural, the undifferentiated is inaccessible to normal patterns of thought, so access can be gained only by means that circumvent the accepted modes of cognition. Conversely, in these circumstances any supernatural revelation of hidden secrets is liable to disclose a world of contradictions and indeterminacies. The more strictly binarity is maintained, the more contradictions and indeterminacies there are to disclose – hence perhaps apocalyptic's affinity with dualism.[146]

Bull self-consciously extends his definition of the apocalyptic beyond its Jewish and Christian origins.[147] In doing so, he contrasts his position with Christopher Rowland's work on apocalypse. Rowland's more traditional approach places a greater emphasis on the genre's Jewish and Christian origins and the shared sense of direct revelation. Yet, his privileging of the original meaning underplays how these ideas are mutated and deployed. The question is not so much what apocalypse meant, but what are the different ways that it has had meaning and what could it mean for us now. Bull does not dismiss the question of origins, but offers an abstract philosophical engagement with theological ideas. He sees apocalypse as an idea that emerges in the process of making sense of the world. What initially appears as divine revelation becomes a logical category employed by humanity in its self-understanding. He uses theological concepts to critique the world. In other words, he does political theology.

As established earlier in this chapter, the world is constituted by the antagonisms of nature, capital, gender and race. These antagonisms are binaries: nature/human, worker/owner, woman/man and white/Black. The disruptive revelation at the heart of Bull's theory of apocalypse no longer has to come from an external divine agent. The apocalyptic revelation comes from the return of the excluded. It is brought about by the socially dead, those who are subjected to 'invisible' forms of violence and those that the world is structured not to see. Such a revelation does not just apocalyptically threaten the existing order; it also illuminates the nature of that order. The revelation of the truth of the world is simultaneously a demand for its end.

Questioning the apocalypse

This chapter has provided an outline of apocalyptic political theology. Political theology, in the narrow sense, is a method of philosophical thinking that uses theological concepts to critique the world. That world is constituted by the material and social relations that can be summarized in terms of nature, capital, gender and race. That world is violent and inescapable, for those relations are not conflicts within the world, but antagonisms that are the world. To envision the end of this world is to consider the traumatic return of the excluded or the interruption of the socially dead. This apocalyptic thinking is not a vision of a new world, but an imagining of the conditions in which a new world would become possible.

Of course, one can reject this account of the world by rejecting the concept of world as such or by disagreeing with the notion of an inescapable world constituted by the divisions of nature, capital, gender and race. There is much more that could be said about this world and this brief account may not be persuasive to everyone; it is clearly informed by a set of social and political views, the defence of which lies beyond the scope of this book. Moreover, it draws upon a range of Spinozist, Hegelian, Marxist, psychoanalytic, post-humanist and other perspectives that share interconnected and interactive ontologies, but differ substantially in how they develop those ideas. While this account of the world is incomplete, it at least shows why the revelation of the nature of the world might be an apocalyptic revelation.

Even for those unconvinced by the specifics of this account, apocalyptic political theology can still offer a critique of the world. For one, it is not dependent upon the details of my discussion of nature, capital, gender and race, but rather a materialist concept of world – the notion that the world is a constructed and cohesive sense of meaning that is not only discursive but also embedded in the inescapable materiality of social, political and economic relations. The world is what allows meaning. It is both what is and what is possible. The features of this world are necessary for us, but they are not necessary as such. Confronted with such a world, the hope of alternatives must pass through the trauma of the end.

This initial summary of apocalyptic political theology has raised three questions that will occupy the rest of this book. First, there is a persistent question about the nature of political theology. In order to philosophically employ theological concepts, it is necessary to develop a political theology that engages in the 'sociology of concepts' and then uses those concepts to think and critique the world. While this chapter differentiated this form of political theology from other broad or sectarian approaches, it remains to be seen how exactly such a political theology operates. What notions of theology and philosophy does such a method require? Is theology subordinated to philosophy? It is for this reason that I turn to Hegel. He not only offers philosophical resources for reflecting on the relationship between theology, politics and philosophy, but those resources are an important part of the history of considering the possibility of dramatic transformations of the world.

Second, while Bull provides some insights into thinking of an apocalyptic disruption without a divine agent, it remains too difficult to envision how this works. If the world is both what is and the possibilities of what is, how can one conceive of novelty? Apocalypticism has been critiqued for its reliance on an external, divine agent. The task for the ensuing chapters is to provide a more detailed account of this immanent apocalypticism. This view of the end maintains the connection between destruction and the possibility of the new, but without the intervention of a transcendent force.

This connection between destruction and novelty is the final question. Apocalypticism, as I will continue to show, is often dismissed as overly pessimistic and fixated on violence and trauma. Even if the above account of the world is convincing, it may be that apocalypticism rushes to the most hopeless conclusions. There are other utopian, messianic or progressive ways of confronting this violent and inescapable world. And, if one is convinced by this apocalyptic view, what then? What does it mean to live apocalyptically? Does it result in a form of quietism or resignation? Or, more worryingly, perhaps it confirms the fears of Lilla, Gray and Svenungsson and leads to totalitarian or absolutist political projects.

2

Implicit political theology: Reading Hegel's philosophy of religion

In the first chapter, I used Lloyd's typology to argue that there is a narrow form of political theology that can be contrasted with both broad (political religion) and sectarian approaches. This narrow approach includes Schmitt, Taubes, Benjamin, Bloch, Agamben and others. I also provided an ontology of the world and argued that this narrow form of political theology offers resources for thinking about why this world should end.

Turning to Hegel as a resource for this work might be surprising for two reasons. First, if Hegel is the Hegel of teleological history and absolute knowledge, it is not immediately obvious what he has to offer to apocalyptic thinking. Further, having defined the world in terms of nature, capital, gender and race, it may seem suspect to turn to someone whose treatment of nature, gender and race is increasingly regarded as deeply problematic.[1] Second, while Hegel offers wide-ranging thoughts on theology, religion, philosophy and politics, much of this work could be described in terms of broad or sectarian approaches to political theology. Hegel thinks religion plays an important social, political and ethical role. He also describes the social, political and ethical consequences of certain theological ideas and offers philosophical reflections on theological doctrines. There is a great deal of literature evaluating Hegel's discussion of these theological themes and that conversation has come to dominate consideration of religion within Hegel scholarship. It could thus seem strange to appeal to Hegel in order to develop political theology in a narrow sense.

This chapter seeks to address both these concerns. First, I argue that there is an established genealogy of apocalyptic thought that draws connections between early Christianity, Joachim, Hegel and Marx. This genealogy is important for those critical of political theology in the broad sense (Lilla, Gray and, to some extent, Svenungsson) as well as those who find Hegel a resource for developing a narrow political theology. Whether Hegel appears as hero or villain in these historical narratives, something – usually unspecified – happens to theology in Hegel. In these narratives, Hegel is positioned between Joachim of Fiore and Marx as a point at which the relationship between politics and theology (or religion) is transformed in a way that is dangerously conducive to extreme political positions. Though some of these genealogies offer simplistic readings of Hegel, they nonetheless capture an underlying truth about his philosophy: he develops a notion of the relationship between philosophy and theology that allows for philosophical experimentation with theological concepts. In this implicit political theology, these concepts become resources for thinking about and against the world.

Second, I offer a detailed account of this implicit political theology through a reading of Hegel's philosophy of religion. The central claim of Hegel's philosophy of religion is that religion is a form of representational thinking. Religion is thus a form of thought and that form of thought is politically significant. Religion shares a truth with philosophy, but this truth is thought differently. It is this relationship between religion as representation and philosophy, and philosophy's subsequent freedom to think the world through religion, that is the root of Hegel's political theological significance. If Schmitt offers the sociology of concepts and Taubes a more inventive critique of the world through theological ideas, then Hegel offers an explanation of how these two approaches are related.

Joachim, Hegel and the end of the world

The critiques of political theology discussed in the previous chapter are rooted in a genealogy of messianic and apocalyptic thought. This genealogy is not unique to Lilla, Gray and Svenungsson but stems from a wider tradition of reflecting on the histories of apocalyptic and millennial movements or shifts in the philosophy of history. Examining this underlining historical narrative will show how Hegel has come to occupy a key role in developing themes within political theology. This genealogy is also key to establishing Hegel's role within Taubes's and Bloch's political theologies. Establishing this role is vital – political theology may entail philosophical experimentation with theological concepts, but it is not a decontextualized experimentation. Placing Hegel in the development of the relationship between apocalypticism and the political provides the necessary backdrop for an analysis of Hegel's implicit political theology and how that method can illuminate Taubes's work.

While the details of this genealogy vary, there are few consistent figures: Jesus, Paul, Augustine and Joachim de Fiore. Thomas Müntzer also frequently makes an appearance. Eventually, this lineage arrived at the events and names associated with modern political utopias or revolutions: the French Revolution, Marx, Communism and National Socialism. This narrative describes a transformation: theological ideas become secular and political. Much in keeping with Schmitt's most popular formulation, the idea of revolution turns out to be a secularized version of eschatological, messianic or apocalyptic ideas. Hegel is a central character in this story. In particular, the connection between his philosophy and the theology of Joachim de Fiore becomes key to understanding Hegel's role in the development of political theology.[2]

One of the most influential historical accounts positing this connection is Norman Cohn's *The Pursuit of the Millennium*.[3] Cohn focuses on European millennial movements between the eleventh and sixteenth centuries and the story he tells is an indicative example of efforts to establish a historical connection between medieval eschatological ideas and twentieth-century political movements. Cohn's work is important for two reasons. First, he describes the general social conditions of millennial movements. Second, he links together Joachim, Hegel, Marx and totalitarianism. The story he tells then becomes a template for later critiques of revolutionary political ideas.

Cohn outlines the social and political contexts conducive to millennial views. These ideas tend to gain traction in communities that experience extreme unbalance as they transition from agricultural to more industrial economies. Previous social orders, built around normalized relations between peasants and lords, begin to break down as social mobility increases. Resultant tensions are only exacerbated by increasing population growth and movement. Cohn concludes that poverty and oppression do not provide a sufficient seedbed for millennialism. It is the insecurity caused by shifts in social and political relations that must be added in order for apocalyptic movements to emerge.[4]

Or, as Yonina Talmon explains, the 'predisposing factor was often not so much any particular hardship but a markedly *uneven relation between expectations and the means of their satisfaction*'.[5] Radical conditions are required for radical ideas to emerge.

Though Cohn does not make the connection, there is a clear parallel between the sociological analysis of these conditions and Hegel's description of the Rabble. For Hegel,

> The lowest subsistence level, that of a rabble of paupers, is fixed automatically, but the minimum varies considerably in different countries. In England, even the very poorest believe that they have rights; this is different from what satisfies the poor in other countries. Poverty in itself does not turn people into a rabble; a rabble is created only when there is joined to poverty a disposition of mind, an inner indignation against the rich, against society, against the government, etc. (*PR*, §244z: 221)

The Rabble does not form as the result of poverty but through a profound sense of alienation.[6] Throughout the rest of Hegel's *Philosophy of Right*, the Rabble appears as something that must be contained and controlled. Apocalypticism emerges at the moment the Rabble move from feeling alienated by society to desiring the destruction of a society that they have come to see as essentially unjust. For Cohn, these conditions result in irrational, revolutionary political fantasies.

> For where revolutionary chiliasm thrives best is where history is imagined as having an inherent purpose which is preordained to be realised on this earth in a single, final consummation. It is such view of history, at once teleological and cataclysmic, that has been presupposed and invoked alike by the medieval movements described in the present study and by the great totalitarian movements of our day.[7]

This connection between medieval movements and contemporary political fantasies is Cohn's second important contribution. His identification of Joachim, a twelfth-century Calabrian prophet, as a key figure in the genealogy of apocalyptic and revolutionary thought continues to shape the construction of this tradition. Joachim is regarded as one of the most significant apocalyptic figures of the Middle Ages and his division of history into three ages forms the connection between more ancient forms of apocalyptic thinking and contemporary political manifestations of that tradition. He prophesized that the defeat of the Antichrist would bring about a spiritual age.[8] This spiritual period, lived out on earth, would be one in which humanity's relationship to law and God was profoundly transformed.

Cohn thinks Joachim would be dismayed by the political gloss his theological vision has received.

> Horrified though the unworldly mystic would have been to see it happen, it is unmistakably the Joachite phantasy of the three ages that reappeared in, for instance, the theories of historical evolution expounded by the German Idealist philosophers Lessing, Schelling, Fichte and to some extent Hegel; in August Comte's idea of history as an ascent from the theological through the metaphysical up to the scientific phase; and again in the Marxian dialectic of the three stages of primitive communism, class society and a final communism which is to be the realm of freedom and in which the state will have withered away.[9]

His description of the connection between the idea of three ages, modern philosophy and the arrival of 'totalitarian' thought and politics means that the irrationalities of millennialism can also be found in contemporary movements. For Cohn, this irrationality is located both in its ecstatic character and its belief in the ability to bring about unlikely or impossible realities. These fantasies, as Cohn so often calls them, are borne of situations in which there are no options. Only the apocalyptic provides a means of organizing and deploying the energies necessary to create hope where none seems possible.

There are reasons to be suspicious of the neatness of Cohn's historical narrative. In particular, his readiness to link Joachim to every political invocation of the number three has been criticized by historians. Marjoree Reeves and Warwick Gould developed a set of criteria by which to determine whether or not a particular figure could be described as a Joachimist. This criteria centred on the questions 'in what forms did a direct knowledge of Joachim's doctrine reach nineteenth-century thinkers, who made conscious use of it, and how did they handle the sources from which they derived their knowledge?'[10] While these questions might seem simplistic, Reeves and Gould were responding to a post-World War II resurgence of interest in Joachim and his connection to contemporary ideas of progress and revolution.[11] Analysis of this connection was and remains problematic due to similarities between Joachim and other prophetic voices. Especially treacherous, in the opinion of Reeves and Gould, is the lazy connection between tripartite divisions of history and Joachim. Citing John Passmore and Henri de Lubac as examples, they describe how Lessing, Fichte, Schelling, Marx, Comte and Hitler have all been connected to Joachim largely by this unstable bridge.[12]

In both its strengths and weaknesses, Cohn's narrative is an illustrative example of the genealogy connecting medieval apocalyptic movements and contemporary politics. He helpfully identifies commonalities between the religious movements and later secular movements. Less helpfully, the actual connection between the two is asserted rather than substantiated. An affinity of ideas does not necessarily indicate an actual connection. The parallels he identifies are significant, but he fails to provide sufficient analysis of how these ideas travel from marginal medieval sects to Stalin. This connection is further weakened by his broad conception of totalitarianism, which includes Fascism, National Socialism and Communism.[13]

Despite these sometimes tenuous connections, Cohn's narrative has become a touchstone for the critique of political theology (in the widest sense of the term). His work is the precursor to that of Lilla and Gray, though Svenungsson provides a corrective account of the relationship between Joachim, German Romanticism and German Idealism.[14] For contemporary critics of fanatical, apocalyptic or 'political theological' ideas, establishing the link between medieval religion and the desire for fundamental social and political change undermines the latter's legitimacy. This strategy appears even in the work of those otherwise disinterested in such political theological issues. Daniel Bell, for example, in his influential argument that liberal democracy has exhausted all political alternatives, writes,

> From the sixteenth-century chiliast, burning with impatient zeal for immediate salvation, to the twentieth-century American labor leader, sunning himself on the sands of Miami, is a long, almost surrealist jump of history. Yet these are antipodal figures of a curving ribbon which binds all movements that have sought to change the hierarchical social order in society.[15]

So Cohn identifies an affinity between ideas but is unable to establish that this affinity is the result of an underlying intellectual tradition. In some ways, whether or not there is an actual historical connection between Joachim and German Idealism is irrelevant. Later political theologians and their critics both construct a tradition tying together these historical movements. For the purposes of reflecting on apocalyptical political theology, Cohn is an important voice in that process of construction. Though he rushes to lump together disparate forms of political movements under the umbrella of totalitarianism, he correctly identifies an anarchic or revolutionary potential within these apocalyptic ideas. In this sense too, he anticipates Lilla, Gray and Svenungsson in objecting to the anti-liberal aspect of apocalypticism. It would be anachronistic to describe Joachim or other apocalyptic movements of the Middle Ages as anti-liberal, but it is the anti-liberal features of contemporary political movements that he traces back to that period. In the most recent edition of *The Pursuit of the Millennium*, Cohn concludes the book by observing that

> There are aspects of Nazism and Communism alike that are barely comprehensible, barely conceivable even, to those whose political assumptions and norms are provided by a liberal society, however imperfect ... Such beliefs seem grotesque, and when one hears them argued they can give one almost the same uncanny feeling as a paranoiac expounding his private systematised delusion. Yet in reality their strangeness springs from the fact that they are rooted in an earlier and forgotten age. However modern their terminology, however realistic their tactics, in their basic attitudes Communism and Nazism follow an ancient tradition – and are baffling to the rest of us because of those very features that would have seemed so familiar to a chiliastic *propheta* of the Middle Ages.[16]

While Cohn establishes a key narrative describing the transmission of this 'ancient tradition', in that version Hegel occupies a marginal position.[17] It is not clear why Cohn differentiates Hegel from the rest of the German Idealists that he claims are influenced by Joachim. The separation is particularly confusing given Cohn's emphasis on Marx, whose understanding of history is clearly developed in relationship to Hegel's philosophy. Whatever reasons for this aspect of Cohn's argument, other tellings of this story offer Hegel a more central role.

Karl Löwith, for example, offers a similar account, though he is concerned with the philosophy of history rather than millenarian movements. He describes his *Meaning in History* as a succinct summary of the philosophy of history as a 'practice'. Löwith understands this practice to consist of the 'systematic interpretation of universal history in accordance with a principle by which historical events and successions are unified and directed toward an ultimate meaning'.[18] He argues that this reading of history is 'entirely dependent on the theology of history, in particular on the theological concept of history as a history of fulfilment and salvation'.[19] Löwith presents the development of this relation between the philosophy of history and theological ideas of history in reverse from Burkhardt to the biblical text. That long historical journey passes through Hegel.

For Löwith, Hegel obscures the fact that his view of history is really just 'the pattern of the realization of the Kingdom of God, and philosophy as the intellectual worship of a philosophical God'.[20] Hegel's history is theological in two senses. First, it preserves the providential directionality of Christianity. Hegel's 'cunning of reason' guides the actions of individuals, who think they are acting of their own will, in order to achieve the realization of absolute reason. In this sense, Hegel's history is 'secretly' Christian, philosophically papering over theological concepts. Second, the figure of Christ is central to Hegel's history. 'With Christ the time is fulfilled, and the historical world becomes, in principle, perfect, for only the Christian God is truly spirit and at the same time man. This principle constitutes the axis on which turns the history of the world.'[21] For Löwith, the connection between the philosophy of history and theology is so profound that Hegel is actually the last philosopher of history. After Hegel, Christianity's dominance of the organization of history begins to break down. Löwith is critical of Hegel's philosophy, arguing that it problematically assumes the possibility of a speculative philosophy realizing the Christian faith or even the possibility of such a realization.[22]

As Löwith argues, these theological aspects of Hegel's philosophy of history have clear parallels to Joachim. *Meaning in History* provides a more thorough description of Joachim's teaching than Cohn and this thoroughness enables a greater understanding of these parallels as well as the important differences between their conceptions of history. While Hegel may adopt a similar pattern, Joachim's version of the end is both more traditional and more radical. He is more traditional in that he preserves a greater continuity with the Catholic church of his age. At the same time, there is a greater anarchism to his final age, which includes 'the liquidation of preaching and sacraments, the mediating power of which becomes obsolete when the spiritual order is realized which possess knowledge of God by direct vision and contemplation.'[23] Like Cohn, Löwith also explains the connection between these ideas and later political moments.

> The political implications of Joachim's historical prophecies were neither foreseen nor intended by him. Nevertheless, they were plausible consequences of his general scheme; for, when Joachim opened the door to a fundamental revision of a thousand years of Christian history and theology by proclaiming a new and last dispensation, he questioned implicitly not only the traditional authority of the church but also the temporal order. His expectation of a last providential progress toward the fulfilment of the history of salvation within the framework of the history of the world is radically new.[24]

Or again, 'Joachim, like Luther after him, could not foresee that his religious intention – that of desecularizing the church and restoring its spiritual fervor – would, in the hands of others, turn into its opposite: the secularization of the world which became increasingly worldly by the very fact that eschatological thinking about last things was introduced into penultimate matters.'[25] For Löwith, this means that German Idealism, Marxism and the Third Reich are all perversions of the original theological intentions of Joachim, but connected to Joachim nonetheless. This connection is the ground of a new kind of history. This new history is contrasted to the view of traditional theology, represented for Löwith, as for Taubes and Bloch, by Augustine. Traditional Augustinian, that is institutional, Christianity writes history with an eye for self-preservation; put differently, the history of Christianity is the history of the Church. Hegel is a Joachimist in seizing upon a different notion of the history of Christianity.

Cohn and Löwith thus offer two versions of the same underlying narrative: the conversion of theological ideas about history into secular political concepts. In both, this development runs from traditional forms of Christianity to Joachim through Hegel to Marx. Both are critical of this tradition, expressing concerns about these connections between the theological and the political.

This same historical narrative, and much of the same interpretation, is shared by those who find these connections resources for critique and hope rather than causes for concern. The anarchic and revolutionary potential that worries Cohn and Löwith energizes Taubes and Bloch. For this latter pair, Joachim plays a central role in a genealogy that leads to Hegel and then fractures into the two alternatives of Kierkegaard and Marx.

Taubes links Hegel and Joachim early on in his discussion of the nature of eschatology (*OE*, 12). While the narrative is the same, Taubes offers his distinctive apocalyptic interpretation of Hegel. After critiquing both historicism, which he associates with conservative Hegelians, and the 'ideology of progress', Taubes offers a rival understanding – an apocalyptic ontology rooted in both the Joachimist tradition and Hegelian philosophy (*OE*, 13). For this apocalypticism, history is the period that stretches between creation and redemption.

In contrast to Löwith, Taubes places Hegel at the periphery of, if not outside, traditional theological understandings of history.[26] If for Löwith, Hegel was the last philosopher of history because he was the last to maintain the Christian notion of universal history, in Taubes's account Hegel and Marx reinaugurate a form of thinking lost due to Christianity's submission to Aristotelian and Scholastic logic (*OE*, 35). This lost form of thinking had also been preserved by others, which Taubes describes in later sections, but it takes on a new, reinvigorated form in Hegel's philosophy. This form of thought is dialectics. 'Dialectical logic is a logic of history, giving rise to the eschatological interpretation of the world' (*OE*, 35). This connection between eschatology and dialectics is not accidental in Hegel's philosophy, but essential to understanding its implications. 'Apocalypticism and Gnosis form the basis of Hegel's logic, which is often discussed but seldom understood. The connection between apocalyptic ontology and Hegelian logic is neither artificial nor an afterthought' (*OE*, 36). Taubes relies on Bauer's famous work to justify this claim, but subsequent research by Laurence Dickey, Cyril O'Regan and Glenn Alexander Magee has continued to develop the understanding of Hegel's relationship to mystical, gnostic and other heterodox traditions.[27]

Taubes presents two interlinked genealogies: one theological and the other philosophical. Like Löwith, he traces this theological tradition back to biblical texts. Taubes works through Daniel, Jesus, the Gospel of John, Paul, into the early Christian church and Origen.[28] In this early Christian period, the focus is on apocalyptic ideas. Following Origen, however, Augustine introduces a fundamental shift in the Christian church's view of eschatology. 'Instead of the concept of *universal* eschatology, *individual* eschatology emerges. The destiny of the soul is central and the End Time is eclipsed from the last day of human life . . . Universal eschatology, which bears within it the expectation of the Kingdom, from now on appears within the Christian sphere of influence as *heresy*' (*OE*, 80). This first section of his theological genealogy concludes with Joachim, who relocates the promises of universal eschatology to a new age. They are inscribed within history rather than beyond it. Taubes is thus in agreement with Svenungsson's description of Joachim's theology as a form of 'non-eschatological apocalypticism'.[29] This transferral breaks with the underlying Augustinian metaphysics that dominated medieval Christianity's understanding of history.[30] His genealogy resumes with Thomas Müntzer before jumping to Lessing's *Education of the Human Race*, the text that transfers the chiliastic sense of history from Joachim to Hegel and German Idealism. For Taubes, Lessing's text 'is the first manifesto of *philosophical chiliasm*' (*OE*, 86). The end of history, Joachim's third age, becomes Hegel's kingdom of the mind. The left Hegelians, like the Joachimists, devote themselves to the realization of this kingdom of the mind on earth. It is this 'on earth' that essentially links Joachim and Hegel, their mutual 'equation of the history of the spirit with the course of world history' (*OE*, 93).

Taubes then shifts to a philosophical history of the same ideas. This history includes Leibniz, Lessing and Kant before again arriving at Hegel.

> Working from the principles of *love* and *freedom*, which are identical in the essence of the spirit, Joachim and Hegel construct world history from the perspective of an end to fulfilment. They both consider the history of the spirit to be synonymous with the course of history. Just as Joachim's exegesis interprets the metaphysical fate of Christ, including the resurrection, in terms of a historical dialectic, Hegel, too, in his philosophy of religion, builds his dialectical, historical speculations on the foundation of death and resurrection. (*OE*, 162)

Taubes concludes his study with the splitting of the Hegelian legacy by Kierkegaard and Marx. He treats both as valid heirs of Hegel, the former turning Hegel's philosophy inward to the subject, the latter directing it outwards into society.[31]

Bloch, like Taubes, claims a strong connection between Joachim and Hegel. His *Atheism in Christianity* is effectively a political theological genealogy, suggesting that Christianity's destiny is its own end. Again, the links between Joachim, Hegel and Marx are essential to this story. Bloch divides Christianity into two basic tendencies: religion of the On-high and religion from below (*AC*, 13–15). These correspond to two contrary aspects of the biblical text: creation and apocalypse. The task taken up by Bloch is the 'detective work' of discerning which texts and ideas fall into each of these categories (*AC*, 57–70). He runs through an analysis of recent (for him) biblical hermeneutics before beginning his own interpretation of the text. Compared to Taubes, Bloch's treatment of both Joachim and Hegel is brief. His reading of the Old and New Testaments, though, is littered with references to Origen, Joachim, Müntzer, Hegel and Marx. Bloch is less focused on drawing actual, historical connections than Cohn, Löwith and even Taubes. Rather, they are presented as key figures of the tradition of realizing Christianity from below in opposition to that of the On-high.

While Bloch's discussion of Hegel is slightly more sustained than his treatment of Joachim, the specifics of neither are of particular concern to him at this point. Bloch is important here not for his insights into Joachim and Hegel but for the interpretation he offers of the tradition as a whole. Bloch develops a reading quite similar to Taubes, though one that remains implicit underneath his reading of the biblical text. If for Taubes, the essential thesis of this genealogy is the ever-greater realization of the identity of the history of spirit and the history of the world, Bloch's insight is the reframing of the history of theological development given this identity. Rather than dismissing mythology or religion, Bloch returns to it convinced of this identity to reread the tradition of Christianity.

What is clear is that for Taubes and Bloch, as well as many others, Hegel transforms theology in a key way. Whether the genealogy connecting early Christianity, Joachim, Hegel and Marx is regarded as a dangerous source of extreme ideas or a resource for utopian or revolutionary ideas, Hegel is there. For Taubes and Bloch, Hegel is not secularizing theological concepts, but the theological is not unadulterated for having passed through Hegel. If he is to be a resource for the development of an apocalyptic political theology, the precise nature of this transformation needs to be made clear. Only with that understanding in place, can I turn to thinking apocalyptically with Taubes and Malabou.

Representational thought: An outline of Hegel's philosophy of religion

Religion in general, and Christianity in particular, are consistent themes from Hegel's early writings through to the end of his life. Across this body of work, Hegel repeatedly returns to the social and political significance of religion as a distinct mode of consciousness. Religion not only plays a key role as a ground for the emergence of philosophy, it is essential to the development and maintenance of the ethical community or *Sittlichkeit*. This ethical community is the end goal of Hegel's political thought and, in many ways, his whole philosophical project.

In order to understand this wider political significance, it is necessary to understand the difference between religion and philosophy. Religion and philosophy share a truth but differ in the way that truth is thought.[32] Whereas philosophy is concerned with truth in its abstract form, religion grasps the same truth in the form of representations. Philosophy's task is to understand this difference. In this sense, philosophical thinking develops out of religion's self-understanding. By tracing this development, the nature of religion, philosophy and their relation will become clearer.

Hegel explains the relationship between representational thought and philosophy by tracing the movement from art through religion to philosophy. In the *Encyclopaedia* he writes,

> Whereas the vision-method of art, external in point of form, is but subjective production and shivers the substantial content into many separate shapes, and whereas religion, with its separation into parts, opens it out in representation, and mediates what is thus opened out; philosophy not merely keeps them together to make a totality, but even unifies them into the simple spiritual vision, and then in that raises them to self-conscious thought. Such consciousness is thus the intelligible unity (cognized by thought) of art and religion, in which the diverse elements in the content are cognized as necessary, and this necessary as free. (*E3*, §572: 302/554–5)

Here, philosophy is the means of raising religious thought to the level of self-consciousness. What religion considers a narrative of separate moments linked together through a process of historical unfolding, philosophy comprehends conceptually and in its unity. From the perspective of religion, these moments are external. For Hegel, the paradigmatic example is the Incarnation. The birth, life and death of Christ and Pentecost are presented as historical events by Christianity. Philosophically they are representations of necessary modes in the development of self-consciousness. The route for attaining this self-consciousness in relation to religious ideas is explained in the following paragraph of the *Encyclopaedia*. 'Philosophy thus characterizes itself as a cognition of the necessity in the content of the absolute representation', which in the religious representations is presented in the form of 'first the subjective retreat inwards, then the subjective movement of faith and its final identification with the presupposed object' (*E3*, §573: 302/555). The story of the Incarnation is really the story of subjectivity that encounters an externality that drives thought inward, beginning a process that culminates with the realization that the God 'out there' is not external at all.

These dense passages are essential to grasping the relationship between philosophy and religion. As much of recent Hegel literature has argued, his main goal is to demonstrate the necessary shape of thought itself.[33] Religious representation is one specific form of thought, consisting of a distinct configuration of self-consciousness, the subject–object relation and the absolute.

Hegel offers a similar explanation at the beginning of the section on religion in the *Phenomenology*. Earlier sections of the text deal with religion, 'although only from the *standpoint of the consciousness* that is conscious of absolute notion; but absolute notion in and for itself, the self-consciousness of Spirit, has not appeared in those "shapes"' (*PS*, §672: 410/495). To use terminology Hegel employs elsewhere, spirit has appeared as object but not yet as subject. Religion in its broadest Hegelian usage, including natural religion, religion in the form of art and revealed religion, marks a decisive move from relating to the absolute as an externality to an understanding of the absolute as something immanent to the sphere of human activity. Terry Pinkard offers a succinct summary:

> Hegel's point is that we regard as divine, as the object of awe and reverence, that which we take to be the 'ground' of all belief and action, and that which we take to have absolute value; the concept of the divine is not at first

identical with the concept of self-founding humanity, but in working out the insufficiencies of its previous accounts of itself, humanity as 'self-conscious spirit' comes to realize that identity, to see the divine as implicit in its own activity of reflection on what it can take as divine.[34]

Again, the same themes are present: religion regards something as external, other and infinite in relation to the finite self. The narrative core of the *Phenomenology* is the gradual realization of the divine within the subjectivity of human community.

So religion and philosophy share a truth. Philosophy understands this truth conceptually and realizes that the divine and human are identical, while religion thinks this truth through representations. 'Representation' is a translation of the German *Vorstellung*, a term that, as is often the case with Hegel, presents some challenges.[35] Miller, in his translation of the *Phenomenology*, uses 'picture-thinking'. While picture-thinking captures an aspect of representation, it has overly visual connotations. I follow Peter Hodgson, Terry Pinkard and others in preferring representation.[36] This alternative term allows for a wider range of meanings. Representations can be ideas or feelings; indeed, representation in both these senses is essential to understanding religion's role in Hegel's philosophy.

Hegel explains this understanding of *Vorstellung* as a mode of spirit's self-consciousness.

> So far as Spirit in religion *represents* itself to itself, it is indeed consciousness, and the reality enclosed within religion is the shape and the guise of its representational thought. But, in this representational thought, reality does not receive its perfect due, viz. to be not merely a guise but an independent free existence; and, conversely, because it lacks perfection within itself it is a *determinate* shape which does not attain to what it ought to show forth, viz. Spirit that is conscious of itself. If its shape is to express Spirit itself, it must be nothing else than Spirit, and Spirit must appear to itself, or be in actuality, what it is in its essence. (*PS*, §678: 412/497–8)

Here, Hegel specifies two key elements of this discussion of religion. First, as seen above, religion culminates in the recognition of the identity of spirit's existence and self-consciousness. Second, representational form of thought is at least initially an obstacle to this goal. Hegel further elaborates this second point at the outset of the *Encyclopaedia*, explaining that representations share the content of thought, but that this content is presented as an 'admixture' with the form of the representation. Thus, while 'the content is *ob-ject* of our consciousness . . . the *determinacies of these forms join themselves onto the content*; with the result that each of these forms seems to give to rise to a particular ob-ject' (*E1*, §3: 26/44). Manifestations of philosophical truths as external objects and historical events means that these truths have a force that often eludes abstract formulations, but the truths of those objects and events can all too easily be confused with the objects and events themselves. This manifestation as a specific object is both the source of religion's force in society and an obstacle to its elevation to thought.

Conceiving of religion as representation means that Hegel's theological reflections take on a distinct role. Religious thought is representational and his discussion of the crucifixion or Pentecost should be understood within that wider philosophical framework. The importance of representation for interpreting Hegel's philosophy of religion can be hard to keep in mind, as Hegel offers extended theological commentary. Indeed, his writing can give the sense that it is theology that should take priority over philosophy (or that his philosophy is deeply theological). For instance, in the introductory materials of his *Lectures on the Philosophy of Religion*, he states that his philosophy is a continuation of natural theology, before claiming that

> God is the one and only object of philosophy. [Its concern is] to occupy itself with God, to apprehend everything in him, to lead everything back to him, as well as to derive everything particular from God and to justify everything only insofar as it stems from God, is sustained through its relationship with him, lives by his radiance and has [within itself] the mind of God. Thus philosophy *is* theology, and [one's] occupation with philosophy – or rather *in* philosophy – is of itself the service of God. (*LPR1*, 84/6)

Hegel provides proofs for the existence of God and explores the doctrines of the Trinity and Incarnation. From examples such as these, it is clear why more theological interpretations of Hegel have dominated Hegel scholarship. The interpretative direction of any reading ultimately hinges on the degree of emphasis placed on the idea of representation. For in the same section of the *Lectures on the Philosophy of Religion*, Hegel goes on to specify that 'the whole of our treatment – indeed, even immediate religion itself – is nothing other than the *development* of the concept, and that [in turn] is nothing other than the *positing* of what is contained in the concept. This positing constitutes the reality of the concept; it elevates and perfects the concept into the *idea*' (*LPR1*, 110–11/30–1). Hegel makes the same point in the *Philosophy of Right*. In a passage particularly relevant to the political theology being developed here, he writes,

> *The essence of the relation between religion and the state can be determined, however, only if we recall the concept of religion.* The content of religion is absolute truth, and consequently the most elevated of all dispositions is to be found in religion. As intuition, feeling, representational knowledge [vorstellende Erkenntnis], its concern is with God as the unrestricted principle and cause on which everything hangs. It thus involves the demand that everything else shall be seen in this light and depend on it for corroboration, justification, and verification. (*PR*, §270r: 242/417)[37]

This relation between representation and concept, religion and philosophy, is the starting point for thinking about Hegel's implicit political theological method. Representations are one relation to truth and philosophy another. If religion, in the course of representing that truth, comes to understand the dynamics of representation, that effects a transition to philosophy. Philosophy then grasps representations *as* representations, in the unity of content and form.

But why is this necessary? A hasty reading might conclude that Hegel is offering an evolutionary account of thought. People were once religious but now, having cast aside useless representations, they can emerge into philosophical light. Yet it is clear that Hegel means something else. Representations continue to be necessary, as the above discussion of their political significance indicates. Understanding this significance, and further grasping the relation between philosophy and religion, requires delving deeper into the nature and function of representations.

Hegel's implicit political theology

Thus far, I have shown Hegel's understanding of religion in relationship to philosophy, emphasizing the importance of his concept of representation. When Hegel discusses religion as representation, he argues that it is both necessary and problematic. It is necessary in that it facilitates the development of self-consciousness, but problematic in that the representations can be confused with the truth they represent. Up to this point, Hegel's insights are helpful for thinking about political theology in the broad sense of political religion.[38] Religious ideas (as well as experiences and affects) are a form of relating to truth and that relationship has political significance. That significance is distinct from, but still related to, the more narrow sense of political theology that I am developing here. I am claiming that beneath Hegel's wider philosophy of religion, there is an implicit political theology. Still rooted in the notion of religion as representation, this more subterranean political theology takes theology as a way of engaging the world.

While there has been a significant amount of work on Hegel's notion of representation, this has focused on religion in isolation from politics. In particular, Malcolm Clark's *Logic and System* and Kathleen Dow Magnus's *Hegel and Symbolic Mediation* both provide a helpful analysis of the function of representation in Hegel's philosophy. Yet, Clark's systematic overview leaves little space for an in-depth consideration of religion, and Magnus concentrates on theological elements without connecting them to politics.[39] Thomas Lewis provides the connection between religion as representation, on the one hand, and philosophy and the state, on the other, but is less concerned with an analysis of the dynamics of representation itself. Taken together, though, Clark, Magnus and Lewis will help clarify the central role of representation in Hegel's implicit political theology.

Clark, Magnus and Lewis are all agreed that representation plays an ongoing and central role in Hegel's philosophical system. To reiterate an earlier point, thought does not dispense with representation after arriving at philosophy. As Clark shows, this creates a tension between a system that is expressed through representations, the 'other' of thought, while simultaneously systematizing the functioning of representations.

> Hence the paradox of Hegel's system: logical thought is at once the whole of philosophy and but a part of it. In Hegel's own terms, logical thought contains its other. That is, true philosophical thought *contains* all reality and is not simply opposed and applied to it. Nevertheless, thought contains reality as its *other*, not merely as a 'confused thought', but as that which reduces the system of pure thought to one part of a greater whole.[40]

Representations and philosophy as pure thought are parts of a whole, a whole that philosophy thinks in its totality, but also a whole that contains the other of pure thought. It is a difficult balance to hold – philosophy thinks the dynamics of thought in its abstractness, comprehending that which it cannot reduce to itself.

Magnus confronts the same problem. Her exploration of representations is written in response to Derrida's critique of Hegel's supposed elision of sensuousness. The specifics of that critique are not key for this present discussion, so suffice it to say that Derrida is concerned that the material ground and ambiguity of any metaphor are domesticated by Hegel's treatment of metaphor.[41] This critique is frequently lodged against Hegel: all of reality is reduced to abstract conceptuality. For Derrida, this allows Hegel to hide 'a fundamental contradiction: self-grounding spirit negates the sensuous element of reality in the same moment that it uses it'.[42] Here, there is a parallel between Clark and Magnus; both explore the ways in which Hegel depicts representations leading to a concept which comprehends that act of representation in its essentiality. While this comprehension places the concept 'above' representation, it does not remove the need for representations. So spirit does not need to negate the sensuous element of reality but can grasp that sensuous element in its otherness to pure thought. That does not presuppose a rejection of that sensuousness, though it does transform the relationship. What both Clark and Magnus show is that Hegel's philosophy has to be read dynamically. It is thought in motion. Any argument that claims representation is somehow overcome or left behind is guilty of freezing Hegel's thought in the moment of the concept rather than continuing to follow the trajectory of pure thought from its abstractness back to its interaction with sensuousness. It is for this reason that the *Phenomenology* can be read as loop. Its conclusion is not an end, but now enables the reader to return to the beginning to comprehend the journey of self-consciousness from the perspective of spirit (*PS*, §20: 11/24).

Put another way, the persistence of representational thinking is sometimes overlooked in thinking about Hegel's understanding of philosophy. As Clark argues,

> Before it can rise above the limitations of mere consciousness and become the infinite, self-relating unity its concept supposes it to be, it must appear to itself as outside of itself. It must, in other words, take on various symbolic

forms. *But even after it recognizes its object as itself in absolute religion, spirit remains in need of the symbolic.* Its discovery of its self-identity does not delete its internal difference; its being as spirit eliminates neither its experience as consciousness nor its need for symbolic representation.[43]

Clark describes this necessity of representation as the return to representation: 'If philosophical thought be seen as abandoning its stake in the familiar world, it is only in order to return to a profounder experience of it. The transition from Vorstellung to thought is itself but an abstraction of the concrete movement which includes no less a return from thought to Vorstellung.'[44]

One of the continuing roles of representation is to provoke thought. In Magnus's reading of Hegel, 'symbols are in a certain sense the negative of thought; they are the material thought must transform in order to be thought'.[45] Or as Clark claims, 'Vorstellung must be seen both as thought and as the "other" of thought.'[46] This otherness is not an externality, though it initially manifests as such. In terms of religion, representations begin as the other in the form of the divine object, then as divine subject, before absolute religion's realization that the consciousness of divine subjectivity is a moment of self-consciousness. This process thus represents spirit's self-alienation into the form of another subject, to which it relates. This transition marks the move from a divine object to divine subject, which prepares the grounds for recognizing the identity of human and divine subjectivity – the becoming substance of subject. Yet all the while, otherness is maintained. The transition is not one of otherness to sameness, but otherness is misidentified as external, to the recognition of otherness as interior.[47]

These statements should be read in light of Hegel's claim that spirit is the unity of identity and difference. Symbolic thought is not completely eliminated in the course of this process. Rather it is maintained as a negativity necessary for the continual activity that spirit *is*. As Magnus explains, spirit

> never gets to the point of being able to 'be' in a simple, immediate, or nondifferentiated way. Spirit's identity *depends upon* the real difference it bears within itself. Its identification is only as true as its difference . . . Spirit never gets to the point of being able to deny or cancel its intrinsic negativity because this negativity is essential to what spirit is. It cannot forget or disregard its internal difference because this difference is the source

and substance of its life. For Hegel, spirit, the ultimate truth of reality, is something that both is there *and* something that *makes itself* be there; it is both immediate and mediated, self-identical and self-differentiating. Spirit is the activity that unites these two dimensions of reality.[48]

This understanding of representation is the ground of Magnus's rejection of Derrida's accusation that Hegel ultimately resolves every negative into a positive. Derrida's reading is in one sense true – Hegel does have a complete system which one could regard as resolving every negative, but only if 'every negative' is taken to refer to contradictions emerging within the categories of thought. 'Both alienation and totality, identity and difference, remain a part of what spirit is. Spirit reconciles these two sides, but, as Hegel points out over and over again, spirit is the continual activity of this reconciliation, not merely the end result of it.'[49] This understanding still allows for negativity, it just comprehends the way negativity 'works' in the broader philosophical system. As I will argue in my reading of Malabou, this insight parallels Hegel's argument for the necessity of contingency and the refutation of critiques of Hegel as a totalizing thinker. Representation marks one of the points at which Hegel asserts the identity of identity and difference: 'the difference intrinsic to the symbol remains within spirit as part of its act of self-identification. Logically speaking, there can be no self-identifying spirit that does not also contain and bear difference within it.'[50] This further clarifies the relationship between representation and philosophy. Magnus and Clark show the ongoing necessity of representation. As Magnus writes, 'we can come to see how the contradictoriness, negativity, and "otherness" inherent to spirit is less an impediment to spirit's self-realization than the condition for it.'[51]

If Magnus and Clark track the mechanics of representation, Lewis draws out the key social and political consequences of this approach to understanding religion. For Lewis, the continuing need for representations is primarily related to the ultimate goal of Hegel's philosophy: the cultivation of an ethical society and the strengthening of the state. Such a society and state requires social cohesion, and religion can be one source of this communal bond.[52] 'Hegel argues that although religious representations do not cognize the truth as adequately as philosophical thinking does, these religious representations are still capable of instilling and expressing the reconciliation necessary for social cohesion.'[53]

The external form that complicates the apprehension of truth is necessary for the cultivation of a bond that goes beyond abstract thought to a form of feeling (*PR*, §270; 244/418).[54] Their externalized form makes representations more accessible than philosophy's abstract formulations, as they are ingrained in rituals and impact communities on an emotional level.[55] It is representations, not abstract thought, that provide the 'existential matrix' of life.[56]

For Lewis, the social function of religion eclipses the traditional sense of a belief in a more or less stable set of dogmatic beliefs.[57] This understanding of religion as representation means that 'God' no longer need refer to a transcendent being and that the question of the existence of God becomes mostly irrelevant. Indeed, what Hegel conceptualizes as religion need not be what is typically conceived of as a religious community or tradition.[58] John Burbidge makes a similar case for an expanded sense of religion. 'It is potentially a universal phenomenon that singular, historical incarnation passes away and becomes universal. So Jesus is now only one among many – the Koran; the founding of Israel, Sri Aurobindo; the Jacobite revolution (or the Paris commune); nature's struggle for survival; the traditional Ojibwa hunter, smoking a peace pipe over the bear he has just killed; Freud's therapies . . . Each has become the focus of stories, because in each all the transcendent and ultimate has become actual.'[59] In this wider notion of religion, God is the representational name of the unity of being and thought.[60] Hegel moves from the divine to the divine concept, claiming that 'this movement of thinking itself, of the concept itself, is that for which we should have the utmost awe. It is at the heart of, in some sense, everything and consequently is appropriately referred to as "divine."'[61] The resulting philosophy of religion develops 'a conception of religion that supports social solidarity for the broader populace'.[62]

Together Magnus, Clark and Lewis provide a description of Hegel's understanding of religion as a politically charged form of thought that enables a different mode of relating to the truth of philosophy. This understanding sheds new light on Hegel's own use of theological concepts, but it still leaves open the question of constructive engagements with those representations. If philosophy can explain how representations have meaning within a community, can it also use representations to make new meaning?

Philosophy and the return to representation

In the course of the discussion, I have argued that representational forms of thought are both necessary and problematic. Representations tend to become divorced from the act of representing undertaken by the subject. This subject then relates to its own representations as external objects rather than tools for reflective practices. 'Religion thus effects a double alienation: The self is alienated from what it conceives to be absolute and from the actual world. The revealed religion partially overcomes this alienation in the cultus, but precisely insofar as it completes this overcoming, it passes from religion into philosophy.'[63]

This transition from religion to philosophy involves a kind of cancellation but also preserves representational thought.[64] Having arrived at philosophy, representations are now viewed in their appropriate light, but continue to function as a moment of that philosophy. As Hegel explains in the *Phenomenology*, spirit maintains the universal determinations of consciousness, self-consciousness and reason, but as moments of the unity that *is* spirit.

> Religion presupposes that these have run their full course and is their *simple* totality or absolute self. The course traversed by these moments is, moreover, in relation to religion, not to be represented as occurring in time. Only the totality of spirit is in time, and the 'shapes', which are 'shapes' of the totality of *spirit*, display themselves in a temporal succession; for only the whole has true actuality and therefore the form of pure freedom in face of an 'other', a form which expresses itself as time. (*PS*, §679: 413/498)

Understanding this relationship, philosophy preserves representational thinking as part of the whole it comprehends.

There are two aspects to the preservation of representational thinking: the representations themselves are preserved as well as representational thinking as such. As Magnus and Clark argue, representations as the other of thought, trouble abstract conceptuality, continuing to drive its movement. It is at this point that the inventive possibilities of Hegel's implicit political theology become clear. It is not only that representations are externalized truths that philosophy can understand as part of self-consciousness. Philosophy can continue to use those representations and engage in other forms of representational thinking.

Put more succinctly, philosophical thought can return to representations and experiment with ever new ways of thinking the world.

The return to representations is not something that Hegel discusses in his major works or lectures. He does, however, explore this idea in his response to Karl Friedrich Göschel, the author of *Aphorisms on Ignorance and Absolute Knowledge* (*Aphorismen über Nichtwissen und absolutes Wissen*).[65] Published in 1829, Göschel argues against the 'ignorance' of Jacobi, the theology of feeling found in those like Schleiermacher and the varieties of theological rationalism that emerge after Kant. While these specifics are not relevant to the present task, Hegel's review of the book provides some interesting reflections on the nature of Hegel's understanding of religion.

In the initial sections of the review, Hegel summarizes the main features of the book, occasionally pausing to offer remarks on the relationship between religion and philosophy. These comments are similar to the arguments found in the *Phenomenology*, the *Encyclopaedia* and the *Lectures on the Philosophy of Religion*. He then addresses a question raised by Göschel on the point of the relation of Hegel's philosophy to scripture.

> The question, namely, is whether this philosophy would not gain in definiteness and clarity in its progress if it were to attach itself more decisively to the Word of God out of which it has developed; if it were to proceed more definitely and in name (i.e., with the naming of names) from the sin which has become manifest to it as abstraction, without the presupposition of which no understanding of the world is possible, without the recognition of which no self-knowledge is possible, and without the transcendence of which no knowledge of God is possible. According to this philosophy itself, it is not thought but representation which is highest. (*RG*, 1:389/377)

Affirming this higher role of representation would allow Hegel's philosophy more clearly to demonstrate its connection to scripture. Hegel acknowledges there is some truth to Göschel's claim, but quickly moves to refute it. The passage warrants citing at length,

> The author has touched on an interesting point – *the general transition from representation to the concept and from the concept to representation, a two-way transition which is already present in scientific mediation*, and which here meets with the demand that it be also expressed in the scientific exposition . . . The present reviewer may, at least with a view to

apologizing for the imperfection of his works in this respect, recall that it is precisely from the beginning, to which the author as well refers, which chiefly imposes the necessity of holding more fixedly to the concept which is expressed in pure thoughts, and which has often been won in hard battle with representation. This at once means the necessity of attaching to the course of the concept's development, of holding oneself more strictly in its tracks so as to win self-assurance with respect to it, and of holding off by force the distractions which the manysidedness makes the danger of yielding something in the methodological strictness of thought too close for comfort. *But greater firmness attained in the movement of the concept will license greater unconcern before the temptation of representation, and at once allow representation to breathe more freely within the overlordship [Herrschaft] of the concept; and to do so with as little fear of its consequences as concern over its [internal] coherence, which – in relation to presupposed faith – need not prove itself free.* (*RG*, 1:390/378–9)[66]

Hegel thus argues that his presentations of the relationship between representation and concept have been pedagogically necessary for the historically situated task of elevating humanity to conceptual thought. As Clark Butler explains in his commentary on Hegel's relationship with Göschel, 'Once the transition from representation to the concept has been made, an enlivening transition from the concept back to representation is permissible. Freer reign can be given for representation to develop under the ascendancy of the concept.'[67]

Shortly after Hegel clarifies the two-way transition between representation and concept, he addresses a common flaw in the critiques of speculative philosophy, namely their one-sided determination.

> Such determinations, as previously indicated, are in part called forth by falsification of the speculative fact and put forth as a complaint against that fact. But they are also in a part advanced as assertions against this fact. Such one-sided determinations, [viewed] as bound up with the matter, are moments of its concept which thus arise, in the course of the exposition of it, in their momentary positions. *The negation of these moments must be exhibited in the immanent dialectic of the concept.* This negation, insofar as such moments have been posited as objections, assumes the guise of their refutation. (*RG*, 1:392/380–1, emphasis mine)

Not only does this reaffirm the emphasis on the dynamic immanent movement of the dialectic, but it also provides a basis for extending Hegel's argument further. The cessation of movement at the concept allows a one-sided determination of the concept itself. Conceptual thought must return to the level of representation in order to be actualized. The abstraction of the concept is not final, but generative.

Here, it is possible to push past Hegel's own stated conclusions. In returning to representations the concept not only allows 'greater unconcern', it enables the transformation of representations. As is clear in his review, Hegel does not see a great need for revising those representations. He is primarily concerned with affirming Göschel's position that scripture may be used to cultivate philosophical thought. I am claiming that it is possible to go further: not only should conceptual thought return to representations, but these representations can be transformed. These kinds of transformations are implicit within Hegel's formulations of Christian doctrines such as sin or the Trinity. Another way of expressing Hegel's heterodoxy is to view these doctrines as transformed by the return from the concept. These transformations are politically significant as convictions about justice, social order and rights mutate in the representational laboratory of political theology.[68] Having understood the necessity of representations, it becomes necessary, as Magnus argues, '*to think through the representations given to us*, regardless of what they are. Only in this way can they become our *own*. Only in this way can they be transformed from something *imposed upon* us to something *determined by* us. To use Hegel's terminology: only this way does spirit's abstract being *in itself* become *for itself* and free.'[69]

Conclusion

Hegel has two interrelated political theologies and understanding religion as representation is essential to both. First, there is a broad political theology that argues for the importance of religion to the life of the state. Second, there is an implicit, narrow political theology that develops an understanding of the relationship between religion and philosophy, allowing for philosophy to inventively and experimentally use theological ideas to think the world.

In the genealogies of political theological themes offered by Cohn, Löwith, Taubes and Bloch, Hegel plays a key role. Something significant happens to theology in Hegel and that transformation remains significant for reflecting on politics today. This transformation involves conceptions of history and the development of dialectical thought, but there is also a shift in the way that Hegel uses theology. Theology becomes a way of philosophically thinking the world. Though it requires pushing past Hegel's own conclusions, I argue that there is a way of reading Hegel as experimenting with theological concepts. That experimentation, along with Schmitt's sociology of concepts, is at the centre of a narrow form of political theology that engages in an inventive use of theology to critique the world. While neither Taubes nor Bloch appeal to Hegel's concept of representation, they engage in this form of experimentation. They both express a lack of concern before representations. Theological concepts become tools of thought, critique and revolution. Both Taubes and Bloch trace the malleability of religious doctrines and then transform Jewish and Christian teachings in order to express more clearly the insights they find in the Hegelian system. Of course, this reformulation is not all they accomplish and both Taubes and Bloch express wariness of Hegelian philosophy.

At the conclusion of the first chapter, I noted three persistent questions that confront apocalyptic political theology. First, there is the issue of political theological method and the relationship between theology and philosophy. This chapter has offered an answer to that question, finding in religious representations the impetus towards philosophical thought as well as the persistent 'other of thought'. Political theology, as a discourse of limits, beginnings and endings, is concerned with the boundaries of what can be defended. In theological concepts such as apocalypse, philosophy finds an other that pushes it to think anew. Thus, in keeping with the opening call for a desecularizing political theology, there is no hierarchy between theology and philosophy. Both are useful for critiquing the world.

That leaves the remaining questions of novelty, trauma and pessimism. If philosophy can return to religious representations and creatively engage them to think the world, how can apocalypticism offer the possibility of an immanent novelty? Taubes will begin to answer these questions, but the possibility of newness is closely followed by the shadow of destruction. Reading Taubes together with Malabou then, will provide insights on the particular form of hope that accompanies the trauma of the end of the world.

3

Spiritual disinvestment: Taubes, Hegel and apocalypticism

Jacob Taubes offers a prime example of what it means to experiment with theological concepts in the sense described by Hegel. His political theology offers a detailed engagement with the histories of theology and philosophy, excavating the sites where concepts have been used and finding within those histories the materials for creative critique. Two key aspects of this political theology consolidate themes developed in my earlier discussions of the nature of the world and Hegel: the notion of working with theological materials and his definition of apocalypse. The first develops the narrow political theological method, as Taubes offers an apocalyptic critique that is immanent and desecularizing. The second expounds the consequences of thinking apocalyptically. Taubes is less convinced of the world's fragility than Schmitt, but more convinced that signs of that fragility should be welcomed. Confronted with the creative potential of destruction, Taubes calls for a disinvestment from the world.

In order to explore Taubes's political theological method and its implications for thinking the apocalypse, I will first outline Taubes's understanding of the relationship between theology and philosophy. In the course of this discussion, the connections to my reading of Hegel in the previous chapter will become clear. This connection opens up an exploration of other Hegelian themes in Taubes's work, including the relationship between the concept and nature, and the ways that Taubes draws out apocalyptic themes in Hegel. Having considered Taubes and this apocalyptic Hegel, I then turn to the nature of Taubes's apocalypticism and the way that his political theology can be read against critiques of apocalyptic thinking. Taubes distrusts the hopes of this world and offers a thoroughgoing negation of everything as it is. This uncompromising negativity recalls anxieties about anti-liberal tendencies of apocalypticism.

Exploring these tendencies in Taubes, alongside Hegel and Schmitt, begins to clarify why Taubes rejects hope in gradual progress or even messianic deliverance. It also illuminates the similarities and differences of his political theology and the work of Schmitt. Taubes defined his political theology against Schmitt's conservative approach and Schmitt will frequently appear as a foil.[1] Finally, I consider parallels between Taubes and transcendental materialist readings of Hegel. These similarities provide the grounds for reading Taubes through Malabou in the subsequent chapter.

An introduction to Taubes

Jacob Taubes was a German philosopher and scholar of religion.[2] In addition to his sole monograph, *Occidental Eschatology*, he wrote a number of articles and essays, many of which were posthumously collected in the volume *From Cult to Culture*. He is perhaps most well-known for his posthumously published series of lectures, *The Political Theology of Paul*. In the introductory remarks to the German edition of *From Cult to Culture*, Assmann, Assmann and Hartwich place Taubes in a distinct line of twentieth-century German cultural criticism, fostered by the Jewish tradition, that draws on the works of Kant, Hegel and Marx. This tradition includes Benjamin, Marcuse, Adorno and Steiner (a tradition that could be expanded to include Bloch).[3] What unites these figures is the development of a form of Jewish thought that is radical, secular and messianic.[4]

Taubes is part of this tradition, but not fully. Unlike the others, he is relatively unconcerned with aesthetics. While he does engage with surrealism, on the whole he remains focused on cult rather than culture.[5] And while Taubes's political theology is not sectarian, it is certainly not secular in any straightforward sense. Anson Rabinbach's description of Bloch's and Benjamin's philosophies as 'both secular and theological' and representing 'an intellectualist rejection of the existing order of things', could equally apply to Taubes.[6] Indeed, the troubling relationship between the secular and theological is one of Taubes's central contributions to political theology.

As might be expected of a Jewish intellectual during this period, his thought is shaped by his experiences during the Second World War. One motivation for the reconfiguration of messianism was an attempt to resist growing Jewish accommodation to German culture, the looming Nazi threat and the aftermath of the War. These concerns are fundamental to Taubes's political theology. He aims to uncover something repressed within his religious tradition, a radicalism lost as religion became a cultural form like any other, and he does so in a context where he is coming to grips with significant intellectual complicity with National Socialism. As he says in a 1952 letter to Armin Mohler, he cannot comprehend 'that both C.S. [Carl Schmitt] and M.H. [Martin Heidegger] welcomed the National Socialist "revolution" and went along with it and it remains a problem for me that I cannot just dismiss by using catchwords such as vile, swinish . . . What was so "seductive" about National Socialism?' (*CS*, 19–20).[7] This dismay is an important motivation in Taubes's desire to reignite an alternative, apocalyptic passion.

The preface to the English edition of *From Cult to Culture* notes that Taubes's exploration of these issues is complicated by his tendency to address specific points in contemporaneous, ongoing debates. Despite the occasional nature of much of this work, clear themes emerge: a dissatisfaction with the world as it is, a complex evaluation of the legacy of modernity and a tension between the desire for the end of the world and a wish to avoid slipping into nihilism. These themes all appear in *Occidental Eschatology*. As seen in Chapter 2, Taubes connects Hegel to Joachim de Fiore, arguing that Hegelian philosophy is the modern expression of Gnostic and apocalyptic theological traditions: '[a]pocalypticism and Gnosis form the basis of Hegel's logic, which is often discussed but seldom understood. The connection between apocalyptic ontology and Hegelian logic is neither artificial nor an afterthought' (*OE*, 36).[8] Taubes's approach is a return to these theological concepts or, to use the Hegelian language developed in the previous chapter, a return to representations. This return is not an attempt to conserve a sacred tradition, but to redeploy these representations anew in an effort to offer a critique of the world.

As already noted, this redeployment of theological concepts means Taubes is neither theological nor secular, but offers a desecularizing political theology. In a 1954 essay on Karl Barth and dialectics, Taubes claims philosophy cannot 'accept the self-interpretation of theology', but 'can try to understand the meaning of divine revelation'.[9] Doing so allows theology to 'serve as a concrete negation of a status quo that the dictatorship of common sense accepts as man's permanent situation'.[10] For Taubes, this concrete negation is theology's central task:

> Theological language is born out of the dualism between the ideal standard and the status quo of man's situation. *So long as this cleavage is not healed, there remains a legitimate task for theology.* But the language of theology itself reflects the cleavage between the ideal and the ruling norms of man and society. In the moment that the ideal standards that theology has put as a judgment upon man and society are realized in the course of human history, the task of theology has been fulfilled . . . *The development of theological language is, therefore, relevant for a philosophy that studies the stages of man's self-realization.*[11]

Not only does Taubes recognize theology's task as concrete negation, he understands the need for the development of theological language and avoids advocating a retrieval of lost theological meanings or pure origins uncontaminated by the developments of modernity. While he describes Jewish and Gnostic apocalyptic thought as tainted by Hellenization, there is no simple process of recovery or return. In his comments on the 're-' of the Reformation and Renaissance, as well as his comments on Kierkegaard's recovery of the early church and Marx's retrieval of the Greek polis, Taubes 'transposes' history into the future.

In the same essay on Barth's theology, Taubes poses the question of the relationship between theology and philosophy and again puts forward a Hegelian position:

> It is true that (as Barth once remarked) all philosophy has its origin in theology. It is, however, possible to turn around the relation between theology and philosophy. Dialectical theology can point to the development of history from theology to philosophy: theology is the origin. But an equally legitimate interpretation of this sequence might be given from the other side: philosophy is the end. If I emphasize the origin, then the later development takes the form of gradual alienation and eclipse of origin. If I emphasize the end, the process of development takes the form of gradual fulfilment. The scheme is the same in both interpretations. At no point does the premise of Barth's pantheology contradict the *scheme* of Hegel's dialectic.[12]

Taubes thus anticipates more recent pronouncements by Žižek and Gianni Vattimo that Christian theology births modernity.[13] Whereas Barth presents this story in an Oedipal light, with philosophy forgetting its origins and returning to kill the father, the Taubesian interpretation sees the story as one of the passing of generations. It is not that philosophy has to return and kill the father, it is simply the case that as one generation is born another dies away.

Taubes presents a similar perspective on the relationship between theology and philosophy in a later essay on 'The Dogmatic Myth of Gnosticism'. Here, he argues for the importance of an allegorical reading of myth. He cautions against a narrow understanding of allegorical readings of myth as simply a form of archaic exegesis. In a wider understanding, allegorical interpretation 'becomes a vehicle for a new understanding of reality that is differentiated from archaic myth. Allegory is a form of translation. *It translates mythic forms, names and the destinies of mythic narrative into concepts.* In allegorical interpretation . . . the mythic template gains a new content.'[14] Moving on to a later Greek, philosophical allegorical interpretation, he argues that this reading 'acts not only as the rationalizing exegesis of archaic myth, but itself turns into the form of representation of a "new" myth'.[15] Continuing the reproductive metaphor, the transformation of the mythic forms, names and destinies is the product of new couplings, diversifying the gene pool. Or more strongly, it is a mutation, the result of the mutual contamination of philosophy and theology.[16]

This emphasis on philosophical interpretations of theological concepts returns to what Agata Bielik-Robson describes as a 'positive, theological evaluation of modernity'[17]:

> Modernity, the age of enlightenment, man's rational empowerment and emancipation, is thus to be defended against itself, against its inner dangers that threaten to overthrow the promise it gave at its onset. The theological definition of modernity, therefore, wholly depends on the right understanding of this precarious promise, which is always threatened to disappear in the course of modern history: the messianic promise of a universal liberation, that is, leaving all the Egypts of this world for good, with its hierarchies, glories of domination and self-renewing cycles of power.[18]

Rather than offering a theological rejection of modernity, as is the case of many of his contemporaries, Taubes offers a theological defence of modernity against its own worst tendencies. This defence of modernity requires the process of developing a new theological language, one which is 'materialist, messianic, historical, emancipatory, focused on the finite life, immanentist and this-worldly'.[19]

It is not only Taubes's Jewish contemporaries who develop theological rejections of modernity; his defence of modernity is one of the points of contrast between his and Schmitt's political theologies. If Schmitt inquires about 'the theological potentials of legal concepts', Taubes looks for 'the political potentials in the theological metaphors' (*PT*, 69). While Schmitt views the secularization of theological concepts as a negative development, Taubes sees his version of political theology as necessary for the development of theological thought. There is a parallel here to Taubes's discussion of Barth. Schmitt is like Barth in offering an understanding of the progression from religion to secular thought as a loss or corruption, whereas Taubes sees philosophy as a *telos* of theological thought. Put another way, Schmitt sees the separation of legal concepts from their theological origins as an abuse of theological ideas. Taubes's political theology provides a constructive method of philosophical engagement with religious texts and history. He sees his work, not as philosophical theology, but as a working with 'theological materials' (*PT*, 69). Taubes argues it is advantageous to experiment more openly with theological materials and rejects Schmitt's claim that theology provides the rules for such experimentation.

As already established, Taubes views religious language, and thus apocalypse, as representations, capable of development and novel usage. Like Hegel, Taubes does not view this development as secularization. While Taubes does not use Hegelian terminology, this development is an immanentization, a revisiting of religious representations from the perspective of the concept. In his view, any attempt at nostalgically employing archaic religious or mythic language is doomed to failure. 'Insofar as the mythical discourse on the gods preserves itself as residues and remainders in the accounts of monotheistic religions of revelation, it retains the weight of a poetic metaphor only. Its power or legitimacy as a religious expression, however, has wasted away.'[20] With the exceptions of Barth and Tillich, Taubes is of the opinion that theology is no longer practiced by the theologians. In his letter to Mohler, he criticizes the theologians of the day and advocates for a wider understanding of theology.

'What is there today that is not "theology" (apart from theological claptrap)? Is Ernst Jünger less a "theologian" than Bultmann or Brunner? Kafka less so than Karl Barth?' (CS, 22). In Taubes's view, much of what passes for theology is precisely this poetic metaphor, trading platitudes for power and legitimacy.

Rather than remaining in this mode of theology, Taubes seeks to renew the development of religious language in order to address the cleavage between humanity as it is and as it could be. In this context, apocalypse is transferred from a chronological feature of revelation, to the revealed temporal and political logic that drives the work of Hegel, Kierkegaard and Marx. As Mike Grimshaw writes, a key question for Taubes is 'how is political theology as a movement to be rethought, for within such a redefinition apocalypse becomes a type of judgment central to any political theology'.[21] Taubes's insight, in Grimshaw's view, is that 'in post/modernity theology, if not sectarian, is the self-reflexivity of modern thought that thinks the unthought of both secularity and "religion"'.[22] This unthought is that which unites secularism and religion in their opposition.

Taubes and Hegel

In more Hegelian terms, Taubes offers a model of theological reflection in which thought has returned from the concept. Understanding Taubes's transformation of the relationship between secularism and religion through Hegel further clarifies Taubes's political theological method. The Hegelian dialectic works by uncovering the unthought commonality that manifests itself as opposition. With regard to religion, this unthought consists in at least three themes. First, as seen in the *Phenomenology of Spirit*'s treatment of superstition and enlightenment, both reason and faith are concerned with pure thought, but in their simplistic forms understand this pure thought in opposition to their self-consciousness. In the initial stages of the analysis of the relationship between Enlightenment and superstition, Hegel argues,

> [The absolute being of the believing consciousness] is pure thought, and pure thought posited within itself as an object or as *essence*; in the believing consciousness, this *intrinsic being* of thought acquires at the same time

for consciousness that is *for itself*, the form – but only the empty form – of objectivity; it has the character of something presented to consciousness. To pure insight, however, since it is pure consciousness from the side of the *self that is for itself*, the "other" appears as something *negative* of *self-consciousness*. (*PS*, §552: 336/299)

This critique of faith, in the simplified form of superstition, is developed in the process of Enlightenment's break from the myth of pure insight.

> One part of this process is the differentiation in which intellectual insight confronts its own self as *object*; so long as it persists in this relationship it is alienated from itself. As pure insight it is devoid of all content; for nothing else can become its content because it is the self-consciousness of the category. But since in confronting the content, pure insight at first knows it only as a *content* and not yet as its own self, it does not recognize itself in it. (*PS*, §548: 333–4/404–5)

Both Enlightenment and superstition mistake their content for something external to self-consciousness, rather than their own self.

Second, there is the representational form of religion. Religion tends to lose sight of its form while secularity forgets the necessity of representations for the actualization of concepts. As Hegel explains the representational form of thought falls short of speculative thought, 'it has the content, but without its necessity... Since this consciousness, even in its thinking, remains at the level of picture-thinking, absolute being is indeed revealed to it, but the moments of this being, on account of this [empirically] synthetic presentation, partly themselves fall asunder so that they are not related to one another through their own notion . . . relating itself to it only in an external manner' (*PS*, §771: 465–6/560). The paragraphs following this one, demonstrate how this transition in form, from representation to concept, is accomplished through representational thinking.

Third, the truth of religion is often forgotten by religion itself. Put in a more Taubesian way, the truth of religion is no longer thought by religion in its predominant institutional or cultural forms. While Taubes does not make use of Hegelian language when describing his political theological method, his work enacts a transition from representation to concept by thinking the unthought of both religion and secularism from the perspective of a philosophy which experiments with religious materials.

Taubes refers to the resulting perspective as a 'transcendental eschatology'. This form of eschatology 'requires that everything be grounded in *subjectivity*, making this the condition of the possibility of cognition, as self-knowledge, self-apocalypse' (*OE*, 132). This eschatology is an internalization that resists depoliticization. 'All apocalypses associated with history or natural occurrences, all sounding of trumpets and symbols of wrath, all global conflagrations and new parodies are only *coup de theatre* and parables; they are simply the orchestral arrangement for the one real apocalypse: the Apocalypse of Man' (*OE*, 132). This passage captures the essential elements of Taubesian political theology – the immanentization of apocalyptic ideas accomplished by the treatment of religious ideas as representations.

Yet, this immanentization of apocalyptic ideas renders these ideas potentially unsuitable for their original ecclesial contexts. One of Taubes's central contributions to political theology is his proposal of expanding the context of theology.

> Perhaps the time has come when theology must learn to live without the support of canon and classical authorities and stand in the world without authority. Without authority, however, theology can only teach by an indirect method. Theology is indeed in a strange position because it has to prove its purity by immersing itself in all the layers of human existence and cannot claim for itself a special realm . . . Theology must remain incognito in the realm of the secular and work for the sanctification of the world.[23]

Theology, stripped of its customary ecclesial authority, must seek out new, 'incognito', activities. As Tina Beattie puts it, theology moves from the queen of the sciences to the court jester, disrupting the forms of hierarchical authority it once exercised.[24] Religious thought, as representation, goes beyond religion.

Taubes finds this alternative activity in the exploration of the gap between what is and what should be. In doing so, he affirms Marx's observation that the critique of religion is the basis of all criticism. The critique of religion is, as Taubes explains, 'the model for a critique of profane existence'.[25] This critique is the critique which religion provides. Yet this critique is self-incriminating. Theology's complicity with that profane existence means that the critique provided by religion entails the critique of religion itself. This initial form of critique persists through the political, economical and technological. 'Every level propagates its own illusory appearances, develops its own apologies, but also forges its own weapon of critique.'[26] Taubes's political theology is the process of transformation described by Marx in his comments on Hegel's *Philosophy of Right*: 'the criticism of heaven turns into the criticism of the earth, the criticism of religion into the criticism of law and the criticism of theology into the criticism of politics.'[27] From theology and religion to law and politics, the concepts of religion, understood in relation to philosophical truth, are still capable of articulating the 'cleavage between the ideal and the ruling norms of man and society'.[28] Political theology does not attempt to explain the political through theological concepts, as in Schmitt. Taubes uses religion not to 'transform the worldly question of industrial society into a theological one; rather, we transform the theological into the worldly'.[29]

This political theology is not wholly Hegelian, however. He follows Marx in questioning the relationship between idea and actuality.

> Individual sections of the *Phenomenology* contain the critical elements for entire realms, like religion, the state, and bourgeois life, but admittedly in an alienated form. For the real process of history is only depicted as the phenomenon of the process, which comes about through self-consciousness . . . Hegel's dialectic is a dialectic of the idea, not of actuality. What Hegel burns in the dialectical fire of the idea is not actual religion, the actual state, actual society and nature, but religion itself as already an object of knowledge, as theology and dogma. It is not the state and society which undergo sublation, but jurisprudence and political science; it is not nature which is sublated in its objectivity, but the natural sciences. (*OE*, 179)

While he is correct to highlight that Hegel is primarily concerned with the concept, he overstates the gap between concept and actuality. Taubes does not offer a fully developed reading of Hegel's wider philosophy, but reading his criticism in the light of that larger context closes the distance between Taubes and Hegel.

This point about the gap between the actual and ideal is also important because it returns to issues fundamental to the ontology of the world developed in the first chapter. There, I argued that Haslanger's social constructivism and Tuana's interactionist ontology could be read in terms of Hegel's notion of spirit. That reading is enabled by transcendental materialist interpretations of Hegel and those interpretations are concerned with precisely this division. If the world is constituted by the interaction of the natural, human-made, social and biological, then ideas can never be merely ideal. Working through Taubes's critique is thus not an attempt to defend Hegel from Taubes but a way of developing a reading of Hegel that brings the two closer together while beginning to draw in the transcendental materialism I am using to account for the world and that will inform the next chapter's discussion of Malabou.

Taubes's critique focuses on the division between idea and actuality, ideal religion and religion as it actually is found in the world. First, Hegel would object to the notion of actual religion, society and nature as objects completely divorced from the process of conceptualization. Taubes's claim is a familiar one: Hegel deals only with ideas, not material, lived reality. It is true, in a sense, that the *Philosophy of Right* is concerned with political science rather than actual politics. What would sublation mean in politics if not a sublation that involves ideas about politics? If Marx attempts to sublate philosophy into a material politics, this move is itself comprehensible from the perspective of a Hegelian philosophy which insists on the actualization of the absolute. In a sense, this understanding makes Hegel the more realistic of the two. Marx sublates philosophy into material reality as part of a process in achieving final resolution. For Hegel, the absolute contains a persistent negativity between thought and reality as immediately given. Thought is always perturbed and reanimated by the other of thought. The absolute does not denote the end of that negativity, but its comprehension.[30]

Second, in the concluding sentence, Taubes claims that it is natural science that is sublated, not nature itself. Again, for Hegel, this statement assumes too great a division between nature and natural science. Abstract reflection on nature includes the material sublation of nature in humanity's creation of its own freedom. The relationship between the abstract and concrete is one of the key themes of transcendental materialism. As Adrian Johnston argues,

> Hegel's emphasis on the need to think substance also as subject reciprocally entails the complementary obligation to conceptualize subject as substance. This reciprocity reflects his post-Spinozist (in both senses of the qualifier 'post-') immanentism in which transcendent(al) subjectivity nonetheless remains immanent to substance in a dialectical-speculative relationship of an 'identity of identity and difference'. Thinking subject as substance, which is a move central to transcendental materialism, involves treating subjectivity and various phenomena tied up with it as 'real abstractions'

> . . . As real qua non-illusory, such abstractions are causally efficacious and, hence, far from epiphenomenal. In Hegelian phrasing, the thought of the concrete apart from the abstract is itself the height of abstraction.[31]

As Johnston explains elsewhere, nature gives birth to a process of denaturalization.[32] Human subjectivity is nature thinking itself.

It is thus possible to accept Taubes's point that political science is not politics as such, but it is a mistake to posit them as completely distinct. The relationship between material and abstract reflection is, as Johnston points out, the identity of identity and difference. This claim is essential to Hegel's definition of philosophy in the *Encyclopaedia Logic*: 'philosophy should be quite clear about the fact that its content is nothing other than the basic import that is originally produced and produces itself in the domain of the living spirit, the content that is made into the *world*, the outer and inner world of consciousness; in other words, the content of philosophy is *actuality*' (*E1*, §6: 29/47). He goes on to explain that the first interaction between consciousness and actuality is experience. Those attentive to experience quickly realize the difference between this transience and the actuality underlying those appearances. The following paragraph is even more explicit: 'right from the start, our meditative thinking did not confine itself to its merely abstract mode . . . but threw itself at the same time upon the material of the world of appearance' (*E1*, §7: 30/49).

Taubes's clear distinction between idea and actuality is also rejected in the *Phenomenology of Spirit*. Here, Hegel critiques both the simple immediacy of the preconceptual as failing to understand the becoming that characterizes actuality. Reason, he insists, must be understood as a purposive activity generated by the immediacy of experience and moving towards the concept.

> The exaltation of a supposed nature over a misconceived thinking, and especially the rejection of external teleology, has brought the form of purpose in general into discredit. Still, in the sense in which Aristotle, too, defines nature as purposive activity, purpose is what is immediate and *at rest*, the unmoved which is also *self-moving*, and as such is subject. Its power to move, taken abstractly, is *being-for-self* or pure negativity. The result is the same as the beginning, only because the *beginning* is the *purpose*; in other words, the actual is the same as its notion only because the immediate, as purpose, contains the self or pure actuality within itself. The realized

purpose, or the existent actuality, is movement and unfolded becoming. (*PS*, §22: 12/26)

Finally, this relationship is also found in Hegel's definition of nature. 'Nature has presented itself as the idea in the form of otherness. Since therefore the idea is the negative of itself, or is *external to itself*, nature is not merely external in relation to this idea' (*E2*, §247: 13/237). Arguing that Hegel is wrong to speak of nature when he really means natural science is to misunderstand the relationship between the two. Taubes's objection to Hegel is understandable, arising as it does from a Marxist tradition of critiquing Hegel's idealism but nonetheless errs in neglecting the Hegelian understanding of the relationship between substance and subject.[33]

Rather than following Taubes in offering these points as critiques of Hegel, one should read Taubes as drawing out the latent principles within Hegel's philosophy. 'The explosive material is already latent in the principle of Hegel. Even though in the Hegelian system the power of the state coincides with the divinations of religion and the principles of philosophy, as he reconciles actuality with spirit, the state with religious conscience, and religious conscience with philosophy' (*OE*, 164). Taubes is not a Hegelian in the sense that he seeks to replicate and clarify Hegel's texts. He is a Hegelian in his creative redeployment of Hegel's philosophy.

The extent of this Hegelianism is clear at the conclusion of *Occidental Eschatology*. He ends with a criticism of all philosophies of return. Kierkegaard, in Taubes's reading, aims to recover early Christianity, while Marx seeks to recover something of the Greek polis. Hegel, though, sees his philosophy as the fulfilment lying at the end of the development of Western history. 'Hegel's fulfilment, however, is a reconciliation of destruction' (*OE*, 192). Hegel stands at the apex of modern thought, destroying modernity for modernity's sake. For Taubes, Hegel writes in a moment of revelation and annihilation at the tipping point between the modern and what will follow.

> This epoch, in which the threshold of Western history is crossed, regards itself primarily as the no-longer [*Nicht-Mehr*] of the past and the not-yet [*Noch-Nicht*] of what is to come. To all weak spirits longing for shelter and security, this age appears wanting. For the coming age is not served by demonizing or giving new life to what-has-been [*das Gewesene*], but by

remaining steadfast in the no-longer and the not-yet, in the nothingness of the night, and thus remaining open to the first signs of the coming day. (*OE*, 193)

Taubes thus offers an argument for uncovering a persistent, latent element that lies within modernity – a willingness to destroy the world as it is in the name of that which it could be. This alternation between affirmation of modernity and call for the destruction of the world presents a persistent tension in Taubes's thought. His embracing of destruction is a clear articulation of a Hegelian apocalyptic political theology, but his focus on 'the nothingness of the night' perpetually comes up against his commitment to modernity as he seeks to navigate between history and apocalypse, progress and providence.[34] He calls for the destruction of the modern world in the name of the values of modernity.

Apocalypticism and the question of history

In the light of this tension, Bielik-Robson argues that one should emphasize Taubes's more eschatological or messianic tendencies rather than accepting his 'self-professed apocalypticism'.[35] Contrary to this position, I claim that it is important to retain the apocalyptic elements of Taubes's philosophy. While agreeing with Bielik-Robson that this tension is problematically unresolved in Taubes's work, it is possible to read texts such as *Occidental Eschatology* as willing the destruction of the world, if world is understood as the material and social relations that I outlined in the first chapter. Evaluating Taubes's apocalypticism requires inquiring further into the nature of that apocalypticism. As already noted, one of the key critiques of apocalypticism has been the notion of an external, divine force breaking into history. Throughout this chapter I have argued that Taubes offers an immanent political theology, opening up the possibility of an apocalypticism without transcendence. It is now time to see if Taubes can fulfil that promise.

At the start of *Occidental* Eschatology, Taubes defines apocalypse as 'in the literal and figurative sense, revelation' (*OE*, 4). Revelation, in turn, is 'the subject of history; history is the predicate of revelation' (*OE*, 7). Seeing this revelation as both concealment and unveiling, Taubes defines the 'apocalyptic principle' as entailing 'a form-destroying and forming power. Depending on the situation and the task, only one of the two components emerges, but neither can be absent' (*OE*, 10). In his lectures on Paul, he explores the consequences of the apocalyptic disposition, claiming that he has 'no spiritual investment in the world as it is' (*PT*, 103). As Bielik-Robson indicates, this final phrase is crucial. Either one emphasizes 'the world' or one focuses on 'as it is':

> If we follow the first apocalyptic possibility, history will only emerge as a passive waiting for an event which will finally lead us out of the world into the original divine Nothingness. But if we follow the latter, history will have a chance to emerge as a process that can finally lead us from the world-as-it-is, that is: naturalised, hierarchised, spatialised, and ideologically stabilised in the cyclical succession of powers.[36]

Bielik-Robson echoes Svenungsson's concerns that apocalypticism entails a break with history rather than an intrahistorical process.[37] For Bielik-Robson, one must choose between apocalypse as revelation and apocalypse as annihilation.[38] The former can take place within history. It can function as an '*operative antinomianism*', a 'traumatising negation' that stops short of 'apocalyptic annihilation'.[39] Whether Taubes's political theology calls for end of the world or its salvation hinges on this question of history.

> What creates history in Taubes's account is neither an annihilating shock awaited by the apocalypticists, nor the inherent norm inscribed into some impersonal 'laws of history', but the antinomian tension, which always presses against the grain, against 'nature', against any progressive normativity. History, therefore, is never a progress, it is rather a disruptive staccato of breaks, awakenings and traumas that never simply evaporate without trace but always leave a disquieting mark that, despite all the 'natural' obstacles, initiates messianic transformation of the world.[40]

If Bielik-Robson is correct, then Taubes is not describing an apocalyptic annihilation, but a negativity that haunts the world. Yet, this reading of Taubes can also be reconfigured within an apocalyptic framework rooted in the conviction that the world cannot be redeemed.[41] In this case, apocalypticism is not so much the end of history, but the end of *our* history. If apocalypse is simultaneous revelation and annihilation, what is revealed are the gaps and fissures which are the sites of a destructive potential. While there may be general problems with apocalyptic political theology, it is important to reflect on Taubes's distinctive immanent, material and finite approach. Thinking apocalyptically from this perspective allows new forms of apocalypticism rather than the rejection of apocalyptic political theology altogether. Apocalypse is no longer something awaited, but an active, negative presence. This negativity is not orientated at messianic transformation – for such transformations are transformations of the violent and inescapable world – but a transformation that passes through annihilation. Apocalypticism is not about replacing what is now with something better. It is about 'opposing the totality of this world with a new totality that comprehensively founds anew in the way that it negates . . . namely, in terms of basic foundations' (*OE*, 9).[42]

This basic foundation, the nature of the world as violent and inescapable, is the revelation that accompanies annihilation. It is only in realizing the horror of the world that one can truly desire its end and only in so desiring that elusive and violent end, see the world in its vicious persistence. Read this way, there is no longer a division between revelation and annihilation in Taubes's apocalypticism. Bielik-Robson places the 'moment of revelation' outside of history; revelation is its initiating otherness. It 'cannot be reconciled with the "natural" course of events . . . messianic belief can be impressed upon human beings only through a violent event called revelation'.[43] This outsideness is a way of describing the otherness of revelation. It is the truth of the world that is inexpressible in the terms of that world. Rather than discussing this otherness in terms of externality, risking the reintroduction of transcendence, this otherness can still be described as immanent to the world. It is, as Bull argues in his Hegelian reading of apocalypticism, that which the world rejects and the positions constituted by the slow, invisible (to many) forms of violence that do not happen in the world, but are the world. Revelation forces one to see the unseen – the exclusions that are constitutive of the world as such.

In this regard, Taubes's political theology is an example of the twentieth-century Jewish messianism described by Rabinbach, characterized by a utopian vision 'of a future which is the fulfilment of all that which can be hoped for in the condition of exile but cannot be realized within it. Redemption appears either as the end of history or as an event within history, never as an event produced by history'.[44] Revelation is something that happens to history rather than is produced by it. As he describes it, the apocalyptic 'element involves a quantum leap from present to future, from exile to freedom. This leap necessarily brings with it the complete destruction and negation of the old order. Messianism is thus bound up with both violence and catastrophe.'[45] The language again suggests a break or fissure within history, addressed from within history, but which is a simultaneously annihilating and founding rather than producing. 'Freedom may occur in history, but it is not brought about by historical forces or individual acts.'[46] There is thus an immanent notion of freedom, but the actualization of this freedom is traumatic.

In both Rabinbach's and Bielik-Robson's reading of Taubes's political theology, two themes emerge. First, in keeping with the earlier discussion of Hegel's implicit political theology, apocalypticism and messianism are not religious concepts that can be merely translated into secular forms of progress and development. They are ways of thinking the end of the world that trouble philosophy. As representations, they think philosophical truth, but from a perspective other to that philosophical thought. Second, while Taubes is able to offer an immanent apocalypticism that avoids relying on transcendent intervention, the complex relationship between revelation and annihilation continues to trouble those who wish to still preserve some continuity with the world. They reject 'the possibility of an optimistic and evolutionary conception of history, of progress, without of course foreclosing the possibility of freedom'.[47] The limitations of this freedom depend on the nature of the world.

This discussion of nature, freedom, history and progress makes clear an essential divide that returns to the opening discussion of the nature of the world and apocalypse. On the one hand, there are liberal, progressive or messianic political theologies that posit a significant degree of autonomy or freedom within the world, but reject critiques of the world as such. The condition of possibility for freedom is the acceptance of the world. To turn away from the world, to disinvest, is to abandon the possibility of changing the world. On the other hand, Taubes's political theology and the version of apocalypticism I am developing here, reverse this relationship. The materially embedded social relations that constitute the world operate as enormous constraints. The possibilities of a better world always remain possibilities of a world that is itself unjust. For this apocalypticism, the condition of possibility for freedom is disinvestment from the world.

Taubes and Bloch

Taubes is not the only one to philosophically discuss theology in these terms. As noted in the introduction to this section, there is a strong link to a broader German political theological tradition. Of this tradition, Bloch is closer to Taubes than most, even though Taubes describes Bloch as 'wishy-washy' (*PT*, 74) and as producing a 'utopia picture-book' (*PT*, 71). Notwithstanding these objections, there remain key points where Bloch supports Taubes's position as well as pushing his more apocalyptic tendencies. In doing so, he tends to maintain greater focus on the concrete aspects of human existence. So, while Taubes might be more concerned with issues of political theological method and philosophical questions, Bloch gives more attention to philosophical and theological understandings of oppression and liberation.

There are three key points at which Bloch can supplement Taubes. First, Bloch offers a similar spatial schematization of political theology. Taubes describes the 'work' of apocalypse as moving in one of two directions. Either it moves from above, revealing 'the central point of God and the world' or 'the centre is revealed from below' (*OE*, 7). For Bloch, theology is an activity that can be practised from On-high or From-below. Describing the institutional forms of Christianity, he writes that 'the religion of the On high had to be kept for the people: the old myth of lordship from on-high which, in Christianity, sanctioned, or at least explained, the unjust distribution of this world's goods with the just distribution of those of the next' (*AC*, 8). Bloch's criticism of the On-high demonstrates his awareness of the ambiguity of religion.[48] Though theology from On-high often comes from 'the church', Bloch is quick to remind his readers that this church is not the Bible (*AC*, 9). The Biblical text provides the undoing of the authority of the institutions which hitherto have appealed to the text in the justification of their actions. The Bible is the source of 'master-ideologies' (p. 12) as well as 'the counter-blow against the oppressor' (p. 13). In order for the Bible to serve its liberating function, it must be read carefully. The reader must engage in the 'detective work of biblical criticism' which demands that one 'identify and save the Bible's choked and buried "plebeian element"' (*AC*, 62). This recalls the ambiguity of the Marxist 'critique of religion' – rather than Bloch urging a critique of the Bible he encourages 'criticism *through* the

Bible' (*AC*, 70).⁴⁹ Such investigative work reveals the dual nature of the Biblical text, 'a Scripture for the people and a Scripture against the people' (*AC*, 70) or, a Bible From-below and a Bible from On-high.

Second, Bloch offers a similar opposition to the world. Speaking of the apocalyptic repetition of Exodus themes, Bloch notes that Israelite Messianism contains a strong antithesis to the world (*AC*, 101). This divestment from the world, to use Taubes's phrase, is presented with a greater Marxist inflection in Bloch than in Taubes. Indeed, Taubes sometimes seems passive in his view of apocalyptic political theology. Though Taubes can envision the end of the world, the result is to 'let it go down' (*PT*, 103). He wonders, with Paul, if 'we should still be rising up against something that is going down anyway?' (*PT*, 40). Bloch is more active, advocating a 'practical chiliasm' in line with earlier movements such as Müntzer's. Yet, for both, there is a conviction that there is a gap between the world and another which is possible. As Bloch writes, 'there is always an exodus from this world, an exodus from the particular *status quo*. And there is always a hope, which is connected with rebellion – a hope founded in the concrete given possibilities for new being. As a handhold in the future, a process which, though by no means achieved, is yet by no means in vain' (*AC*, 107). Apocalyptic thought is thus opposed to the world as it is, in the name of the world that might be.

> A theory of religion based on *wish ipso facto* passes over into another, Utopian dimension, which does not cease to exist in the subject even when the illusion of an hypostasized Beyond is shattered. Indeed the subject, aware of itself now, and powerful, gains in stature from it, till it stands above nature itself. The idealism reflected in the now pulverized Other-world is revealed as the fruit of purely human powers of transcending which, far from going beyond nature, operate within it. (*AC*, 195)

Here, Bloch expresses the Hegelian understanding of nature articulated above. Spirit is not the abolition of nature, but the transcending arch of freedom which emerges from its material ground.

This apocalyptic focus is also central to Bloch's understanding of a Jesus who preaches that 'there will be no time for tranquil observation: the Kingdom will break through suddenly, in a single all-transforming bound' (*AC*, 118). He opposes any attempt to suggest that this kingdom is an internal one in the hearts of believers (*AC*, 117) or that the world as it is now will continue in some form. 'This world must pass away before the next.' (*AC*, 119). Bloch, attuned to the ambiguity of 'this world', specifies that

> Whenever the words 'this world' and 'the other world' appear ... 'This world' means the same as 'the present aeon'; 'the other world' means the same as 'the better aeon' ... What is meant is eschatological tension, not some sort of geographical separation from a fixed This-world here and a fixed Beyond there. The only real thing now about this world is its submergence in the next. (*AC*, 119)

Further, the coming of Christ as Messiah is a 'new eschatological Exodus, overthrowing all things from their beginning to their end: *the Exodus into God as man*' (*AC*, 123). The repetition of exodus marks not only an apocalyptic break within history – it is an apocalyptic event within the concept of God.

Third, despite the title *Atheism in Christianity*, Bloch is not arguing for atheism in any normal sense of the term. Rather, he proposes a form of desecularizing political theology. The questions posed by religion, such as the problem of evil, determinism or ultimate meaning, remain important questions for atheism. It must respond to these issues if it 'is not just the unhistorical unrealistic folly of optimism, or of equally unhistorical nihilism, with man as a laughable begetter of illusion ... and with the alien specter of death all around us, and that gorgon of cosmic inhumanity which can never contain any shred of concern for man' (*AC*, 107). He presents a path between the continuation of religious belief as it has hitherto been experienced and an absolute rejection of all things religious. In a similar way to Taubes's critique of modernity for modernity's sake, or the critique of rabbinic Judaism for Judaism's sake, Bloch could be said to engage in the critique of theism for religion's sake. Joining Taubes in offering a theology which is 'materialist, messianic, historical, emancipatory, focused on the finite life, immanentist and this-worldly',[50] Bloch offers a vision of a new heaven and new earth in which the 'Christ-impulse' can 'live even when God is dead' (*AC*, 167). If '[a]theism-with-concrete-Utopia is at one and the same time the annihilation of religion and the realization of its heretical hope' (*AC*, 225), then 'with-concrete-Utopia' sufficiently modifies the term atheism so that it avoids slipping into the virulently anti-religious rhetoric associated with New Atheism and other contemporary rejections of religion.

Bloch and Taubes are far from being in total agreement, however. Most notable is their divergent views of Paul. For Taubes, Paul represents a transvaluation of values, the establishment of a new covenant-community and the vehicle of an apocalyptic message. For Bloch, Paul twists the Hebrew Scriptures in order to explain that Christ is the Messiah because of the cross, rather than in spite of it (*AC*, 156–9). This understanding of Jesus's death gives rise to the

> *patience of the Cross* – so praiseworthy an attitude in the oppressed, so comfortable for the oppressors; a sanction, too, for the unconditional and absolute *obedience to authority*, as coming from God. Every theology of hope which might have placed itself in the front rank of change opted instead for conformity when it accepted these ideas – an acceptance whose convenient passivity broke the fine edge of Jesus' own hope. (*AC*, 161)

This harsh rhetoric does not prevent Bloch from acknowledging that Paul played a crucial role in the development of Christianity; Bloch simply places much more emphasis on Jesus, whose message he believes was obfuscated by the preaching of Paul. Christ is the usurper, the one who disrupts the On-high and rejects any association of divinity with mastery or lordship. Bloch also develops his philosophy in a more explicitly Marxist direction. While Taubes refers to Marx in his essays and at the conclusion of *Occidental Eschatology*, it would be inaccurate to describe Taubes as a Marxist. Bloch on the other hand, not only identified his philosophy as Marxist, he was active in Communist circles.[51] Perhaps due to these involvements, Bloch's apocalypticism is manifested in a more active and overtly political fashion.

Even with these differences, Taubes's Hegelian tendencies, used to develop an apocalyptic political theology, are further enhanced by occasional Blochian supplementation. Both their work arises out of a conviction that the rational critique of false consciousness had not succeeded in impeding fascism. They both argue for a recommencement of utopian myth-making in order to create an imaginary capable of resisting the world. They engage in this myth-making, or myth-retelling, by developing philosophies that employ theological concepts in the development of immanentist and materialist political theologies. Or, put in more Hegelian language, they both return to representations to think the world and its end.

Anti-liberal tendencies in Hegel, Taubes and Schmitt

Taubes and Bloch think the end of the world, but they think this end in different ways. Taubes is more sceptical than Bloch about the sources of hope that can be found in the world. For Taubes, the source of hope in the world is its end. To understand how Taubes's apocalypticism goes further than Bloch's utopianism, it is useful to return to the comparison of Taubes and Schmitt. The latter two share a suspicion of the limits of politics (recalling the distinction between politics and the political discussed in the first chapter). This suspicion emerges in their critiques of liberalism. They both recognize a need for the political beyond politics, but their opposing views of the nature of the political is what distinguishes Taubes's anarchic apocalypticism from Schmitt's authoritarian conservatism. Considering the differences in their forms of anti-liberalism will thus clarify the nature of Taubes's apocalypticism as well as further elaborate the connections to Hegel's philosophy.

The first difference is the competing directions of their political theologies. As already noted, Taubes describes two forms of apocalypticism, operating from different directions. One reveals 'the central point of God and the world' from above, while for the other 'the centre is revealed from below' (*OE*, 7). Corresponding to these two movements of apocalypse are two political theologies. As Taubes says in a 1986 lecture, 'Carl Schmitt thinks apocalyptically, but from above, from the powers that be; I think from the bottom up' (*CS*, 13). For Schmitt, political theology is about containing a destructive force. This containment from above returns to the earlier discussion of the *katechon*. Taubes defines the *katechon* as the 'retainer [*der Aufhalter*] that holds down the chaos that pushes up from below' (*PT*, 103). Taubes, when he fully embraces the apocalyptic spirit, welcomes this chaos. Grimshaw suggests that perhaps this insight is precisely what liberal Christianity has sought to cover up – its apocalyptic core. Schmitt's exception becomes 'the sign in the secular society of liberal modernity of the apocalyptic power that exists, that is referenced by both exception and miracle, that reminds us that what we believe to be the case, the norm, is in fact only fragile and transitory'.[52] For both, this anti-liberalism focuses on the potential of an apocalypse, though Schmitt is concerned with constraining this potential while Taubes aims to unleash it.[53] Taubes's anti-liberalism comes about in his critique of modernity, but in the name of a fuller version of the modern project. Schmitt's anti-liberalism attempts to contain forces of social disruption that Taubes sees as necessary for the realization of this alternative modernity.

It is important to note that anti-liberalism does not necessarily imply a rejection of the accomplishments of liberalism. The critique of liberalism is similar to Marx's critique of capitalism. The *Communist Manifesto* includes a list of the great achievements of capitalism: 'machinery, application of chemistry to industry and agriculture, steam-navigation, railways, electric telegraphs, clearing of whole continents for cultivation, canalisation of rivers, whole populations conjured out of the ground'.[54] Similarly it is possible to make a list of the achievement of liberalism: the articulation of equal rights (even if the implementation lags behind) or the universal declaration of human rights. Hegelian anti-liberalism is not a rejection of these advancements but a rejection of the naturalization of liberalism. As Taubes says in a 1986 address,

> I really would like to be liberal; don't you think that I would like it? But the world is not so made that one can be liberal. For that is at the cost of others; the question is who pays the cost, and the third and fourth worlds, the fifth and sixth worlds that are approaching, they will not be liberal at all, but brutal demands will be made there. The question is, how does one deal with them, when one starts to deal with them? If you work only at this liberal level of democracy, you just don't see what happens in history. (*CS*, 38)

In Grimshaw's commentary on Taubes's correspondence with Schmitt, he argues that, for Taubes,

> liberalism involves, in the end, a denial of the cost others suffer by our being liberal. That is, liberalism is not a neutral state of affairs, nor a neutral society, but a claim that is inherently oppositional and judgmental, with associated decision and implementations, and such decisions are primarily focused on the benefits to the victors in what is seen as the inevitable march of human progress. Taubes's point is that liberal democracy fails to see what happens in history, which is a history of brutality. In short, liberals have too high a view of humanity and human nature, views that a realistic encounter with and examination of human history would quickly overturn.[55]

Taubes rejects liberalism in the name of a greater form of liberation. Not only does this anti-liberalism have Hegelian antecedents, but Taubes's relationship with Schmitt plays out a tension internal to Hegel's own work.

There are at least two ways in which Hegel demonstrates an anti-liberal tendency. First, the most direct critique of liberalism comes in Hegel's *Philosophy of Right*. As Karin de Boer argues, while Hegel sees the achievement of individual freedom as an essential goal, his primary focus is 'the structures that allow a modern state to establish itself as a rational whole'.[56] True freedom is something attained by the community of spirit, not something that functions at the level of the individual. As Hegel writes, 'society is not dispersed into atomic individuals, collected to perform only a single and temporary act, and kept together for a moment and no longer. On the contrary, it makes the appointment as a society, articulated into associations, communities and corporations, which although constituted already for other purposes, acquire in this way a connection with politics' (*PR*, §308: 294/476).[57] De Boer makes this point specifically in opposition to those who read Hegel as emphasizing individual freedom and uses Robert Pippin as one of her examples. As Pippin explains in *Hegel's Practical Philosophy*, he sees the rational exchange of reasons as a central theme of Hegel's philosophy. Freedom, for Hegel, 'consists in being in a certain reflective and deliberative relation to oneself (which he describes as being able to give my inclinations and incentives a "rational form"), which itself is possible, so it is argued, only if one is also already in certain (ultimately institutional, norm-governed) relations to others, if one is a participant in certain practices'.[58] Pippin works from this starting point to the conclusion that Hegel's 'suspicions about moral individualism, an ethics of conscience, etc., should not obscure the fact that he also wants to defend, in his own way, the supreme importance of an individual's free, reflective life, however much he regards it as a necessarily collective achievement'.[59] It is this passage that triggers de Boer's concern, for in her reading the state is not the means by which individuals achieve their own rational goals, but an expression of the rational whole to which 'the ultimate interests of citizens ought to coincide'.[60] The first anti-liberal tendency within Hegel's philosophy is thus found in this relationship between the individual and society. The needs of society as a whole are primary.

Second, and somewhat at tension with the first, is the anti-liberalism that is continued in Taubes and Bloch. While Bloch in particular shows the same concern for the formation of a community of shared will, both Taubes and Bloch are more suspicious of institutions than traditional Hegelianism would allow. If de Boer's focus on anti-liberal elements of Hegel's *Philosophy of Right* leads to a stronger role for the state, this alternative anti-liberalism seeks new forms of the social whole. Both objections to liberalism are rooted in a rejection of individualism as the basis of society but differ in that one is more accepting of the presently existing social whole than the other. For Taubes, there is an anti-politics to apocalypticism (remembering that anti-politics can be ultra-political). This anti-politics differentiates apocalypticism from utopia as 'utopia belongs to essentially politicized man and merges from the political spirit. The state is the vessel for the fulfilment of this concept of humanity . . . Even the ideal of utopia needs to take its bearings from the real state' (*OE*, 135). Taubes contrasts that utopianism with an anarchic chiliasm that is dissimilar to the form of politics continued even in the most concrete forms of utopianism. Though the coming kingdom may be associated with a place (such as Jerusalem) at a fundamental level it is 'not being inaugurated, but it is coming. It is not found in any location, but it is happening [*es ereignet sich*]. It is not being discovered, but it is expected' (*OE*, 136).

While Bloch does not develop as clear an anti-politics as Taubes, *Atheism in Christianity*'s invectives against theology from On-high are not only aimed at ecclesial authorities; they also target the collusion between those authorities and the state. He describes Job as one of the heroes of the Bible, for he realized that 'piety was not to be confused with conformity to law and order' (*AC*, 19). This conformity with the law as manifested by the state is problematic because it involves submission to that which is imposed from On-high. Much of Bloch's critique of institutional religion is rooted in Christianity's abandonment of its liberating message as religion from below. 'There was always opium there for the people – in the end it tainted their whole faith. If the Church had not always stood so watchfully behind the ruling powers, there would not have been such attacks against everything it stood for' (*AC*, 47). Bloch is led to the Hegelian conclusion that whatever form of social organization emerges in his concrete utopia, it must not contain the alienation of a state that is defined in contradiction to its people.

Thus, though Bloch is critically contrasting his concrete utopianism with other forms of utopian thinking and is firmly opposed to the world as it is,

Taubes's apocalypticism goes further. Bloch still finds hope in the world, while Taubes performs the more difficult balancing act of a materialist eschatology that wavers between hope and nihilism.[61] Such an apocalypticism is not rooted in the hope for the resolution of problems within the world but in a desire for the end of the antagonisms that *are* the world. As Frank B. Wilderson III argues, the only end to such antagonisms is the destruction of one side, which read in a Hegelian vein, means the destruction of both – one through the other.

While Taubes offers an apocalyptic condemnation of the world that goes further than Bloch or Hegel, there is still this tension between hope and nihilism. At times, Taubes makes his lack of investment in the world seem easy. Recalling the discussion of Cohn and Hegel, though, it is important to bear in mind the rarity of truly apocalyptic energy. Apocalyptic challenges to social order do not begin, even under substantial oppression, until elements within a community are convinced that they have no future from the perspective of that order. Only then do the fractures within that order begin to appear. As noted in that earlier discussion, it is for this reason that Hegel remains worried about the Rabble. The Rabble refuses or is unable to adapt to the political limitations of particular community. 'Poverty in itself does not turn people into a rabble; a rabble is created only when there is joined to poverty a disposition of mind, an inner indignation against the rich, against, society, against the government, etc' (*PR*, §244z: 221/389). As Brooks argues in his reading of the Rabble, an essential component of being a member of a society is the conviction that problems are best resolved within the limits of a political system.[62] Within liberalism, for example, there is no resolution between individual freedom and equality. Managing that tension *is* liberalism. To refuse either side completely is to abandon liberalism. Engaging in this refusal, when combined with economic, social and political alienation, generates the position of the Rabble.

Hegel does not have a solution to the threat of the Rabble. He considers charity, holds out the possibility of economic mobility and even suggests colonialism might be a temporary solution (*PR*, §245–6: 221–2/390–1). For Hegel, the problem is that the system of production and ownership which he accepts as given – that is capitalism – necessarily produces the Rabble. This position is based on the rushed conclusion that 'despite an *excess of wealth* civil society is *not rich enough*, i.e. its own resources are insufficient, to check excessive poverty and the creation of penurious rabble' (*PR*, §245: 222/390).

Even if Taubes sometimes makes apocalypticism look a little too easy, both his and Schmitt's political theologies are attune to, if not grounded on, the possibility of collapse represented by the Rabble. It could all go down. The difference is the direction from which they think that possibility. Taubes does not discuss the exception in the same way as Schmitt, but they both are concerned with the moment of the suspension of the normal. For Schmitt, the normal is suspended in the name of the normal. It is an act of preservation. For Taubes, it initiates the end. It carries on the theological legacy of Paul who 'fundamentally negates law as a force of political order. With this, legitimacy is denied to all sovereigns of this world, be they imperatorial or theocratic.'[63] It is an act of disinvestment. For Schmitt, it is a political act carried out by the sovereign in the name of the law. For Taubes, it is the existential 'apocalypse of man' expressed in the theological language that marks the cleavage between the world as it is and the world as it should. It happens rather than is directly enacted.

Transcendental materialist readings of Hegel: From Taubes to Malabou

In the course of this chapter I have offered an overview of Taubes's political theology. In so doing, I have shown how Taubes continues key Hegelian themes, contrasted Taubes's political theology with Schmitt's, but also shown that they each offer their own version of an anti-liberal political theology. In the next chapter I will continue developing Taubes's political theology through an engagement with Malabou. In order to provide context for that engagement, it is important to understand Malabou's relationship to transcendental materialism and how the transcendental materialist reading of Hegel relates to the reading of Taubes and Hegel I have been offering thus far.

Transcendental materialism is most strongly associated with the work of Adrian Johnston, who uses the term to name Žižek's distinctive reading of German Idealism, Marxism and psychoanalysis.[64] He not only uses this term to interpret Žižek but goes on to develop his own version of a transcendental materialist philosophy. In so doing, Johnston has collaborated with Malabou and the two share many of the basic philosophical positions: non-reductive materialism, creative rereadings of German Idealism and an appreciation for the growing body of literature connecting biology, neuroscience and psychoanalysis.[65] In the first chapter, I claimed that transcendental materialism is one approach to thinking the nature of the world, bringing a Hegelian perspective to the same conceptual issues identified by Tuana and Haslanger. In the following chapter, Malabou's rejection of transcendence and her materialist understanding of trauma will be key to further exploring apocalypticism.

There are three specific themes in Taubes that connect to transcendental materialist readings of Hegel. First, Taubes repeatedly refers to the importance of grounding political theology in material reality. He cautions against 'crass-materialism', which is circumvented through a Hegelian mediation of materialism and idealism. Hegel himself does not perform this mediation, but Hegel's philosophy is part of the transcendence of self-alienation that allows this mediation to occur. Citing Marx's view of communism as 'the complete return of man to himself as a social (i.e., human) being' Taubes adds that 'Communist naturalism or humanism is different from both idealism and materialism; at the same time it is the truth that binds them together' (OE, 182). Noting the Hegelian language, he quotes the *Philosophic and Economic Manuscripts of 1844*, in which Marx further claims communism as 'the genuine resolution of the conflict between man and nature and between man and man – the true resolution of the strife between existence and essence, between objectification and self-confirmation, between freedom and necessity, between the individual and the species. Communism is the riddle of history solved, and it knows itself to be this solution.'[66]

This binding together of idealism and materialism is mirrored in Johnston's definition of transcendental materialism. This philosophy claims that

> [t]he break induced by the more-than-material subject splitting off from its material origins is irreparable, opening up an impossible-to-close gap, a nondialecticizable parallax split. The transcendental materialist theory of the subject is materialist insofar as it asserts that the Ideal of subjective thought arises from the Real of objective being, although it is also simultaneously transcendental insofar as it maintains that this thus-generated Ideal subjectivity thereafter achieves independence from the ground of its material sources and thereby starts to function as a set of possibility conditions for

forms of reality irreducible to explanatory discourses allied to traditional versions of materialism.[67]

Johnston develops this materialism further than Taubes, but the emphasis on achieving independence from the material origins of the subject is another way of articulating spirit's relation to nature.[68] The possibility of a freedom arising from material reality, maintaining a dialectical relationship to that material reality, but without recourse to any form of transcendent being, is a concern of both Taubes's and Bloch's apocalyptic political theology. Whatever the representations of God and apocalypse mean for Taubes, they are materially manifested. To repeat Bielik-Robson's description, Taubes's political theology is 'materialist, messianic, historical, emancipatory, focused on the finite life, immanentist and this-worldly'.[69]

Second, and on a related note, Taubes claims that Hegel's ontology moves from the metaphysical to the transcendental: 'They do not take nature as a norm but the production of man: history. Human creativity is placed above nature.'[70] Johnston does not state his position in opposition to nature but celebrates a similar production of the transcendental from its material basis. This point recalls the above discussion of Taubes's understanding of nature and freedom.

Finally, Taubes wants to preserve a kind of incompleteness to Hegel's philosophy. Taubes's understanding that 'Hegel, like Joachim, conceives of the course of world history as a progression and, consequently, as a constant negation of any system that currently exists' (*OE*, 166) parallels Johnston's observation that 'the reconciliation achieved by absolute knowing amounts to the acceptance of an insurmountable incompleteness, an irresolvable driving tension that cannot finally be put to rest through one last *Aufhebung*'.[71] Hegel's philosophy is complete in its grasping of its inherent incompleteness. Hegel's system is comprehension of the logical and therefore necessary nature of the material being which gives rise to the reasoning subject. The closed nature of Hegel's thought refers to the systematic conceptualization of the shape of this restless spirit.

That this comprehension is still a form of closure is necessary to an adequate understanding of Hegel's project. If there is only a persistent failure and reconstitution, then thought is trapped in the position of the unhappy consciousness. It is not enough for philosophy to be dialectical; dialectics must lead the subject to self-consciousness. Hegel, summarizing the sections leading up to religion in the *Phenomenology of Spirit*, makes this point: 'Then there was the self-consciousness that reached its final "shape" in the Unhappy Consciousness, that was only the *pain* of the Spirit that wrestled, but without success, to reach out into objectivity. The unity of the *individual* self-consciousness and its changeless *essence*, to which the former attains, remains therefore, a *beyond* for self-consciousness' (PS, §673: 410/495). Religion is the next step in realizing the unity of the subject with that beyond, first as a unity with an other, then as a unity with an other that is also the subject. The distinctive form of alienation experienced by self-consciousness engaged in religious thought is a necessary stage for the development of philosophical thought.[72]

While Johnston is generally resistant to theological appropriations of philosophy,[73] Taubes's political theology, with a God that '*comes into being* through history, through antithesis and negation, through *corruptio*, through suffering and formlessness' (OE, 101), provides a compatible theological reading of Hegel's philosophy. For Taubes, political theology must be done in a new philosophical framework, with categories that 'are transcendental and not metaphysical'.[74] In this regard, Johnston's position is the reversal of Göschel's. If Göschel asks Hegel if it would not be better to root philosophical concepts more directly in biblical imagery, Johnston suggests that this imagery is too risky. Political theology, following the legacy of Taubes and Bloch, echoes Hegel's reply to Göschel – absolute knowing instills the confidence necessary to return to representations. Taubes's turn to theology is thus the opposite of Schmitt's. As Boer argues, faced with the opposition of politics and theology, the answer is not to abandon theology. Rather, 'we take the move from theology to politics all the way, push it through to its dialectical extreme. And, in doing so, we would end with theology: not a going back to theology as Schmitt argued, but a theology beyond the initial opposition, one that is the next step, thoroughly politicised and materialised.'[75] Taubes experiments rather than returns.

This chapter has worked through the basic elements of Taubes's political theology with particular focus on both the role of Hegelian ideas and the contrast between Taubes and Schmitt. Taubes's apocalyptic political theology emerges as a critique of modernity for modernity's sake – a willingness to let loose apocalyptic fervour on a society which he felt did not live out the ideal of modern freedom. Navigating the tension of both affirming the modern world and calling for its destruction, I then supplemented Taubes's political theology through comparing and contrasting his work with Bloch's own treatment of eschatological themes. Reading Bloch alongside Taubes, it becomes clear that the latter pushes past the hope of concrete utopianism to a more difficult position. This political theology requires a delicate balance between hope and nihilism, revelation and annihilation. This discussion also shows the extent to which Taubes exemplifies the Hegelian practice of returning to representation and using theological concepts to think the world at the edge of the limits of philosophy.

Taubes thus advances the attempt to address the remaining questions that trouble apocalyptic views of the world. Both Taubes and Bloch offer a reading of apocalypticism that rejects transcendence in favour of an immanent and materialist account. There is a possibility of newness, even a newness that is not a possibility of this world, but that possibility is not external. Yet questions still remain. First, why does apocalypticism insist on the connection between this immanent novelty and violence or trauma? Second, what does it mean to live apocalyptically? To answer these questions, I now turn to Malabou.

4

Plastic apocalypticism

Reading Taubes, with help from Bloch and Schmitt, offers an initial articulation of an apocalyptic political theology. Taubes's thoroughgoing negativity is an example of what it means to reject the world and all its possibilities. While this political theology provides a good starting point, it does not fully respond to two persistent questions that present themselves when attempting to develop an apocalyptic account of the world. First, why does apocalypticism insist on the connection between the possibility of a possibility not of this world and traumatic violence? Second, what does it mean to live apocalyptically? To answer these questions, Taubes's 'materialist, messianic, historical, emancipatory, focused on the finite life, immanentist and this-worldly' political theology must be further developed.[1] More traditional forms of apocalypticism require an external, transcendent agent as the source of novelty. Reading Taubes and Hegel, I have argued that it is possible to experiment with theological materials and offer an immanent account of apocalypticism. But how does such an immanent account offer a genuine novelty rather than just a more extreme reconfiguration of the world? And if it is possible to develop an immanent apocalypticism, why not also argue for a more peaceful form of apocalypticism? Only having resolved these questions can the question of apocalyptic living be addressed.

The questions of immanence, novelty and trauma are also main concerns of Catherine Malabou's work on plasticity. Malabou develops her concept of plasticity through Hegel, she rejects messianic approaches to the new and she does so within a materialist reframe work amenable to the concept of world developed earlier.[2] Reading Taubes through Malabou offers a way of further connecting this concept of world and an immanent, materialist form of apocalypticism. Taubes offers a political theological alternative to messianism that can be read in terms of Malabou's most strident forms of destructive plasticity and Malabou offers a philosophical exploration of the challenges of such a traumatic form of novelty.

I begin by linking Malabou's concept of plasticity to the readings of Hegel discussed in previous chapters, before turning to the parallels between Malabou's understanding of plasticity and Taubes's understanding of apocalypse as revelation and annihilation. To draw out how Hegel is helpful in articulating this understanding of apocalypticism, I return to Malcolm Bull's work on Hegel and apocalypse, as well as explore the connection between plasticity and Hegel's understanding of contingency. What might initially seem like mystical longing or utopian hopefulness in Taubes or Bloch, when read in conjunction with Hegel, can be understood in terms of possibility and contingency. Through these themes, Malabou explains the role of a distinctively explosive and traumatic form of change, providing further resources for considering the link between apocalypticism and violence.

Malabou, Hegel and plasticity

In the preface of the *Phenomenology of Spirit*, Hegel describes speculative thought as the negation of the form of standard propositions: '[T]he general nature of the judgment or proposition, which involves the distinction of subject and predicate, is destroyed by the speculative proposition, and the proposition of identity which the former becomes contains the counterthrust against the subject-predicate relationship' (*PS*, §61: 38/59). He uses the example of the statement 'God is being' to illustrate his point. In this proposition, the subject disappears into the predicate. Instead of grasping the unity of the proposition, the two terms are seen as accidentally connected. In contrast to this form of the proposition, Hegel claims that philosophy must work towards 'the goal of plasticity' (*PS*, §64: 39/60). Rather than the rigid understanding of the proposition, the movement, which is the unity, of the statement must be rendered explicit. 'This return of the notion into itself must be *set forth*. This movement which continues what formerly the proof was supposed to accomplish, is the dialectical movement of the proposition itself. This alone is the speculative *in act*, and only the expression of this movement is a speculation exposition' (*PS*, §65: 39–40/61). The comprehension of the concept in its movement is the definition of truth.

A similar understanding of plasticity appears in Hegel's preface to the second edition of the *Science of Logic*. 'No subject matter is so absolutely capable of being expounded with a strictly immanent plasticity as is thought in its own necessary development' (*SL*, 40/5:30). Here, he expands the use of the term, using it not only to describe the form of the discourse, but the process of discourse itself. 'A plastic discourse demands . . . a plastic receptivity and understanding on the part of the listener' (*SL*, 40/5: 31).

These references, along with Hegel's discussion of the 'plastic arts', are the inspiration for Malabou's concept of plasticity. Plasticity indicates three traits that are shared between subjectivity, the dialectical process and being itself. As she explains in *The Future of Hegel*, the term names the capacity of 'being at once capable of receiving and of giving from' (*FH*, 8) and 'an explosive material . . . that can set off violent detonations' (*FH*, 9). Plasticity is itself a plastic term indicating 'concrete shapes in which form is crystallized (sculpture) and to the annihilation of all form (the bomb)' (*FH*, 9). While philosophy has conceptualized malleability and transformation, it is this destructive form of plasticity that Malabou argues has been under theorized (*OA*, 4).

The concept of plasticity emphasizes the dynamic nature of Hegel's dialectical method. For Malabou,

> The dialectical process is 'plastic' because, as it unfolds, it makes links between the opposing moments of total immobility (the 'fixed') and vacuity ('dissolution'), and then links both in the vitality of the whole, a whole which, reconciling these two extremes, is itself the union of resistance (Widerstand) and fluidity (Flüssigkeit). The process of plasticity is dialectical because the operations which constitute it, the seizure of form and the annihilation of all form, emergence and explosion, are contradictory. (*FH*, 12)

This passage succinctly encapsulates Malabou's contribution to the task of understanding apocalypse in an immanent and materialist way. The world is a dynamic whole composed of both resistance and fluidity, the granting of form and the destruction of form.

The applications to apocalyptic political theology become clearer when this discussion of the dialectical process turns to the issue of temporality. Recalling Hegel's use of plasticity to describe the true nature of the relationship between subject and predicate, Malabou argues that plasticity characterizes the relationship of substance and accident. Accident can designate *continuation* in both senses of the word, as *consequence*, that is, 'what follows' in the logical sense, and as *event*, that is, 'what follows' in a chronological sense. Self-determination is thus the relation of substance to that which happens. Following this line of thought we understand the 'future' in the philosophy of Hegel as the relation which subjectivity maintains with the accidental. (*FH*, 12)

The future, for Hegel, is not merely the present that has not yet happened. In this understanding '[t]ime is a dialectically differentiated instance; its being divided into definite moments determines it only *for a moment*' (*FH*, 13). Put another way, the future is constituted by a moment of abstraction, a schematization of moments itself subject to the threefold determinations of plasticity. For Malabou, understanding the future this way is a shift from the vernacular meaning of time to an 'anticipatory structure' constitutive of subjectivity (*FH*, 13). This anticipation is not the simple teleology often attributed to Hegel's philosophy of history but a structure which she defines as 'to see (what is) coming' which is 'the interplay, within Hegelian philosophy, of teleological necessity and surprise' (*FH*, 13).

This understanding of plasticity is a conceptual resource for thinking apocalyptically without the teleology that accompanies eschatological, messianic and apocalyptic ideas. Malabou's understanding of the future acknowledges the primacy of Hegel's understanding of possibility.[3] What is possible is actual and the becoming of the actual is its necessity. At the same time, there are those things that become necessary. Or, put another way, their necessity is their becoming. And this necessity, like the future, is a moment. Necessity may be undone. This affirms the basic necessity of contingency – there is nothing unconvertible. Nothing is beyond change except the system of knowing which grasps the fundamental concepts inherent to that change. Everything is plastic.

> To state that nothing is unconvertible amounts to claiming the philosophical necessity of the thought of a new materialism, which does not believe in the 'formless' and implies the vision of a malleable real that challenges the conception of time as a purely messianic process. It means that we can sometimes decide about the future . . . which means that there is actually something to do with it, in the sense in which Marx says that men make their own history. (*PD*, 77)

The concepts of plasticity and 'to see (what is) coming' allow Malabou to articulate an understanding of the future in which the future is not necessarily present now.

This understanding of plasticity recalls the earlier analysis of the contrast Boer draws between eschatology and apocalypse. Rooted in a study of biblical genres, Boer argues that apocalypse is defined in part by the seeing of the future. This vision is one of the reasons that Boer prefers eschatology over apocalypse. Yet, eschatology does not imply the same sense of destruction or annihilation. Malabou's understanding of plasticity provides language for speaking about the seeing of a future that brings with it the possibility of explosive plasticity. It is this relationship between the future and destruction that ties together Taubes, Bloch and Malabou. This destructive revelation does not reveal the future in any fixed sense, but that what is now necessary, the world, may become impossible and the impossible, indeed unthinkable, may become necessary.

> For Hegel, philosophical tradition refers to two things simultaneously: 'to the movement through which a particular accident . . . becomes essential (i.e. it becomes *fate*), and to the way a destiny, standing for the essential, then actualizes itself in its accidents, i.e. in its epochs and stages. Whether one is prior to the other is not something that can be known. This is what Absolute Knowledge *knows*. Hegelian philosophy assumes as an absolute fact the emergence of the random in the very bosom of necessity and the fact that the random, the aleatory, becomes necessary.' (*FH*, 163)

Necessity characterizes a moment of thought, not the course of thinking itself. In a sense, necessity flies at dusk. The possible only becomes necessary as it becomes actual, but that actuality is always contingent (*SL*, 550–3/6:213–17). Awareness of necessity's late arrival changes the subject's relationship to the future, foregrounding the underlying contingency.

Plastic apocalypticism: Taubes and Malabou

Malabou's plasticity can be used to read Taubes in two primary ways: in terms of his political theological method and as a way of understanding the nature of apocalyptic disruption. First, Taubes's returning to experiment with theological representations can be taken as an example of plastic reading. If Taubes defines the enduring significance of theology as the discourse which names the difference between humanity as it is and as it could be, Malabou's plasticity identifies the nature of Taubes's relationship to the traditions that furnish his key terms and concepts. Recalling Rabinbach's description of twentieth-century German Jewish messianism's 'language-work', Taubes and Bloch have a plastic relationship to the apocalyptic traditions whose texts proliferate their writings.

> The plastic reading of a text is the reading that seeks to reveal the form left in the text through the withdrawing of presence, that is, through its own deconstruction. It is a question of showing how a text lives its deconstruction . . . It is a matter of revealing a form in the text that is both other than the same *and* other than the other, *other than metaphysics, other than deconstruction.* A form that is the fruit of the self-regulation of the relation between tradition and its superseding and which at the same time exceeds that strict binary terms of this relation. (*PD*, 52)

Like Taubes and Bloch, Malabou sees value in speaking with traditions, subversively appropriating concepts. Plasticity recognizes the negativity within being itself as the motor of thought, tracing the movement between tradition and novelty and exposing the tensions within the present in order to open up spaces for something new. This emergence from within the tradition, an immanent critique or deconstruction, is the central theme that Taubes and Bloch both trace back to Joachim. What makes Bloch and Taubes particularly useful for the development of political theology is their rejection of returning to an untarnished origin. They are not engaged in political theologies of recovery, but of (re)invention.

Second, and more importantly, Taubes's understanding of apocalypticism can itself be interpreted as plastic. Recall that in *Occidental Eschatology* Taubes writes, '[t]he apocalyptic principle combined within it a form-destroying and forming power. Depending on the situation and the task, only one of the two components emerges, but neither can be absent' (*OE*, 10). As shown in the previous section, Malabou understands plasticity as 'the union of resistance and fluidity . . . The process of plasticity is dialectical because the operations which constitute it, the *seizure of form and the annihilation of all form*, emergence and explosion, are contradictory' (*FH*, 12). The resonance between the two formulations is clear, and using plasticity to understand some of the implications of Taubes's apocalypticism further clarifies key issues in his political theology.

For example, in the previous chapter, I discussed Bielik-Robson's objection to Taubes's apocalypticism: the willingness to see it all go down inevitably contradicts his desire to defend modernity against its own worst tendencies. I argued that his willing the annihilation of the world as it is should be taken as the annihilation of the world *as it is*, rather the destruction of the world *tout court*. Here, Malabou is helpful in calling for readings of texts that give rise to their plastic processes of metamorphosis (*PD*, 52). In this sense, metamorphosis names a process which, in its plasticity, is annihilation, but always an annihilation which is forming (*OA*, 74–5). In the development of an immanent and materialist apocalypticism, the destruction of the world is an end, but such an end is always also a beginning. The question of what begins is beyond a plastic apocalypticism. The world is all that is. In order for something else to be possible, the world and all its possibilities must end. Equipped with Malabou's terminology, it is possible to understand Taubes as calling for the destruction of the world as a plastic process of metamorphosis in which annihilation, explosion and emergence are joined in contradictory relation.

With these two primary confluence between apocalypticism and plasticity in mind, I now turn to the persistent questions that follow the apocalyptic – questions of immanence, alterity, novelty and trauma. If apocalypticism in the broadest sense of the term has been used to indicate a shared 'conceptual framework . . . endorsing a worldview in which supernatural revelation, the heavenly world, and eschatological judgment played essential parts',[4] plasticity can help further define the nature of revelations that are not divine, revolutions that are earthly not heavenly and the consequences that might follow judging the world itself to be unjust.

The problem of novelty and the rejection of the transcendent

When considering Taubes's use of apocalyptic ideas, the most pressing concern is apocalypticism's reliance upon transcendence and its tendency to encourage passivity. Both these tendencies take emphasis away from human agency. The result is what Bloch refers to as the patience of the cross in which the temporal suffering of the present is only a momentary distraction from eternal paradise (*AC*, 161). Against this idea, the young Hegel writes in condemnation of 'the innumerable hypocrites in any church' who embrace ascetic ideals, privileging those who 'have mastered all the requisite knowledge' and who 'live and move in church activities' (*ETW*, 138/181–2). This form of Christianity 'has taught men to despise civil and political freedom as dung in comparison with heavenly blessings and the enjoyment of eternal life' (*ETW*, 138/182). For Hegel, it fell to those who would think philosophically about religion to overturn this form of religion: 'it has been reserved in the main for our epoch to vindicate at least in theory the human ownership of the treasures formerly squandered on heaven' (*ETW*, 159/209). If Hegel, Bloch and Taubes reject this form of passivity, a hope rooted in the arrival of salvation from a transcendent agent, what then is the source of this new possibility?

In order to understand how Hegel, Taubes and Malabou together can address this problem, I will first consider Taubes's own work on immanence, before returning to Malabou's reading of Hegel, her rejection of messianism and how this develops Taubes's apocalyptic insights. Reading Hegel and Taubes through Malabou while using Taubes to draw out the apocalyptic themes of Hegel and Malabou will further clarify the nature of plastic apocalypticism.

Taubes and immanence

In Taubes's view, 'theology describes the external horizon of alterity, which in negation and alienation took a stand against culture as the sphere of familiarity and whose antagonistic force he intends to strengthen in a time in which Christian, particularly Protestant, theology in its conventional understanding has long since been incorporated into culture as one of its domains among others'.[5] Theological discourse functions as an other to philosophy, recalling the idea of representations as the other of thought. This otherness is originally derived from theology's concern with transcendence and Taubes takes it as his task to argue for a form of theological critique that rejects that transcendent guarantor and instead engages in an immanent opposition of cult to culture.

In a review of the first volume of Paul Tillich's systematic theology, Taubes discusses Tillich's symbolic topology. Rather than directing theology outwards, to the external, Taubes sees Tillich as 'mining the depths'. 'The "depth" of reason expresses something that is not reason but that precedes reason and is manifest through it. That which transcends reason is not located "beyond" reason, but the arrow of transcendence points "downward" into its depths. The depth of reason is interpreted as "substance" that appears in the rational structure of reality.'[6] Taubes does not offer an evaluation at this point, only noting the importance of depth as an ontological symbol. In the following section, however, he connects his summary of Tillich to Hegel. Taubes reads the *Phenomenology of Spirit* as developing a logos-theology in which what becomes 'explicit in theology is the spirit that recognizes itself; it is reason united with its own depth.'[7] This logos relocates the word that was external to humanity, placing it within the movement of the dialectic. Theology allows humanity to speak of its self-alienation before it realizes its own role in that process. Achieving this recognition results in a 'Gnostic theology of knowledge' which 'has its source in the Alexandrian theology and in the speculations of Joachim of Fiore'.[8] Hegel's thought is simultaneously theological and philosophical, 'but it is not a theology in the supernaturalistic sense, for it does not locate the spirit outside of man. In Hegel's logos-theology the symbols are finally translated into immanent categories.'[9]

In a later work on surrealism Taubes offers a similar perspective, highlighting the importance of the issue of these spatial terms. Questioning the prefix *sur* of surrealism, he asks 'how the vertical schema of Gnosticism must fundamentally transform itself if it is to become visible in the circumference of post-Copernican immanence'.[10] While acknowledging that it is also possible to argue for a horizontal schema, Taubes advocates interpreting the *sur* in terms of the vertical. Initially adopting the vertical schema might appear to be an affirmation of the transcendent, but Taubes clarifies,

> In Gnosticism, the pneumatic Self, which stands in opposition to the world in all its forms, must guarantee its unworldliness though an unworldly God beyond the cosmos. *This is in a certain sense nothing other than the great projection of the revolutionary uncovered non-worldly self.* The surrealist revolt takes place against the infinite world established in modern science of nature and technology that is experienced as a system of domination and

coercion, but in its breakout from this endless system of worldly coercion, it cannot invoke the guarantee of a God beyond the world.[11]

A key claim to Taubes's discussion of surrealism is his exploration of its emphasis, shared by Gnosticism, against the coercion of the necessary, understood variously as common sense, the natural and the status quo.

If Taubes's theology involves recognizing alterity, but this alterity cannot be transcendent in the usual sense of the external or non-human, an alternative notion of alterity is required. The beyond or alterity indicated by theological representations, now rendered as immanent categories, signifies not an external alterity but 'an "intensity" of the immanent'.[12] Taubes's reading of Tillich and Hegel brings to mind the earlier discussions of secularization. Hegel does not offer a story of secularization in which religion is presented as outdated superstition. Rather religion is an essential moment in the development of spirit that recognizes itself as the agent of its own alienation. The result is not a cessation of alienation but an understanding of that alienation as key to the form of knowledge that is absolute knowing.

Immanence and apocalypticism: Against messianism

Just as Taubes is concerned with defining an immanent apocalypticism, Malabou too rejects transcendence. Her exploration of immanence and temporality comes in response to Derrida's 'messianism without a messiah'. Her objections are twofold. First, she rejects transcendence in the form of an external alterity:

> And with no irruptive transcendence, there is no open door to the pure event. Nor any messianism. Nothing happens except self-transformation. From modification to metamorphosis, from migration to modification, the torsions, *volte-faces*, and reversals of a single impossibility of escaping unfold . . . there is no outside, nor is there any immobility. The plasticity of unavoidable transformation. The lifeline of a radical transformation without exoticism. (*PD*, 44)

Malabou writes of a plasticity that, like the destruction and deconstruction that came before it, does not operate as an external force but emerges from within – an 'alterity that does not come from a yonder' (*PD*, 67). Plasticity denotes forms of novelty that emerge within an immanent plane.

Malabou's stressing of the immanent in her reading of Hegel is not only a rejection of the Derridian or Levinasian messianic preservation of the transcendent, it is also an argument about the nature of the Hegelian absolute. Malabou wants to keep a strong reading of this concept, maintaining with Hegel that there is nothing outside the absolute (*FH*, 4). She cites the opening sections of the *Philosophy of Mind* to support her position: 'Mind is, therefore, in its every act only apprehending itself, and the aim of all genuine science is just this, *that mind shall recognize itself in everything in heaven and so on earth. An out-and-out other simply does not exist for mind*' (*E3*, §377z: 1/9–10).[13] This position is maintained throughout Hegel's work. In addition to the oft-cited '[t]he true is the whole' from the preface to the *Phenomenology of Spirit* (*PS*, §20: 11/24), there is Hegel's explanation of the absolute in the *Encyclopaedia of Philosophical Sciences*:

> [T]he absolute idea is the universal, but this universal is not merely the abstract form that confronts the particular contents as something-other; on the contrary it is the absolute form into which all determinations, the whole fullness of the content posited by it, have returned. In this perspective, the absolute idea is to be compared with the old man who utters the same religious statements as the child, but for whom they carry the significance of his whole life. Even if the child understands the religious content, it still counts for him only as something outside of which lie the whole of life and the whole world. (*E1*, §237z: 304/389)

In the *Science of Logic*, he clarifies that the absolute is not an external logical form, divorced from and applied to the 'real' world.

> Accordingly, what is to be considered here as method is only the movement of the *notion* itself, the nature of which movement has already been cognized; but *first*, there is now the added *significance* that the *notion is everything*, and its movement is the *universal absolute activity*, the self-determining and self-realizing movement. (*SL*, 826/6:551)

Malabou, through her reading of Hegel, requires neither transcendence nor a transcendent understanding of the absolute 'because plasticity works on and within the body of the systematic exposition, without ever extending above it or overdetermining it ... it is revealed as the concept capable of accounting for the incarnation, or the incorporation, of spirit' (*FH*, 18). This understanding of the absolute returns to themes addressed in the earlier reading of Hegel.

The absolute may be complete and closed, but only in the sense that it is a complete understanding of incompleteness and a closed system in the sense that it accounts for the negativity that can never be overcome.

For Hegel, this extends to the most fundamental ontological level. In the *Science of Logic*'s section on the doctrine of being, he examines the relationship between being, nothing and becoming. Pure being and pure nothing are identical, each passing over into the other.[14] Yet their identity is mobile, as they are both the same and 'absolutely distinct' at the same time (*SL*, 82–3/5:83). The name of this relationship, in which being and nothing are both same and different, is becoming. This transition is the introduction of dialectic as 'the higher movement of reason in which such seemingly utterly separate terms pass over into each other spontaneously' (*SL*, 105/5:111). Having established that the 'dialectical immanent nature of being and nothing' (*SL*, 105/5:111) manifests their unity in becoming, Hegel turns to the precise nature of this becoming as coming-to-be and ceasing-to-be. As one might expect, a similar pattern emerges. The two are not externally related as sublations of the other. Rather, 'each sublates itself in itself and is in its own self the opposite of itself' (*SL*, 106/5:112). The finite is defined as limited, which establishes the infinite by way of contradiction. Yet, the infinite too is defined by its other, the finite, making it finite as well. Finite and infinite 'are just as much essentially *connected* by the very negation which separates them' (*SL*, 140/5:153). Hegel claims that thought

> passes from the finite to the infinite. This transcending of the finite appears as an external act . . . Owing to the inseparability of the infinite and finite . . . there arises a limit; the infinite has vanished and its other, the finite, has entered. But this entrance of the finite appears as a happening external to the infinite, and the new limit as something that does not arise from the infinite itself but is likewise found as given. And so we are faced with a relapse into the previous determination which has been sublated in vain. But this new limit is itself only something which has to be sublated or transcended. And so again there arises the void, the nothing, in which similarly the said determinateness, a new limit, is encountered – *and so on to infinity*. (*SL*, 141/5:154)

He calls this understanding of the infinite the spurious infinite, against which he poses an alternative notion – affirmative infinity. 'The infinite, therefore, as now before us is, in fact, the process in which it is deposed to being only *one* of its determinations, the opposite of the finite, and so to being itself only one of the finites, and then raising this its difference from itself into the affirmation of itself and through this mediation becoming the *true* infinite' (*SL*, 148/5:163). This true infinite is in fact a becoming that has become further determined from the moment of abstract becoming which characterized the relationship between being and nothing. This infinite does not move in a line but through self-negation.[15] The infinite is defined by contradiction.[16]

Thus, even though it is natural that eschatological ideas give rise to fixation on the transcendent as the location of the infinite and the source of hope, Hegel's philosophy no longer requires this transcendence. Representing the absolute as subject, a key step in the development of consciousness encourages the identification of the absolute as 'a fixed point to which . . . the predicates are affixed by a movement belonging to the fixed point itself', but this fixity implies externality, whereas grasping the dynamics of the absolute reveal its 'actuality is self-movement' (*PS*, §23: 13/27). Malabou's rejection of a transcendent understanding of the absolute, coupled with her insistence that there is nothing outside the absolute, follows this reading of Hegel. Defining the infinite as self-negation means there is nothing outside of the infinite. The spurious infinite 'has the fixed determination of a *beyond*, which cannot be reached, for the very reason that *it is not meant* to be reached, because the determinateness of the beyond, of the *affirmative* negation, is not let go' (*SL*, 142/5:156). The finite thus 'perpetually generates itself in its beyond', unaware of its role in generating the infinite against which it defines itself (*SL*, 143/5:156).

In rejecting a transcendent understanding of the absolute, Malabou is arguing for an immanent absolute within the boundaries of history. It is only such an understanding of the absolute that can be constitutive of human freedom. As Stephen Houlgate argues,

> Human beings' own needs, therefore, drive them to the recognition that they are essentially self-conscious, social animals who are able to find freedom only in self-conscious community with other human beings. This initially unintended course of action is, in Hegel's view, rational and necessary and is nothing other than the course of action to which human beings are driven by their own free activity. We are thus not at the mercy of some transcendent Absolute, but we are guided by the logic that is immanent in our own activity.[17]

Thus, while Hegel is clear that the absolute is not God, the concept of God provides the means of thinking God as subject, which is a key stage in recognizing the unity of God with the subject that knows God. That unity moves consciousness from consciousness of the absolute to the absolute's self-consciousness in the subject. This self-consciousness, in turn, is Hegel's basis for a conception of freedom. Consequently, Malabou offers a helpful means of conceiving of novelty within the immanent sphere, while maintaining a strong understanding of the absolute, complementing the political theologies of Taubes and Bloch who both see religion, as a mode of thought, playing a vital role in the cultivation of human freedom.

Malabou's second critique of messianism stems from her opposition to the notion of time as a 'purely messianic process', a kind of fulfilment of destiny, whether this destiny be the divine of traditional religion or the messianism of humanism (*PD*, 76–7). For Malabou, both must be rejected as rooted in a notion of the future as merely a 'that which is to be present' – the rigidity of a future that can only be awaited. She, like Taubes, rejects messianism or any form of apocalypticism that entails a 'passive waiting for an event which will finally lead us out of the world' and instead sees the potential for 'a process which can finally lead us from the world-as-it-is'.[18] This process depends on the plasticity of an immanent apocalypticism, 'the movement of the constitution of an exit, there, where no such exit is possible ... plasticity renders possible the appearance or formation of alterity where the other is absent. Plasticity is the form of alterity without transcendence' (*PD*, 66).[19]

In rejecting this notion of the future, Malabou also dismisses attempts to graft Hegel's philosophy on to the narrative of the translation of eschatology into progress. As with Taubes, this reading of Hegel is the antithesis of Löwith's understanding of Hegel's role in the development of the philosophy of history. In Malabou's reading of Hegel, Löwith is both right and wrong. He is right to describe Hegel as central to the transformation of theological concepts of temporality into 'secular' philosophy. He is wrong to see this transformation as a crude translation of salvation history into the myth of progress.[20] Malabou's reading is thus helpful to political theology because it opens up an alternative to a dominant trope in the genealogy of radical politics: namely that Christian apocalyptic and millenarian theologies become secularized in the works of Hegel and Marx, inevitably leading to totalitarianism. The guaranteed

Kingdom of God, the telos of history, is transformed into the inevitable realization of a particular political or social order. Malabou, by foregrounding plasticity, allows us to affirm Hegel's role in transforming theological concepts while rejecting this genealogy. In doing so, she provides further conceptual resources for conceiving apocalypticism within immanent and materialist political theologies.

A Blochian supplement

As in the previous chapter, Bloch's development of apocalyptic thought in relation to Hegel provides a useful supplement to this discussion of Malabou and Taubes. In the *Future of Hegel*, Malabou refers to Derrida's description 'of a certain simultaneity of the non-simultaneous, in which the alterity and identity of the now are maintained together in the differentiated element of a certain same-ness' (*FH*, 15), later drawing a parallel to Hegel's description of the synthetic unity of time as a negative unity (*FH*, 47). This negative unity of time already disrupts the consistency of a present which is displaced into the past and future as the present that was and the present that will be, respectively (*FH*, 3).

As explained earlier, Malabou is developing a concept of the future that is not merely 'that which is to come' and arises not out of the transcendent alterity of the messianic, but through the identity of identity and alterity. When discussing temporality, Bloch uses the term 'non-contemporaneity' to describe this dialectical identity.[21] The now is contaminated with futures of incomplete pasts, structural remnants of the not-yet-resolved, a capacity to both transform and destroy the now, not as an external force intruding from without, but as a negativity constitutive of any and every now.[22]

> Not all people exist in the same Now. They do so externally, through the fact that they can be seen today. But they are thereby not yet living at the same time with the others ... Various years in general beat in the one which is just being counted and prevails. Nor do they flourish in obscurity as in the past, but contradict the Now; very strangely, crookedly, from behind. (*HT*, 97)

These non-contemporaneous remnants become irrational features of any new rationality. These contradictions, 'non-desires for the Now' (*HT*, 108), are revelations of plasticity and plastic revelations. Attention to these non-contemporaneous moments becomes the basis for a new apocalyptic political theology, one in which apocalypticism denotes the capacity for rupture that is constitutive of all nows. Apocalypticism is shorn of its associations with teleology, in the sense of a linear progression towards a determined end. 'History is no entity advancing along a single line . . . it is a *polyrhythmic and multi-spatial entity, with enough unmastered and as yet by no means revealed and resolved corners*' (*HT*, 62). The future is not-yet, though not a not-yet present, but a not-yet as the indication of the capacity to transform, rupture or remain the same. It is an alterity within history rather than an 'alterity . . . from a yonder' (*HT*, 67).

For Bloch, this not-yet is a horizon rather than a determinative content – it represents an unfulfilled past which is contemporaneous but not simultaneous with the present. In Bloch's framing, the excess that pushes these movements out of the merely social or political is the non-contemporaneity of the situation. Structural remnants of the not-yet-resolved past combine with an accumulated rage at the present. The rage is then funnelled through these elements, or in Bloch's terms the 'subjectively non-contemporaneous contradiction activates this objectively non-contemporaneous one' (*HT*, 109). Bloch develops this theory of non-contemporaneity while discussing the persistence of messianic and millenarian motifs.[23] Socialism, he claims, has broken away from its theological origins, but 'may pay respect to the dreams of its youth' in the process of fulfilling the substance of those dreams and casting off its illusory elements (*HT*, 118).

This Blochian supplement to Taubes's and Malabou's reading of Hegel, also returns to transcendental materialist themes discussed above. In Johnston's work, transcendental materialism is concerned with 'the immanent genesis of the transcendent', a genesis which is, 'in short, a self-sundering material *Grund* internally producing what (subsequently) transcends it'.[24] The immanent genesis of the transcendent echoes Bloch's clearest statement on immanence and transcendence, his notion of transcending without transcendence: 'As the abolition of every On-high which has no place for man; as a transcending with revolt, and equally a revolt with transcending – but without transcendence' (*AC*, 57).[25] As Bloch explains, this transcending without a transcendent is 'the leap from the Kingdom of Necessity to that of Freedom', which is yet another iteration of the Hegelian understanding of the immanent genesis of freedom from nature. Bloch's insistence on transcend*ing* rather than the transcend*ent* only further clarifies Johnston's formulation of the transcendental materialist understanding of freedom.

These two features of Bloch's philosophy, non-contemporaneity and transcending without transcendence, are related. As Ben Anderson notes, Bloch offers

> a unique type of materialism that . . . enables us to sense how the complex movement, and emergence, of hope enacts topologies of space–time in which plural 'goods' or 'betters' are synchronous and non-synchronous with matter rather than existing elsewhere (in another space) or else when (in another time). The result is that there is no need for an other-worldly form of transcendence that would intervene in the world from a position 'out there' or 'up there'.[26]

Though Bloch explains the possibilities opened by non-contemporaneity, it is still unclear how one exploits this disjointed time. Just because everything could be otherwise does not mean everything will be otherwise. Understanding the possibility of other possibilities requires an investigation of the relationship between necessity and contingency.

Contingency and plastic apocalypticism

If plasticity, in the domain of temporality, indicates a relationship to the future as 'to see (what is) coming', the present becomes what Bloch describes as non-contemporaneity. As seen in the previous section, the present is a disjointed collection of nows. Translated into more Hegelian language, Malabou, Taubes and Bloch advocate for a greater appreciation of possibility within Hegel's philosophy. Understanding this possibility and its implication for Malabou's notion of plasticity and apocalyptic political theology requires a more detailed consideration of contingency and necessity in Hegel. Working through these concepts also connects this formulation of apocalypticism to recent developments in continental philosophy, particularly in the work of Slavoj Žižek, Markus Gabriel and Quentin Meillassoux.[27] This more recent work repeats an earlier concern in the study of Hegel, seen most clearly in the work of Stephen Houlgate and John Burbidge. I will look at this earlier work first, before turning to points of connection with the work of Žižek and Gabriel, and then concluding by returning to Malabou, Taubes and the development of apocalyptic political theology.

The necessity of contingency

Hegel defines the relationship between actuality, possibility and contingency in the section on the doctrine of essence in the *Science of Logic*:

> [F]irst of all, since the actual and the possible are *formal differences*, their relation is likewise merely *formal* and consists only in the fact that the one like the other is a positedness, or in *contingency*.
>
> Now since in contingency, the actual as well as the possible is *positedness*, they have received determination in themselves; the actual thereby becomes, secondly, *real actuality* and with it equally emerges *real possibility* and *relative necessity*.
>
> Thirdly, the reflection of relative necessity into itself yields *absolute necessity*, which is absolute *possibility* and *actuality*. (SL, 542/6:202)

In other words, the relationship between actuality and possibility is contingency. Stated in a formula familiar to the *Logic*, 'This *absolute unrest* of the *becoming* of these two determinations [actuality and possibility] is *contingency*. But just because each immediately turns itself into its opposite, equally in this other it simply *unites with itself*, and this identity of both, of one in the other, is *necessity*' (SL, 545/6:206).

As Houlgate explains in his essay on this section, for Hegel, 'although being *is* immediacy and *is* there, it is not *just* that, but – in being what it is – is in fact the process of emerging and of actualizing what it is'.[28] Actuality, in the vernacular sense of 'the stuff that is', is for Hegel simply immediacy. Hegel has an expanded view in which actuality 'is thus always the actualizing of possibility; and possibility taken by itself is in its turn always actuality that is *not yet* actualized, and so is the possibility *of* actuality'.[29] The possibility of actuality is always also the possibility of non-actualization – all possibility thus entails contingency. In Houlgate's reading, as 'possibility *must* take the form of contingency, it is apparent that not only contingency but also *necessity* arises from the ideas of actuality and possibility'.³⁰ What is this necessity? It is contingency.

This contingency does not denote a free-for-all. There is no abstract contingency as such, only contingencies of possibilities defined by a state of given conditions. A real possibility is defined by its 'determination, circumstances and conditions' (*SL*, 547/6:208). Real possibility is posed against a real actuality.

> Now this is the posited *whole* of form, it is true, but of the form in its determinateness, namely, of actuality as formal or immediate, and equally of possibility as an abstract in-itself. This actuality which constitutes the possibility of something is therefore not *its own possibility*, but the in-itself of *another* actual; it is only itself the actuality which ought to be sublated, possibility as possibility only. Thus real possibility constitutes the *totality of conditions*, a dispersed actuality which is not reflected into itself but is determined as being the in-itself, but the in-itself of an other, and as meant to return back into itself. (*SL*, 547/6:209)

Or, as Houlgate explains '[b]ecause necessity has its source in what *possibility* cannot but be, all that can be understood by necessity at this point is the necessity *of* contingency'.³¹

If Hegel allows for contingent events in the realms of nature and history, it does not necessarily follow that he allows for contingency within concepts as well. It is conceivable that Hegel would allow for contingency in world events but not in the nature of the concept. Further, Hegel describes his logic as necessary. In the preface to the second edition of the *Science of Logic*, he argues that philosophy displays thought 'in its own immanent activity or what is the same, in it its necessary development' (*SL*, 31/5:19). Houlgate argues that a contingent thing only emerges from a possibility necessarily: 'since all contingent circumstances and condition are themselves rooted in prior conditions and give rise to subsequent conditions, it is clear that the whole course of contingency itself must be necessary. But, if the whole course of contingency is necessary, then there can be no real *contingency* in the world at all, since things, could not be otherwise than they are.'³²

As Houlgate acknowledges, this view of contingency would seem to coincide with the most teleological readings of Hegel. For the purposes of apocalyptic political theology, it would lend itself to the view that unseen or impersonal forces are directing history towards a predetermined end. Yet Houlgate makes clear that a further step is needed in order to comprehend the relation between contingency and necessity. Insisting on the primacy of necessity, in the manner suggested above, overlooks the contingency of necessity: 'specific "necessary occurrences" are contingent upon the antecedent conditions, and the whole course of real necessity is itself contingent upon what there actually is or happens to be as a whole. Indeed, the whole course of real necessity *is* simply what there actually and contingently is.'[33]

This brings Houlgate to a conclusion that resonates with my earlier discussion of nature and freedom. Hegel's understanding of freedom is constituted by a negation of nature. The realization of that freedom is a contingent event. Real necessity describes the realization of possibilities in nature. So, rather than being a determinist, Hegel 'is in fact simply a *realist* who thinks that the world takes the contingent course it takes until human beings intervene and tease out new possibilities from the conditions they encounter – possibilities which are actually contained in those conditions, but which would not be actualized without human intervention'.[34] The interactionist ontology discussed in Chapter 1 calls for extending the capacity to reveal new possibilities beyond the agency of humans, but the underlying point remains the same: freedom consists of the transformation of the possibilities of the world. Apocalyptic political theology focuses on the way that these transformations remained trapped within the possibilities of the world unless they are rooted in the world's end.

There is still one more layer to Hegel's understanding of contingency and necessity – Hegel's concept of absolute necessity. In the concluding pages of the section on actuality, Hegel defines absolute necessity as 'the truth into which actuality and possibility as such, and formal and real necessity withdraw ... that being which in its negation, in essence, is self-related and is being. It as much simple immediacy or *pure being* as simple reflection-into-self or *pure essence*' (SL, 552/6:215). In short, absolute necessity is '*immediate* simplicity, it is *being*' and this simple immediacy is 'absolute negativity' (SL, 552/6: 215). As Houlgate explains,

> absolute necessity determines nothing other than the unavoidable fate *of* all contingent things, namely that they will end. The paths laid down by

absolute necessity and contingency thus do not constitute two distinct sets of events in the world, but rather form *one* course of events which, in one respect, is wholly contingent and dependent on what there actually is, and in another respect, is structured by the absolute necessity of negation. Absolute necessity and contingency do not stand in relation to one another, therefore, nor does one underlie the other; rather, they are one and the same process.[35]

Absolute necessity is thus finitude – the passing away of all contingent being. This necessity is not only a logical or formal necessity. The grasping of the absolute necessity of the passing away of all finite things is a key element of the development of human freedom. 'The necessity that is inherent in freedom is not just the formal necessity of contingency, nor just the real necessity that follows from given conditions; nor is it sheer, absolute necessity that just *is* because it is. It is a fourth form of necessity that is *internal* to freedom itself – the necessity that there is because human beings have the *real* capacity for free self-determination.'[36]

Houlgate ultimately concludes that humanity necessarily becomes self-conscious and develops self-determining freedom because that is the nature of humanity. Yet, the process of this development occurs through contingent historical events. Nor is this form of necessity characterized by the absoluteness that characterizes the necessity of the passing away of finite things. Thus, 'the necessity which is immanent in freedom and which is at work in history cannot be *all* powerful, but must remain exposed to contingencies that it does not control.'[37] Necessity does not necessarily endure. Hegel's philosophy, in affirming the absolute necessity of finitude, acknowledges that 'self-conscious freedom in the state and civil society is itself ultimately subject to the *absolute necessity* of destruction.'[38] It is undeniable that his more optimistic statements about the course of history have had greater influence in the dominant interpretations of his philosophy, but this solemn conclusion is nonetheless an unavoidable consequence of his logic.

This brief summary of Houlgate's treatment of contingency in Hegel offers some resources for the immanentization of the apocalypse constitutive of Taubes's and Bloch's political theology. There is an emphasis on the contingency of the present form of human existence and a break from any notion of impersonal forces of history bringing about a promised utopia, millennium or heavenly community. Houlgate's reading makes clear that, for Hegel, everything must pass away.

Contingency all the way down?

John Burbidge offers an important alternative to Houlgate's reading of the same sections. In his reading he argues for a deeper contingency than Houlgate. While I will show that he does not allow for the categorial necessity required by Hegel, he develops the theme of contingency in a series of formulations amenable to the apocalyptic reading of Hegel being developed in this chapter. In Burbidge's formulation, by the time the *Logic* has advanced to the end of the section on actuality, the actuality has been transformed, shifting from what is to one of many possible actualities.[39]

Burbidge not only announces this more fundamental contingency, he claims that Hegel's understanding of contingency is necessary for serious philosophical engagement for history.

> What distinguishes a theory that takes history seriously is that, within its purview, singular actuals as novel and unique initiate general possibilities. These possibles as universals are not considered to be necessary prior conditions, underlying what is ultimately significant in the actual as individual. Rather, singular actuals provide the necessary condition for the universals generated through reflection and debate. Prior to an action, these general possibilities have no status at all. What uniquely happens is created – coming to be, as it were, out of nothing.[40]

For Burbidge, taking history seriously means beginning with the actual. What is possible is determined by the actual, but not the actual as it immediately appears. Philosophical thought, through its exposures of contradictions, unveils possibilities previously hidden and exposes the inherent finitude of any system, but these invisibilities are, in a sense, necessary. 'This is what is really necessary: this dynamic process where contingencies emerge to disrupt totalities, introducing abrasion. The resulting new universality cannot be anticipated, for it will emerge only from the conflict. Yet it will, in Hegel's final sense, be necessary as the end result of the contingent processes. Such necessity can never be deduced a priori from known prior conditions.'[41] From the apocalyptic perspective, the end of the world will have been necessary.

In pushing for a more fundamental level of contingency, Burbidge connects self-consciousness' awareness of this contingency to Hegel's discussion of the death of God in the later sections of the *Phenomenology of Spirit*. He focuses his reading on §785, shortly before the transition from revealed religion to absolute knowing. Just prior to this key section, Hegel discusses 'the coming into existence of God's individual self-consciousness as a universal self-consciousness' through Christ's sacrifice (*PS*, §784: 475/570). The death of God as 'man', 'is *abstract* negativity, the immediate result of the movement which ends in spiritual self-consciousness' (*PS*, §784: 475/570).

Burbidge picks up Hegel's argument as Hegel explains the implications of this transition:

> The death of the Mediator is the death not only of his *natural* aspect or of his particular being-for-self, not only of the already dead husk stripped of its essential notion, but also of the *abstraction* of the divine notion . . . The death of this representational thought contains, therefore, at the same time the death of the *abstraction of the divine notion* which is not posited as self. The death is the painful feeling of the Unhappy Consciousness that *God Himself is dead* . . . This feeling is, in fact, the loss of substance and of its appearance over against consciousness; but it is at the same time the pure *subjectivity* of substance, or the pure certainty of itself which it lacked when it was object, or the immediate, or pure essence. This knowing is the inbreathing of the spirit, whereby Substance becomes subject, by which its abstraction and lifelessness have died, and Substance therefore has become *actual* and simple and universal self-consciousness. (*PS*, §785: 476)[42]

The experience of the death of God is essential to the emergence of absolute knowing from representational thought. It is only by virtue of this experience that 'spirit is *self-knowing* spirit' (*PS*, §786: 476/419). Though Burbidge does not emphasize the point, the link between contingency and the experience of the death of God starts from the representational understanding of religion. The death of God, the significance of the story of Christ, is the historical enactment of the relationship between the universal, particular and singular. The death of God as mediator is 'the death of the abstraction of the divine essence: the death of the absolutely reliable, transcendent standard that made life worth living, the death of everything the self has stood for and everything that has defined the meaning of existence'.[43]

The crucifixion is the death of any transcendent guarantor. It represents the collapse into immanence. While Burbidge does not develop this line of thought, the resurrection and Pentecost come to represent the birth of the community of spirit that assumes the task of freedom – the rational self-determination at the heart of *Sittlichkeit*.

> [I]t is precisely this dissolution of all stability that heralds the possibility of absolute knowing. This goal of all epistemology can no longer be a confident claim to certain conclusions, nor a comprehension of everything in its essence. It can only be a flux, pure subjectivity, aware of the past that has brought it to the present, accepting the present as the dynamic life it can only enjoy, but leaving open the future. Though the next stages will emerge from the present, there are no essentials that will have to be maintained. Any aspect may be put in question. Contingencies will surprise us.[44]

As Burbidge considers the significance of this understanding of contingency, the connection to apocalyptic thought becomes even clearer:

> [S]omeone comes along who is not content to fit into the status quo, who sees very clearly the failures and the inadequacies of the current state of affairs, and who is moved to act. Passion erupts in the committed action of the few who are grasped by the demands of the age; and whose station places them at a critical juncture. They plunge forward, threatening the fragile stability of the social order. Where that happens, and where their passionate acts articulate the unexpressed restlessness of many others, history is ruptured. The comfortable social order is recognized as one-sided, needing correction. But correction does not come piecemeal. Order shatters in revolutionary turmoil. Rebellion evokes resistance and counter attack. Even if the challenge is ultimately defeated, the future will never be like the past. For the new social order will have built into its fabric new conventions that do justice to those passions worn out in the struggle.[45]

This level of disruption, the explosiveness of unexpressed restlessness, escapes the limits of social reasoning. Burbidge's reading does not close off the role of social reasoning. It includes those processes, but sets them atop an absolutely contingent ground. It is the contingency of this ground that is at the heart of apocalyptic fervour. It is possible that it could all be different.

Yet, Burbidge makes clear that contingency is not synonymous with randomness. As he argues elsewhere, the novel is novel only with respect to what precedes it. The comparison establishing novelty is thus a determination establishing continuity between the new and the old. 'History develops; it does not haphazardly skip to unrelated stages.'[46] Apocalypses are always specific endings. The relationship between the actual, possible, contingent and necessary is only manifested in the movement of thought. To use Hegel's language from the preface to the *Phenomenology of Spirit*, 'the whole is nothing other than the essence consummating itself through its development. Of the absolute it must be said that it is essentially a *result*, that only in the *end* is it what it truly is; and that precisely in this consists its nature, viz. to be actual, subject, the spontaneous becoming of itself' (*PS*, §20: 11/24). For Burbidge, this arriving at the result never ceases.

While Houlgate and Burbidge initially appear to offer quite similar accounts of the role of contingency in Hegel's *Logic*, they differ in regard to the depth of this contingency. For Houlgate, it is not contingent that there is anything at all or that humanity knows the way it knows, only that things are the way they are. For Burbidge, Hegel's contingency is more pervasive. This point of contention is also at the centre of the difference between Markus Gabriel's and Žižek's reading of contingency in German Idealism. Žižek, like Burbidge, sees contingency at the heart of Hegel's openness to the future. 'What if the wager of [Hegel's] dialectic is not to adopt the "point of view of finality" toward the present viewing it as if it were already past, but, precisely, to *reintroduce the openness of the future into the past*, to *grasp that-which-was in its process of becoming*, to see the contingent process which generated existing necessity?'[47] He also presents a similar understanding of the relationship between contingency and necessity, arguing that '*the very process through which necessity arises out of necessity is a contingent process*.'[48] And like Burbidge, this contingency goes all the way down.

> Only if the encompassing unity is contingency can we claim the subject's discovery of necessary truth is simultaneously the (contingent) constitution of this truth itself, that to paraphrase Hegel, the very return to (rediscovery of) eternal Truth generates this truth. So, far from being an "essentialist" who develops the entire content out of the necessary self-deployment of the notion, Hegel is – to use today's terms – the ultimate thinker of autopoesis, of the process of the emergence of necessary features out of chaotic contingency, the thinker of contingency's gradual self-organization, of the gradual rise of order out of chaos.[49]

Žižek, then, shares Burbidge's strong notion of contingency, in which '[n]ecessity is thus nothing but the "truth" of contingency, contingency brought to its truth by way of (self-negation)'.[50]

Gabriel, on the other hand, agrees with Houlgate's assessment that, for Hegel, contingency has its limits. On the issue of contingency, this point differentiates Hegel and Schelling. Hegel includes contingency, but there is a necessity to the logical system, the categories, which comprehend that contingency. For Schelling, however, it could all be different, or not be at all.[51] Put alternatively, Hegel has a concept of absolute necessity but not absolute contingency. The form of being is necessary and this form includes the necessary passing from being to nothing of the various contingent contents that fill that form.

Conclusion

The reading of Hegel developed here finds the greatest resonance with Burbidge's reading but with the qualification that contingency cannot extend all the way down to Schelling's depths. As Houlgate explains, modern subjects

> bring our own categories to bear on our experience and view nature and history through these categories just as any civilization does. The categories we employ – or at least should employ – are, as we have seen, categories such as freedom, development and self-determination. But these categories are not just conventional categories; they are not just the product of technological changes or of 'paradigm shifts' which are ultimately a matter of chance . . . The categories of modern consciousness are historical products, but they are not therefore intrinsically limited categories because they are the categories through which we have become fully aware of our historicity and freedom.[52]

These categories are necessary, though the historical path to the derivation of those categories is contingent. These categories are necessary for being self-conscious of the historical character of human activity at this moment in history. They are categories necessary for understanding the present. They do not exhaust that present. It is important to remember that annihilation, for all of its destructiveness, is still a possibility of the world. It is simply the only possibility that opens up the possibility of the emergence of new possibilities.

With this one qualification from Houlgate, however, Burbidge offers a thorough reading of Hegel's notion of contingency, stemming from readings of both the *Science of Logic* and the *Phenomenology of Spirit*, leading to an open understanding of the future and drawing upon Hegel's understanding of religion. The reading of Taubes and Bloch developed in the previous chapter, along with Malabou's understanding of plasticity, is granted greater conceptual clarity when supported by Burbidge. This clarity is especially evident with regard to Bloch's concepts of the not-yet and concrete utopia, and the synthesis of Taubes and Malabou in plastic apocalypticism.

Contingency clarifies the relationship between the not-yet and concrete utopia. As Bloch explains, concrete utopia differs from more traditional forms of utopianism.

> Concrete utopia is therefore concerned to understand the dream of its object exactly, a dream which lies in the historical trend itself. As a utopia mediated with process, it is concerned to deliver the forms and contents which have already developed in the womb of present society. Utopia in this no longer abstract sense is thus the same as realistic anticipation of what is good; which must have become clear. There is a processive-concrete utopia in both basic elements of the reality discerned by Marxism: in its tendency, the tension of what is due though hindered, and in its latency, the correlate of the not yet realized objective-real possibilities in the world. (*PH*, 2: 623)

As noted in the last chapter, Taubes dismisses Bloch's utopianism. This dismissal is understandable – the *Principle of Hope*'s encyclopaedic survey of symbols of hope, at times, seems excessive. The underlying theory of concrete utopia, however, is an apocalyptic rendering of the relationship between the actual, possible and contingent. It is the contingency of what is that justifies the belief that it could be different. Taubes's acknowledgement of the more tenuous relationship between the potential nihilistic and messianic forms of embracing contingency provides a balance to Bloch's optimism, but Bloch's concrete utopia allows for a kind of strategizing that does not directly arise from Taubes. Put another way, Taubes offers an important survey of the situation and considerations of the consequences of actions while Bloch more directly demands action within the situation.

For Bloch, this orientation to the future is not divorced from one's relationship to the past. As Žižek explains, this requires the application of the concept of contingency to the philosophy of history. The resulting understanding of history is remarkably similar to Bloch's notion of non-contemporaneity:

> the task of a true Marxist historiography is not to describe the events the way they really were (and to explain how these events generated the ideological illusions that accompanied them); the task is rather to unearth the hidden potentiality (the utopian emancipatory potential) which was betrayed in the actuality of revolution and in its final outcome (the rise of utilitarian market capitalism).[53]

This parallel becomes even clearer when Žižek describes the cunning of reason as functioning 'to explain how these betrayed radical-emancipatory potentials continue to "insist" as historical "specters" that haunt the revolutionary memory . . . so that the later proletarian revolution should also redeem (lay to rest) these past ghosts. These alternative versions of the past which persist in a spectral form constitute the ontological "openness" of this historical process.'[54]

Bloch's concrete utopia is thus an aspiration arising from a consideration of the non-contemporaneousness of the present situation. In more Hegelian language, concrete utopia is the utopian impulse rooted in actuality. This actuality is one characterized by the absolute necessity of contingency. The possibility of novelty, the apocalyptic potential, emerges from actuality, not from beyond. Apocalypticism, in this understanding, does not await the transcendent but engages in the act of transcending.[55] As Burbidge explains,

> whenever we consider the actual world as a totality on its own, we find it to be a world within which determinate actualities emerge and become necessary and sufficient conditions for other actualities, but whatever does in fact emerge is permeated by contingency. This is the nature of necessity when we consider the total picture – what Hegel calls 'absolute necessity' – and it requires, as a defining feature of its complex dynamic, that there be contingencies.[56]

Grasping this actuality returns the conversation to Malabou's understanding of plasticity. Plasticity denotes the manners of change conceivable within the contingency of necessity. That is, given that everything could be different (except the categories), plasticity announces the modes of transformation that may occur. Things may be moulded through processes of reform or exploded through apocalyptic movements. Both will result in the emergence of new forms in a process of perpetual transformation.[57] This consistency of form as such, though the form of form may change, is derived from the materialism common to Taubes and Malabou. There is only this world, this actuality. Given the contingency of that actuality, new organizations of that actuality may come, but it will involve the re-organization of the material that is now.

This re-organization, as Malabou shows, requires going beyond gradual transformations to grasp destructive plasticity. Contingent does not mean arbitrary and the disruption of what has become necessary is cataclysmic.[58] It is the end of the world. Or rather it is the ending of *a* world, but a world which can only appear as *the* world. Malabou has been critical of the messianic obsession with ending, but apocalyptic ending is 'not the end of time itself'.[59] Rather, it seeks to think in the wake of the 'collapse of messianic structures', no longer having anything 'to do with the tenacious, incurable desire to transform what has taken place' (*OA*, 88–9). The possibilities of novelty beyond such transformations are necessarily traumatic.

This discussion of Malabou, Taubes and Hegel results in a notion of plastic apocalypticism. Malabou's understanding of plasticity as the ability to give form, to receive form and to annihilate form provides additional philosophical resources for thinking about the nature of apocalypticism. Her reading of Hegel offers a way of conceiving of novelty within the immanent plane. This understanding of plasticity is strikingly similar to Taubes's definition of apocalypticism. When read in light of Hegel's understanding of necessity and contingency, it becomes possible not only to see, with Taubes, the possibility of it all going down but also to insist that it may, eventually, have been necessary.

5

Pessimism and hope in apocalyptic living

This book began with an account of the world and has subsequently worked through Hegel, Taubes and Malabou to think about that world's end. While apocalypticism has historically been associated with the breaking in of a transcendent power that simultaneously reveals the divine truth and destroys the world, Hegel, Taubes and Malabou, together, provide a way of thinking apocalyptically without that transcendence. Through concepts of plasticity and contingency, it becomes possible to consider a resolutely negative orientation to the world, focused on the possibility of possibilities not of that world. This immanent account of novelty provides a peculiar kind of hope. There is the possibility of something different, but that possibility requires passing through annihilation.

In the first chapter I identified a series of questions that accompany apocalypticism. While the ensuing chapters have addressed questions about the nature of political theology, true novelty without transcendence and the fact that this novelty necessarily is accompanied by destruction, it remains to be seen what 'disinvesting in the world as it is' means for life in that world. How does one live in a world that must end? How does a process of active disinvestment in the world function? To begin to answer these questions, I draw on the conceptual resources of plastic apocalypticism while engaging with the queer theory of Lee Edelman and Frank B. Wilderson III's Afro-Pessimism. The result is not a set of answers but perhaps the beginning of a strategy for living negatively.

Living with the absence of alternatives

The most frequent challenge to apocalyptic ideas, after the problem of violence, is the question of alternatives. If the world is so bad, what does a good world look like and how might it be brought about? The underlying assumption is that there is an ethical or political duty to provide a concrete plan for how things will be different in this new world.

In responding to this challenge, it is important to begin by reiterating that the rejection of the world does not require insisting that nothing good has ever happened in the world. Schmitt, in the course of his critique of liberalism, makes this point.

> There are certainly not many people today who want to renounce the old liberal freedoms, particularly freedom of speech and the press. But on the European continent there are not many more who believe that these freedoms still exist where they could actually endanger the real holders of power. And the smallest number still believe that just laws and the right politics can be achieved through newspaper articles, speeches at demonstrations, and parliamentary debates.[1]

Liberalism, modernity and the Enlightenment have produced understandings of rights, freedom and equality that are undeniably valuable. Yet, at the same time, it is far from clear that these philosophical traditions are the *only* ones capable of producing such understandings or that their distinctive conceptualizations of rights, freedoms and equality are capable of addressing the structuring antagonisms of the world. For Schmitt, the defence of these traditions can also function as a distraction as they 'wear down great enthusiasm into chatter and intrigue and kill the genuine instincts and intuitions that produce a moral decision'.[2] To succumb to the demand for alternatives is to become trapped by affirmation and to get lost in the chatter and intrigue. Put another way, it is to reinvest in this world through faith in its possibilities.

The narrative of these improvements is not as straightforward as it may initially seem. One way of reading 'progress' in history is to argue that the legal and political orders that operate in the world have resulted in important developments: greater rights from women, increased tolerance of a wide range of sexual orientations and decreased racially motivated violence and discrimination. Surely, these victories are evidence that these legal and political orders work? They are the preconditions of emancipation rather than obstacles to its realization.[3] Again, rejecting the world does not mean overlooking those important developments, the concrete differences they have made in the lives of people or the sacrifices through which those developments were wrought. Yet it is nonetheless possible to read this 'progress' in a different way. These developments were not the result of straightforward legal appeals and political processes, but a complex mixture of these approaches alongside violence, violation of the law and political revolution. The eventual accommodation is an example of the *katechon* at work. Abstract gender and racial equality can be achieved provided that concrete equality remains taboo. The state as the agent of abolition is better than slaves being the authors of their own liberation. Greater acceptance of homosexuality is possible provided that this homosexuality is not *too* queer. Preserving marriage and the nuclear family is worth the risk of expanding who has access to those institutions. Changes will be allowed so long as order is preserved and chaos is contained. These accommodations, to those who oppose them, may initially seem to be defeats. In truth, the opposite is the case. Ultimately, they are reaffirmations of the power of that legal and political order.[4] The end of slavery can now be celebrated at the expense of the shame that slavery ever existed in the first place. Previous injustices can be recast as a misapplication of principles now corrected through the same political order that re-establishes itself as the arbiter of justice.

Arguing against these legal and political orders is not an opposition to greater rights for women, increased tolerance of a wide range of sexual orientations and decreased racially motivated violence and discrimination. Rather, this opposition is motivated by the desire for concrete rather than abstract equality and for the possibility of relationships no longer dictated by what Butler famously names the heterosexual matrix.[5] If the world is structured by the antagonisms of nature, capital, gender and race, however, this concrete equality and these reconfigured relationships are not possible. A world in which appropriation, distribution and production are no longer fundamentally determined by this set of antagonisms is not a better world – it is a different world.

This insistence on the limitations of the world only returns the conversation to the demand for alternatives. Apocalypticism refuses this blackmail of affirmation from the outset. How can one offer an alternative to the world from within the world? There are the only possibilities of the world, and any attempt to formulate alternatives remains trapped by the logic of that world.[6] Apocalypticism does not assume that it is possible to adopt a position 'above our material complexity' or to take 'an angelic view of the world'.[7] Rather than offer a solution on the basis of this assumed knowledge, it only offers a refusal. It 'negates this world in its fullness' (*OE*, 9).

Apocalypticism thus attempts to defend this negative position against 'the trump card of affirmation' – the question '[i]f not this, what?'[8] This question makes profound assumptions about the nature of this 'this'. It is a *katechonic* question, implying that the choices are between the gradually improving or progressing world and an existence of violence and chaos. The question elides that the world is already maintained by perpetual violence that is often slow and invisible (to many). The choice is not between violent destruction and peace, but between different distributions of violence. As China Miéville writes, 'We don't have to have an alternative, that's not how critique works. We may do . . . but if we don't that no more invalidates our hate for this, for what is, than does that of a serf for her lord, her flail-backed insistence that this must end.'[9] The demand for alternatives assumes the ability to know what should be hoped for and, indeed, how to best hope. Plastic apocalypticism is not a discourse of articulated hopes, though. Rather, it is the hope in the possibility of being able to one day hope. It is the conviction that the end is enough to hope in without having to also articulate the beginning that will follow.

This refusal severs one of the links posited between apocalypticism and totalitarianism. As discussed earlier, one objection to apocalyptic political theology is that politics with apocalyptic origins results in the violent imposition of a new world. Setting to one side the assumption that theological origins somehow infect later political movements, the link between some utopian visions of a new world and violence must be acknowledged. Even in Thomas More's version, utopia is the consequence of conquest.[10] The violence of plastic apocalypticism is not the violence of imposing a new vision, though. Rather, the plastic apocalypticism developed here distills apocalypticism to its negative essence. It is an anarchic unleashing more than a planned imposition. Nothing is imposed because there is not yet the position from which to think new beginnings. For now, the end is enough.

Pessimism and surrender

If the demand for an alternative is one standard response to apocalyptic ideas, the other is the accusation of self-indulgent pessimism and surrender. Apocalypticism breeds quietism. Indeed, Taubes himself endorses a version of this resignation. In his analysis of Paul's first letter to the Corinthians, he summarizes the Apostle's position as one that rejects the need for any kind of revolution. What is the point if it is all going down anyway? Taubes agrees with Paul, replying, 'Demonstrate obedience to state authority, pay taxes, don't do anything bad, don't get involved in conflicts' (*PT*, 54). A defence of apocalypticism and the accompanying pessimism thus requires a notion of pessimism that is not merely surrender.

This defence of apocalyptic pessimism is particularly important as the injunction to hope is reaching a new crescendo. These demands are often accompanied by the condemnation of pessimism. Rebecca Solnit's *Hope in the Dark* is emblematic in this regard: 'the world often seems divided between false hope and gratuitous despair. Despair demands less of us, it's more predictable, and in a sad way safer.'[11] For Solnit, the position that everything is horrible, while potentially a self-satisfying anti-authoritarian position, is ultimately just the inversion of the notion that everything is or will be fine.[12] In opposition to this easy despair, she advocates a hope found in contingency. The future remains unknown and actions, of individuals and groups, can shape that future. Hope, in her view, lies between optimism and pessimism. Both these options are passive – whether things will ultimately be fine or it will all go down. Only hope entails action.[13]

There is an active form of pessimism that can be contrasted with the version that Solnit rejects.[14] Both Edelman's queer theory and Wilderson's Afro-Pessimism argue for forms of pessimism that are not merely resignation. Neither Edelman nor Wilderson frame their work in terms of political theology, but apocalyptic political theology can learn from the resolute negativity that animates their positions.[15] They both, in different ways, reveal the difficulty of opposing the world. The fact that their arguments are radical within and marginal to contemporary queer and Black politics and theory is indicative of the extent to which the promise of the world continues to be the source of hope. Both show the complexity of the 'epistemological violence necessary to undo a social order'.[16]

Edelman argues for an anti-politics that rejects the absorption of the queer into heteronormative forms of life. While mainstream activism celebrates the increased visibility of LGBTQ people, gay marriage, the right to adopt and, to varying extents, greater legal protection against discrimination, Edelman highlights the cost of these victories. Queerness has been captured. It has moved from the shadowy regions of parks and bus stations into the bright light of pride parades with floats sponsored by banks and fast-food restaurants.[17] 'Queer' used to signify something dangerous – a threat to family and society. The progress of the last few decades has been achieved on the condition of disarmament.

Edelman is an example of someone who insists on continuing to fight, not only against heteronormativity, but against the reproductive futurism that he finds at the heart of its vision of subjectivity, family, social relations and politics – a vision that he memorably describes as the 'fascism of the baby's face'.[18]

> Rather than rejecting, with liberal discourse, this ascription of negativity to the queer, we might, as I argue, do better to consider accepting and even embracing it. Not in the hope of forging thereby some more perfect social order – such a hope, after all, would only reproduce the constraining mandate of futurism, just as any such order would equally occasion the negativity of the queer – but rather to refuse the insistence of hope itself as affirmation, which is always affirmation of an order whose refusal will register as unthinkable, irresponsible, inhumane.[19]

Edelman reiterates that this vision of queerness is not an oppositional identity taken up to undo the dominant order. Such an oppositional identity could too easily take on an inverted heroism, opposing that order so as to save some aspect of it. Rather, Edelman argues that his rejection of the future is offered 'in opposition to politics as the governing fantasy of realizing, in an always indefinite future', some vision of reality.[20] For Edelman, the oppositional nature of this identity is essential. Queerness is positional rather than substantive.[21] The queer political gesture (rather than gesture of queer politics) is to reject substantive political identity as such. In embracing this position and rejecting the fantasy of identity, queerness begins to disrupt the configuration of past, present and future represented by the demand for endless reproduction. As Edelman points out, this disruption begins with the rejection of actual biological reproduction. In foregrounding non-productive sex, Edelman is refusing to invest in the future.[22] He is disinvesting from the world in the name of 'having a life'.[23]

Edelman's vision of a queer anti-politics is not without its issues. It can look like indulgent individualism in the guise of radical resistance to the Symbolic precisely at a moment when it seems more difficult than ever to articulate collective visions of disruption.[24] Abandoning the future can also seem like a capitulation to a capitalist mode of time: history has ended and all that remains is an endless cycle of alienated labour and consumption.[25] These themes are taken up in José Esteban Muñoz's queer utopian response to Edelman. Drawing on Bloch's work, Muñoz agrees with Edelman's rejection of the world but argues that this queer refusal is accompanied by 'an insistence on potentiality or concrete possibility for another world'.[26] Muñoz describes a queer negativity, but one which is more utopian than what I am describing as Edelman's queer apocalypticism. Put another way, if Edelman offers an anti-utopian critique, Muñoz provides an anti-antiutopianism. 'Radical negativity, like the negation of negation, offers us a mode of understanding negativity that is starkly different from the version of the negative proposed by the queer antirelationist. Here the negative becomes the resource for a certain mode of queer utopianism.'[27] His queer futurity is a response to the dangers of the political nihilism he finds in Edelman.[28] In keeping with his use of Bloch, Muñoz's utopianism is not a teleological advancing towards an already known end, however. Much as with the earlier description of Hegel's absolute, he argues utopia should be understood as part of a method rather than a defined goal.[29] Utopia is not about the successful journey to a prescribed future but the process of failing one's way to the new. In that failure there is potentiality.[30]

There is also the question of whether or not Edelman's attempt at offering an account of queer negativity is capable of avoiding slipping back into affirmation. Malabou argues that as 'freedom becomes tied to the possibility of saying yes to no. Absolute negation is thus affirmative in principle' (*OA*, 74). While it may be possible to maintain a 'singular insistence on jouissance' and 'forsakes *all* causes, *all* social action, *all* responsibility for a better tomorrow or for the perfection of social forms', what motivates this abandonment?[31] The difficult work of forsaking is an act of political self-destruction that refuses 'enslavement to the future.'[32] While Edelman is more adamant about what life is not rather than what it is, there is in this declaration something like Muñoz's notion of an open and indeterminate potentiality.[33]

Malabou describes this as 'the *negative possibility*' (*OA*, 75). There is a power to the negative that can be read as a peculiar form of hope. Not a hope in the future but a hope in impossible possibilities of the present. Not specific impossible possibilities but impossible possibilities as such. As the concept of plasticity shows, annihilation is still a forming. There will be a future. This future cannot be reproduced as it does not exist, nor can it be produced as its conditions of possibility are not discernible in the present.[34] Its condition of possibility is the end – it is a possibility indistinguishable from annihilation. This is queer hope as disinvestment in the world. It is a hope for the possibility of *a* future that requires first rejecting hope for *the* future of the world. The unintelligibility of queer being does not abandon hope of being understood, but refuses to be understood here and now.[35] There is an impossible possibility of a queer futurity that 'is animated by a future desire only perceptible ("perhaps") – not recognizable – now'.[36] Rather than no future, there is no future for *this*. There is no future without the passage through the apocalyptic trauma that provides the conditions for the impossible possibility becoming possible.

This question of impossibility and possibility is also central to Wilderson's work. As Edelman is concerned with the structural position of queerness, Wilderson is concerned with the positionality of Blackness. For Edelman, the rejection of queerness is central to both the libidinal and political economy of a capitalism that is heteronormative. For Wilderson, the gratuitous violence and subjugation of Black bodies is even more fundamental to these economies. The liberation of the worker, the housewife and the queer, cannot be extended to the positionality of the slave.[37] 'The Black', for Wilderson, indicates an impossibility of the world. This position is a form of anti-subjectivity.[38] As already discussed in the first chapter, he sees this impossibility, the exclusion of Blackness from the human, as foundational to the world. Given the nature of this world, then the only option is its rejection. 'Where there are Slaves it is unethical to be free.'[39] One must refuse, to the extent that it is possible, to be reduced to this world.

This pessimism about the possibility of inclusion in the world is not mere resignation. It requires work, but it is not work for a solution. No solution is possible. The demand for solutions is the same as the demand for alternatives. The assumption is that one must have an answer to critique the problem. Again, apocalypticism simply refuses this demand. Sometimes refusing is all you can do. Even this refusal is not complete. Living apocalyptically is the constant investigation of what it means to engage in this refusing, of cultivating habits of refusal and of developing the capacity to sustain this refusal as a mode of negatively being in the world.[40] It is a pure negativity, not interested in refusing in favour of a determinate alternative. It is a willingness to see 'an undoing . . . for its own sake'.[41]

This undoing is violent. It is the kind of change that requires plasticity of the explosive kind. For Wilderson, life in the world is intimately attached to violence. It is the only way that Blackness can refuse to be made an object. A Black person can only appear 'under the "cleansing" conditions of violence. Only when real violence is coupled with representational "monstrosity", can Blacks move from the status of things to the status of . . . of what, we'll just have to wait and see.'[42] The negation of the world is always met with violence. It is therefore not a question of violence and non-violence, but whose violence directed at whom and for what purpose. In Saidiya V. Hartman's conversation with Wilderson, she describes his analysis of negation as 'the captive's central possibility for action, whether we think of that as a radical refusal of the terms of the social order or . . . an embrace of death'.[43] For Wilderson, this life of negation is still life. 'We have tremendous life. But this life is not analogous to those touchstones of cohesion that hold civil society together. In fact, the trajectory of our life (within our terrain of civil death) is bound up in claiming – sometimes individually, sometimes collectively – the violence of which Fanon writes about.'[44] As Fanon shows, that violence cannot make a wrong world right, nor can taking up violence be the direct and intentional creation of genuinely new possibilities. Violent revolution, like all revolution, is still a possibility of this world, but refusing the wrong world is not a peaceful activity.[45]

Pessimism thus entails some resignation and some surrender of agency, but what matters is what is resigned and what is surrendered. It is the possibility of solutions to the problems of the world that is abandoned, because it is the world itself that is the problem. Attempting to solve this problem always entails taking up the mantel of agency or power as it is defined by the world. Those who take up this mantel in order to solve the problem are often unaware of the extent to which they are the problem too.[46]

Edelman and Wilderson each offer a form of pessimism, an analysis of anti-relational or non-relational positions and a consideration of the implications for thinking about the world and its future. Solnit's insistence on hope still persists, however. After all, she is clear that hope is not a belief that everything is going well or taking up tasks that seem destined for success. One hopes for the good because it is good, not because it is likely.[47] In her vision, '[h]ope is not a door, but a sense that there might be a door at some point, some way out of the problems of the present moment even before that way is found or followed. Sometimes radicals settle for excoriating the wall for being so large . . . rather than seeking a door.'[48] Here, Solnit reaches a position that is nearing the apocalyptic version of hope I have been developing. Indeed, she even draws upon Bloch in outlining her definition of hope. Yet her hope is still a hope for a solution, even if that solution is not necessarily conclusive and definitive. These more tentative solutions, important though they may be, are still solutions within the world. They are ultimately rendering the world structured by the antagonisms of nature, capital, gender and race more tolerable.

The hope that Solnit is describing, from this perspective of a world structured by antagonisms, are examples of what Lauren Berlant calls cruel optimism. This is a hope that is dependent on an 'attachment to compromised conditions of possibility'.[49] This hope provides the subject a sense of being and purpose. To lose the object of hope is to risk dissolution, groundlessness. Yet it is precisely this dissolution and groundlessness that marks the possibility of new possibilities. Only after the hopes of this world have been abandoned and the world itself has fallen away, will it be possible to witness the emergence of new hope. To repeat what is now becoming a refrain, the only hope is for an end and that hope is enough, for now.

This active pessimism, a persistent refusal, is the non-quietist version of disinvesting from the world. Not becoming fixated on the false hopes of the world requires effort. One must have strategies for forging the kind of autonomy that Bifo argues comes from refusal. 'Do not take part in the game, do not expect any solution from politics, do not be attached to things, do not hope.'[50] Yet, even in his argument, as is often the case, the urge to abandon hope is followed by a warning not to abandon the revolution, even if that revolution is vague, unformed and far from sure of success.

An understanding of disinvestment drawing on Edelman and Wilderson abandons even this hope. That does not amount to an abandonment of agency or a form of resignation, however. Pessimism is not so much resignation as the recognition that there is no possibility of victory. The questions of agency and hope are incomplete questions. The real question is the agency to do what? Hope for what? The task is neither to redeem the present world nor to offer something new, but to recognize that this world is not worth perpetuating and to find agency and hope in that act of abandonment. There is still the possibility, though no guarantee, of finding 'something beautiful or generative or sustaining in the pessimistic and the negative'.[51]

Living towards the end of the world

This discussion of abandoning hope in the world inevitably returns to the question of violence. Throughout this book I have argued that apocalypticism does not have to entail the violent imposition of a vision of a new world. While that desire has animated other political visions, a plastic apocalypticism drawing on Hegel, Taubes and Malabou has a different relationship to violence. On the one hand, it recognizes trauma as the condition for the immanent emergence of novelty. On the other hand, it does not seek to bring about this new. It operates with an awareness that any attempt to bring about the fundamentally new can only be the realization of possibilities of this world, a world whose possibilities continue the antagonistic divisions that apocalypticism seeks to escape. As Malabou argues, 'Transformation is a form of redemption, a strange salvation, but salvation all the same. By contrast, the flight identity forged by destructive plasticity flees itself first and foremost; it knows no salvation or deception' (*OA*, 12).

What is more, even if it were possible to envision the kind of act that could result in a new world, such an act would lie beyond any ethical or political justification. Such an event would be sufficiently cataclysmic that to even desire such an event is itself problematic. The suffering of the world is overwhelming, but its annihilation will be no better. Indeed, terms like 'better' no longer function in considerations of the apocalyptic. There is only must. Yet, it is also problematic to not desire such an event, for to do so is to will the continuation of the violence of the present. To oppose the apocalyptic end is to desire the comfort of familiar forms of violence rather than the uncertainty of the traumatically new. In this tragic dilemma, how is one to live?

First, this life entails abandoning the hope of living rightly.[52] The possibility of solutions has been forsaken and now the hope for absolution should be too. Clearly not all positions in the world bear the same culpability for the world, but apocalypticism is not oriented towards the desire to evade the blame that adheres to one's position.

Second, apocalypticism is not the apocalypse. There may be no fiery end. If the Anthropocene, as discussed in the first chapter, took some 150 years to arrive, the end of that era may come at a similar speed. The violence of the world is often slow and the violence of its undoing may be so as well.

Finally, the constant investigation of what it means to engage in this refusing, of cultivating habits of refusal and of developing the capacity to sustain this refusal as a mode of negatively being in the world may also not be dramatic. In *Fear and Trembling*, Kierkegaard (or Johannes de Silentio) contrasts two opposing positions: the knight of infinite resignation and the knight of faith. Both these positions are offered in the course of exploring Abraham's ethical dilemma and the theological suspension of the ethical.[53] To explore the options of resignation and faith, Kierkegaard offers the example of fated lovers, forbidden from realizing their love. The knight of infinite resignation dwells in the pain and torment of the inability to be with the one he loves.[54] The knight can only sublimate his desire. It becomes 'the expression of an eternal love, would assume a religious character, would be transfigured into a love of the eternal being, which true enough denied the fulfilment but nevertheless did reconcile him once more in the eternal consciousness of its validity in an eternal form'.[55] The knight of faith also experiences this pain and also goes through a process of sublimation. Yet this knight goes one step further, declaring 'I have faith that I will get her – that is, by virtue of the absurd, by virtue of the fact that for God all things are possible.'[56]

Both these positions can be considered in relationship to apocalyptic subjectivity. First, like the knight of infinite resignation, one can be overwhelmed by the horror of his world and live into this horror. It can become one's experience of the entire world and even sublimated in political or artistic ways. Second, like the knight of infinite faith, one can preserve hope in the possibility of the impossible: the world could be redeemed.

I am arguing for a third possibility: the knight of apocalyptic pessimism. Both of Kierkegaard's knights are assured of their desire. It is only the means of realizing that desire that remain elusive. The knight of apocalyptic pessimism has no such assurance. She does not seek to overcome the obstacle to the object of her desire but rejects the world that is itself the obstacle to desiring rightly. She does not trust that with God, all things are possible – there is no God that acts in such ways and she is not interested in the impossible becoming possible *within* the world. The knight of infinite faith desires something that makes sense. The knight of apocalyptic pessimism hopes the peculiar hope for the possibility of the impossible that cannot be expressed in the grammar of the world.[57]

Yet, like the knight of faith, the knight of apocalyptic pessimism still must exist in the world. There is nothing else to do. When Taubes describes himself as not being 'spiritually' invested in the world, it is because there is no other means of disinvesting. Part of the horror of the world is its inescapability. Between the two knights, however, there is still a difference. Kierkegaard's knight of faith

> finds pleasure in everything, takes part in everything, and every time one sees him participating in something particular, he does it with an assiduousness that marks the worldly man who is attached to such things. He attends to his job. To see him makes one think of him as a pen-pusher who has lost his soul to Italian bookkeeping, so punctilious is he. Sunday is for him a holiday. He goes to church. No heavenly gaze or any sign of the incommensurable betrays him; if one did not know him, it would be impossible to distinguish him from the rest of the crowd, for at most his hearty and powerful singing of the hymns proves that he has good lungs.[58]

Unlike this knight of faith, the knight of apocalyptic pessimism begins to detach from 'such things'. She is not like the knight of infinite resignation, knowable by his 'walk', but she is no longer spiritually invested in the world as it is.[59] Kierkegaard's description can be rewritten in the light of the world that the knight of apocalyptic pessimism refuses. She votes, but realizes that the institutions maintained by voting are also instruments of oppression (better a little less oppression while awaiting the end). She seeks ecological justice, but with the full knowledge that such justice is inconceivable so long as there is a humanity conceived as relating to an othered nature. She refuses patriarchy, all the while knowing that this gesture occurs within a patriarchal world.

The knight of apocalyptic pessimism rejects the hope of politics. She disinvests, but without any alternative investment possibilities. This disinvestment is a form of anti-politics, but, as I argued in the first chapter, some anti-politics is ultra-political. Alberto Toscano makes this point in his discussion of Eric Hobsbawm's analysis of millenarian movements. Hobsbawm, having discussed a variety of modern political movements that echo themes from medieval millenarianism, claims that these movements are 'pre-political'.[60] Toscano reads this 'pre-political' as 'ultra-political'. Or, put differently, it is the ultra-political as pre-politics or the political demand that exceeds any existing politics. 'The world-denial and hope for radical transformation that is the "archaic" response to capitalism as cultural catastrophe and dispossession can also translate into an "impractical and utopian" approach to politics.'[61] It is this intensely negative disposition and fervent utopian desire which mark out millenarianism's significance. 'Paradoxically, the very fanaticism that makes it difficult to identity their "rational political core" is, in the last instance, their rational political core. Millenarian utopianism is a *sui generis* political realism.'[62] Likewise, apocalypticism, in its anti-politics, is an expression of the impossibility of political action.

Living and thinking apocalyptically thus changes nothing and it changes everything. This conclusion is unsatisfactory, but so is the world. It offers no solutions, only practiced refusal. The knight of apocalyptic pessimism can only await the end that must come, but does so knowing that the world has an incredible ability to persist.

The end

In a now infamous speech, former US President Jimmy Carter declared 'a crisis of confidence'. He claimed that this crisis 'strikes at the very heart and soul and spirit of our national will. We can see this crisis in the growing doubt about the meaning of our own lives and in the loss of a unity of purpose for our Nation. The erosion of our confidence in the future is threatening to destroy the social and the political fabric of America.'[63] He went on to argue that this confidence was at the foundation of the American project. 'Confidence in the future has supported everything else – public institutions and private enterprise, our own families, and the very Constitution of the United States . . . We've always believed in something called progress.'[64] He argued that the loss of confidence in the future disconnects Americans from their past. The consequences were profound – declining productivity, evaporating faith, the loss of values and the dissolution of the nuclear family. Carter was right. He saw brewing chaos and urged America to function as *katechon*. The world depends on hope in the future. The future is *everything*. The rejection of the future is a hope for *nothing* – a hope for the end. But that is still a kind of hope.

In the course of this book, I have argued that there is an inescapable world constituted by slow and invisible (to many) violence. This violence is the violence of antagonisms, material and social, along the dividing lines of nature, capital, gender and race. History has seen improvements along those divisions – changes that have improved the lives of many. Yet, that does not change the persistence of those antagonisms. The world has seen changes, but the world itself has not changed. Such a change is impossible to think, but it is possible to imagine the end. Drawing on a narrow conception of political theology, I have sought to creatively reread the potential of apocalyptic thinking. Drawing on Hegel, Taubes and Malabou, I have argued for an apocalypse that is immanent, material and desired for its own sake. I have concluded by exploring what it might mean to live pessimistically and offering the figure of the knight of apocalyptic pessimism, arguing that her directionless refusal can provide a model for this peculiar form of hope. For, though hoping in the end is a strange and difficult task, the end is enough. It is all there is. For now.

Notes

Introduction

1 Carl Schmitt, *Theory of the Partisan: Intermediate Commentary on the Concept of the Political*, trans. G. L. Ulmen (New York: Telos Press, 2007), 48. See also Schmitt's view of Hegel's relationship to Marx in the translator's comments in Carl Schmitt, *The Crisis of Parliamentary Democracy*, trans. Ellen Kennedy (Cambridge: MIT Press, 1998), 106n.16.
2 Gilles Deleuze and Felix Guattari, *A Thousand Plateaus: Capitalism and Schizophrenia*, trans. Brian Massumi (London: Bloomsbury, 2013), 218.

1 Philosophy, Political Theology and the End of the World

1 Carl Schmitt, *Political Theology: Four Chapters on the Concept of Sovereignty*, trans. George Schwab (Chicago: University of Chicago Press), 36.
2 Schmitt's definition of political theology can be ambiguous and shifts over time. At points he seems to want a stronger form of political theology than the methodological version described here, even as that methodological approach continues to dominate his work. On these ambiguities and the way that others have approached them, see Benjamin Lazier, 'On the Origins of "Political Theology": Judaism and Heresy between the World Wars', *New German Critique* 35, no. 3 (2008): 147.
3 Schmitt, *Political Theology*, 45.
4 Schmitt, *Political Theology*, 36.
5 This work is clearest in Schmitt's study of liberalism and democracy in *The Crisis of Parliamentary Democracy*, trans. Ellen Kennedy (Cambridge, MA: MIT Press, 1998), his study of the emergence of international law in *The Nomos of the Earth in the International Law of the Jus Publicum Europaeum*, trans. G. L. Ulmen (New York: Telos, 2003) and his analysis of the changing nature of warfare in *Theory of the Partisan: Intermediate Commentary on the Concept of the Political*, trans. G. L. Ulmen (New York: Telos, 2007).

6 Schmitt's membership in the Nazi party and his efforts to justify and legitimate National Socialism necessarily colours any discussion of his work. This complicated legacy has been and continues to be evaluated. This work has been biographical, including Reinhard Mehring's *Carl Schmitt: A Biography*, trans. Daniel Steer (Cambridge: Polity, 2014) and Gopal Balakrishnan's *The Enemy: An Intellectual Portrait of Carl Schmitt* (London: Verso, 2000). In a more theoretical vein, a number of volumes have assessed his work in light of his political affiliations. In particular, the collections of essays edited by Chantal Mouffe (*The Challenge of Carl Schmitt* (London: Verso, 1999)), and more recently by Jens Meiehenrich and Oliver Simons (*The Oxford Handbook of Carl Schmitt* (Oxford: Oxford University Press, 2016)), catalogue Schmitt's continued impact on political theology, philosophy and theory. This influence is not always welcome. See, for example, Mark Neocleous, 'Friend or Enemy? Reading Schmitt Politically', *Radical Philosophy* 79 (1996): 13–23. For an overview of some of this recent literature, see Peter C. Caldwell, 'Controversies over Carl Schmitt: A Review of Recent Literature', *The Journal of Modern History* 77, no. 2 (2005): 357–87. As even Schmitt's contemporaries noted, the fact that themes from his work offer some explanation for his support of the Nazis does not change the significance of the problems he identifies. Both Benjamin and Taubes thought that Schmitt had isolated something essential about the political as such. Benjamin says as much in a letter to Schmitt (*CS*, 16–7). On Benjamin's view of Schmitt see Horst Bredekamp, 'From Walter Benjamin to Carl Schmitt, via Thomas Hobbes', *Critical Inquiry* 25, no. 2 (1999): 247–51. While Schmitt's support of the Nazi's clearly perplexed and troubled Taubes, in the end there was still an affinity between the two. Taubes writes, 'As an apocalyptic spirit I felt and still feel close to him. And we follow common paths, even as we draw contrary conclusions' (*CS*, 8).

7 Massimo Cacciari makes a similar point in his *The Withholding Power: An Essay on Political Theology* (London: Bloomsbury, 2018), 5. Hussein Ali Agrama goes even further, arguing that political theology already operates within a secular 'problem-space' rendering it incapable of adequately questioning secular politics. See *Questioning Secularism: Islam, Sovereignty, and the Rule of Law in Modern Egypt* (Chicago: University of Chicago Press, 2012), 226–7. As Adam Kotsko points out, one of the distinctive features of Taubes's work on Paul is that he does not view Paul as somehow analogous to the political or even a biblical figure that becomes political, but as political himself. See 'The Problem of Evil and the Problem of Legitimacy: On the Root and Future of Political Theology', *Crisis & Critique* 2, no. 1 (2015): 291–2. Taubes does not think all theological ideas or figures are political in the same way, but his approach reflects a murkier, more dynamic relationship between always already related political and theological spheres. Taubes's political theology is closer to what Agrama calls asecularity,

'a situation not where norms are no longer secular or religious, but where the questions against which such norms are adduced and contested as answers are not seen as necessary' (Agrama, *Questioning Secularism*, 186).
8 Ted A. Smith, *Weird John Brown: Divine Violence and the Limits of Ethics* (Stanford, CA: Stanford University Press, 2015), 12.
9 Vincent Lloyd, 'Introduction', in *Race and Political Theology*, ed. Vincent Lloyd (Stanford, CA: Stanford University Press, 2012), 5–9.
10 Michael Kirwan, *Political Theology: A New Introduction* (Minneapolis, MN: Fortress, 2008), ix. For other theological perspectives on political theology, see William T. Cavanaugh, *Theopolitical Imagination* (London: T & T Clark, 2002), and Peter Scott and William T. Cavanaugh (eds), *The Blackwell Companion to Political Theology* (Oxford: Blackwell, 2004).
11 Kirwan, *Political Theology*, xiii.
12 Andrew Shanks, *Hegel's Political Theology* (Cambridge: Cambridge University Press, 1991), 153.
13 It is a different conversation in a literal sense. Despite both he and I offering some version of a Hegelian political theology, Shanks does not cite Schmitt, Taubes (admittedly a less well-known figure) or other key figures of this narrower political theology. He mentions Benjamin, but the discussion is of his philosophy more generally rather than his key contributions to political theology. This observation is not a critique of Shanks, but an indication of the gap that occurs between different approaches to political theology.
14 Take, for example, Clayton Crockett's *Radical Political Theology: Religion and Politics after Liberalism* (New York: Columbia University Press, 2011) or Hent de Vries and Lawrence E. Sullivan's collection *Political Theologies: Public Religions in a Post-Secular World* (New York: Fordham University Press, 2006). While many of the essays in the latter are concerned with the sociology of concepts and a 'narrow' political theology, the volume as a whole is framed as a reflection on the 'return to religion'. The political theologies of Schmitt, Benjamin, Taubes and Agamben offer something that extends beyond this interest in religion to reflections on the nature of the political as such.
15 Mark Lilla, *The Stillborn God: Religion, Politics, and the Modern West* (New York: Vintage Books, 2008).
16 Lilla, *The Stillborn God*, 8–9.
17 Lilla, *The Stillborn God*, 17–18.
18 Lilla discusses Taubes, Schmitt and Benjamin in *The Reckless Mind: Intellectuals in Politics* (New York: New York Review of Books, 2016), but he does not frame his critique in terms of political theology.
19 John Gray, *Black Mass: Apocalyptic Religion and the Death of Utopia* (London: Penguin, 2008).

20 Gray, *Black Mass*, 13.
21 Though Gray critiques revolutionary ideas and connects them to religious origins, he also questions simplistic secular solutions (*Black Mass*, 366–8).
22 Anthony Paul Smith and Daniel Whistler describe this form of post-secularism as 'theological postsecularism' in their 'What Is Continental Philosophy of Religion Now?', in *After the Postsecular and the Postmodern: New Essays in Continental Philosophy of Religion*, ed. Anthony Paul Smith and Daniel Whistler (Newcastle upon Tyne: Cambridge Scholars, 2010), 14–16. For a prime example of this triumphalist theological post-secularism, see Phillip Blond's 'Introduction: Theology before Philosophy', in *Post-Secular Philosophy: Between Philosophy and Theology* (London: Routledge, 1998), 18.
23 On asecularity, see note 7. Though Peter L. Berger has used the term desecularization to discuss the 'return of religion' ('The Desecularization of the World: A Global Overview', in *The Desecularization of the World: Resurgent Religion and World Politics*, ed. Peter L. Berger (Grand Rapids, MI: William B. Eerdmans, 1999), 1–18), I am using the term to indicate a process of dismantling the distinction between religion and the secular. In this sense, desecularization is to secularism as decolonization is to colonialism.
24 Jayne Svenungsson, *Divining History: Prophetism, Messianism and the Development of the Spirit*, trans. Stephen Donovan (Oxford: Berghahn Books, 2016), xiii.
25 Svenungsson, *Divining History*, 12.
26 Svenungsson, *Divining History*, 22–3. Throughout the book, Svenungsson is concerned about the externality of the apocalyptic. For example, she returns to this point in her critique of Badiou (p. 158). There is a real question about the nature of the apocalyptic 'agent' and this agent's relationship to the world (and whether apocalypticism even requires such an agent). As I will argue in Chapter 4, one of the advantages of Malabou's plasticity is that it offers a way of thinking immanent, traumatic novelty. Plastic apocalypticism has no need of external, divine intervention into the world.
27 Svenungsson, *Divining History*, 176, 179. She points to the revolutions in views of gender and sexual orientation as examples of the law serving as the precondition of emancipation (p. 195).
28 While some of the political theologians discussed here do discuss theocracy, this anarchic, mystical form of theocracy is unrelated to the fundamentalist version that animates critiques of political theology. See Lazier, 'On the Origins of "Political Theology"', 154–5.
29 Svenungsson, *Divining History*, 195.
30 This section is deeply informed by the social constructivism of Sally Haslanger's *Resisting Reality: Social Construction and Social Critique* (Oxford: Oxford

University Press, 2012) as well as Nancy Tuana's essay 'Viscous Porosity: Witnessing Katrina', in *Material Feminisms*, ed. Stacy Alaimo and Susan Hekman (Bloomington: Indiana University Press, 2008), 188–213. Neither Haslanger nor Tuana is concerned with defining a 'world' (and indeed may resist this term), but they both capture what Tuana describes as the materiality of the social (p. 188). Combined with Haslanger's conviction that the socially constructed can be real and objective (*Resisting Reality*, 184), their work illuminates the historical process by which ideas, beliefs and attitudes exceed mental function and become the actual material ground of experience as such. In this regard, their work is similar to Adrian Johnston's transcendental materialism, which I return to below. For more on Johnston see my 'Transcendental Materialism as a Theoretical Orientation to the Study of Religion', *Method & Theory in the Study of Religion* 29, no. 2 (2017): 133–54.

31 For an overview of the concept of the world from German Idealism to postmodernity, see Sean Gaston, *The Concept of the World from Kant to Derrida* (London: Rowman & Littlefield, 2013).

32 Markus Gabriel's critique of the concept of world is particularly significant, given that it is offered in the process of developing a new realist philosophy that draws, in part, on German Idealism. Gabriel's objection is twofold. First, the world is the ultimate horizon of human experience. As such there is nothing from which the world can be differentiated. Nothing forms the background against which the world can be perceived. Strictly speaking, this means the world does not exist. Second, 'world' implies totality or unity. Gabriel argues that this unity is an illusion. See his *Fields of Sense: A New Realist Ontology* (Edinburgh: Edinburgh University Press, 2015), 187–9. A version of this argument is also the basis of his *Why the World Does Not Exist*, trans. Gregory Moss (Cambridge: Polity, 2015). Gabriel's rejection of the concept world is developed through a critique of constructivism (as well as other forms of metaphysics). This critique is aimed at forms of constructivism that reject realism, so Haslanger's account – both constructivist and realist – circumvents these criticisms. As will become clear as this chapter progresses, using Haslanger and Tuana allows one to theorize a dynamic and contentious unity that has a permanence worthy of the title 'world'.

33 The German *die Erde* may mean either 'earth', in the sense of soil or ground, or 'the Earth', in the sense of the planet. There is an ambiguity in Schmitt's usage, and I have elected to follow the translators and critical literature in rendering this 'the earth' rather than 'the Earth'. In later sections, I deal with scientific literature where there is less ambiguity and accordingly shift to 'the Earth'.

34 Schmitt, *Nomos of the Earth*, 67.
35 Schmitt, *Nomos of the Earth*, 327.
36 Schmitt, *Nomos of the Earth*, 78.

37 Schmitt, *Nomos of the Earth*, 70. On the foundational nature of *nomos* see Robert Cover's 'Nomos and Narrative', in *Narrative, Violence, and the Law: The Essays of Robert Cover*, ed. Martha Minow, Michael Ryan and Austin Sarat (Ann Arbor: University of Michigan Press, 1993), 95–172. Drawing on the work of Peter Berger, Thomas Luckmann and Karl Mannheim, Cover argues, '[t]his nomos is as much "our world" as is the physical universe of mass, energy, and momentum. Indeed, our apprehension of the structure of the normative world is no less fundamental than our appreciation of the structure of the physical world. Just as the development of increasingly complex responses to the physical attributes of our world begins with birth itself, so does the parallel development of the responses to personal otherness that define the normative world' (p. 97).
38 See G. L. Ulmen's introduction to Carl Schmitt, *Nomos of the Earth*, 23.
39 Schmitt, *Nomos of the Earth*, 44–5.
40 Schmitt, *Nomos of the Earth*, 44–8.
41 As Johnston argues, ideas have real and traceable effects on their material ground. See Adrian Johnston, *Adventures in Transcendental Materialism: Dialogues with Contemporary Thinkers* (Edinburgh: Edinburgh University Press, 2014), 14, 18.
42 Schmitt, *Nomos of the Earth*, 78.
43 Schmitt, *Nomos of the Earth*, 59–60.
44 Julia Hell, '*Katechon*: Carl Schmitt's Imperial Theology and the Ruins of the Future', *The Germanic Review: Literature, Culture, Theory* 84, no. 4 (2009): 290.
45 Schmitt, *Nomos of the Earth*, 178.
46 Hell, '*Katechon*', 310.
47 Schmitt, *Nomos of the Earth*, 51–2.
48 Hell, '*Katechon*', 289–93.
49 Carl Schmitt, *The Concept of the Political*, trans. George Schwab (Chicago: University of Chicago Press, 2007), 28.
50 Schmitt, *Concept of the Political*, 33. See Hell, '*Katechon*', 292–3.
51 Daniel Colucciello Barber, 'World-Making and Grammatical Impasse', *Qui Parle: Critical Humanities and Social Sciences* 25, nos 1–2 (2016): 180.
52 Schmitt, *Nomos of the Earth*, 355.
53 Charles W. Mills points out that the racial categories that govern the process of appropriation, settlement and distribution can themselves be subject to political theological analysis. See *The Racial Contract* (Ithaca, NY: Cornell University Press, 1997), 54–5.
54 Frantz Fanon, *The Wretched of the Earth*, trans. Richard Philcox (New York: Grove, 2004), 6.
55 For an overview of the Anthropocene, see Will Steffen et al., 'The Anthropocene: Conceptual and Historical Perspectives', *Philosophical Transactions of the Royal*

Society of London A: Mathematical, Physical and Engineering Sciences 369, no. 1938 (2011): 842–67.

56 Steffen et al., 'Anthropocene', 849–50.
57 Andreas Malm and Alf Hornborg, 'The Geology of Mankind? A Critique of the Anthropocene Narrative', *Anthropocene Review* 1, no. 1 (2014): 63.
58 Jason W. Moore, 'The End of Cheap Nature, or, How I Learned to Stop Worrying about "The" Environment and Love the Crisis of Capitalism', in *Structures of the World Political Economy and the Future Global Conflict and Cooperation*, ed. Christian Suter and Christopher Chase-Dunn (Berlin: LIT, 2014), 285–314. See also Philip Goodchild, 'Debt, Epistemology and Ecotheology', *Journal for the Study of Religion, Nature and Culture* 9, no. 2 (2004): 160.
59 Moore, 'End of Cheap Nature', 288.
60 Dipesh Chakrabarty, 'Climate and Capital: On Conjoined Histories', *Critical Inquiry* 41, no. 1 (2014): 11.
61 Dipesh Chakrabarty, 'The Climate of History: Four Theses', *Critical Inquiry* 35, no. 2 (2009): 217. It should be noted that Chakrabarty is not responding to Malm, Hornborg or Moore directly but rather to critiques of the Anthropocene more generally.
62 In addition to the succinct summary of these issues provided by Malm and Hornborg's essay, see Andreas Malm's *Fossil Capital: The Rise of Steam Power and the Roots of Global Warming* (London: Verso, 2016), 39ff., as well as his 'Who Lit This Fire? Approaching the History of the Fossil Economy', *Critical Historical Studies* 3, no. 2 (2016): 215–48.
63 Throughout the remainder of this chapter, I will refer to 'material and social relations' for the sake of specifying that I am addressing both. As will become clear, however, this distinction is only analytical – there are no social relations that are not also material.
64 Malm and Hornborg, 'Geology of Mankind?', 66–7.
65 Schmitt also makes this connection between the division of land and the ordering of people: '*nomos* is the immediate form in which the political and social order of a people becomes statically visible – the initial measure and division of pasture-land, i.e., the land-appropriation as well as the concrete order contained in it and following from it' (*Nomos of the Earth*, 70).
66 Silvia Federici refers to both enclosure and colonialism as forms of 'land expropriation' to mark that, even absent direct force, land was seized (*Caliban and the Witch: Women, the Body and Primitive Accumulation* (Brooklyn, NY: Autonomedia, 2004), 68).
67 Federici, *Caliban and the Witch*, 74.
68 Federici, *Caliban and the Witch*, 74–5.
69 Federici, *Caliban and the Witch*, 75.

70 Federici, *Caliban and the Witch*, 74.
71 Federici, *Caliban and the Witch*, 97.
72 Federici, *Caliban and the Witch*, 97.
73 Federici, *Caliban and the Witch*, 97.
74 Federici, *Caliban and the Witch*, 75.
75 Federici, *Caliban* and the Witch, 86–9.
76 Federici, *Caliban and the Witch*, 194.
77 Federici, *Caliban and the Witch*, 184. Emphasis in original.
78 Federici, *Caliban and the Witch*, 164–5.
79 Karen J. Warren identifies eight connections commonly asserted within ecological feminist thought: historical and causal, conceptual, empirical and experiential, epistemological, symbolic, ethical, theoretical, and political (praxis). See her 'Ecological Feminist Philosophies: An Overview of the Issues' in *Ecological Feminist Philosophies*, ed. Karen J. Warren (Bloomington: Indiana University Press, 1996), xi–xvi. The body of literature exploring these issues is vast, but Val Plumwood's argument that ecofeminism provides an 'integrated framework' for critiquing the 'network of dualisms' that makes up Western culture is particularly important given Malcolm Bull's understanding of apocalypticism taken up below (Val Plumwood, *Feminism and the Mastery of Nature* (London: Routledge, 1993), 1–2).
80 Maria Mies, *Patriarchy and Accumulation on a World Scale: Women in the International Division of Labour* (London: Zed Books, 2014), 76.
81 Federici, *Caliban and the Witch*, 102. See also her account of the relationship between European forms of patriarchy and private property imposed upon the indigenous people of the New World (p. 111).
82 In her analysis of witch-hunts, Federici describes the construction of a notion of women as 'weak in body and mind and biologically prone to evil' (*Caliban and the Witch*, 186).
83 Federici, *Caliban and the Witch*, 200.
84 Federici, *Caliban and the Witch*, 179–80. It was 'the colonised native Americans and the enslaved Africans who, in the plantations of the "New World," shared a destiny similar to that of women in Europe, providing for capital the seemingly limitless supply of labor necessary for accumulation' (p. 198).
85 Federici, *Caliban and the Witch*, 198–9. Adam Kotsko explores the political theology of both gender and race in regard to the devil in his *The Prince of This World* (Stanford, CA: Stanford University Press, 2016), 127–9, 157–64, 200–1. Similarly Falguni A. Sheth uses Schmitt to describe the racialization of the enemy. For Sheth, the 'unruly' racial other is the enemy that must be contained, disciplined or eliminated. See her *Toward a Political Philosophy of Race* (Albany: State University of New York Press, 2009), 32.

86 Frank B. Wilderson, III, *Red, White & Black: Cinema and the Structure of U.S. Antagonisms* (Durham, NC: Duke University Press, 2010), 11.
87 See, for example, Jared Sexton's 'The Social Life of Social Death: On Afro-Pessimism and Black Optimism', *Intensions* 5 (2011): 1–47.
88 Wilderson, *Red, White & Black*, 18. Elsewhere, Wilderson describes the position of Blackness this way: 'Human Life is dependent on Black death for its existence and for its conceptual coherence. There is no World without Blacks, yet there are no Blacks who are in the World. The Black is indeed a sentient being, but the constriction of Humanist thought is a constitutive disavowal of Blackness as social death; a disavowal that theorises the Black as degraded human entity: i.e., as an oppressed worker, a vanquished postcolonial subaltern, or a non-Black woman suffering under the disciplinary regime of patriarchy. The Black is *not* a sentient being whose narrative progression has been circumscribed by racism, colonialism, or even slavery for that matter. Blackness and Slaveness are inextricably bound in such a way that whereas Slaveness can be disimbricated from Blackness, Blackness cannot exist as other than Slaveness' ('Afro-pessimism & the End of Redemption', The Occupied Times, 30 March 2016. Available at: https://theoccupiedtimes.org/?p=14236 [accessed 7 July 2017]).
89 As Wilderson argues, 'the slave makes a demand, which is in excess of the demand made by the worker' ('Gramsci's Black Marx: Whither the Slave in Civil Society?', *Social Identities* 9, no. 2 (2003): 230).
90 Wilderson, *Red, White & Black*, 20. See also Jared Sexton's explanation of the difference between the exploitation of labour and the position of the slave in 'The *Vel* of Slavery: Tracking the Figure of the Unsovereign', *Critical Sociology* 42, nos 4–5 (2014): 8.
91 Nancy Fraser, 'Expropriation and Exploitation in Racialized Capitalism: A Reply to Michael Dawson', *Critical Historical Studies* 3, no. 1 (2016): 163–78. I am grateful to Jeremy Posadas for drawing attention to this parallel argument in Fraser's work.
92 Wilderson, *Red, White & Black*, 58.
93 Frantz Fanon, *Black Skin, White Masks*, trans. Charles Lam Markmann (London: Pluto, 1986), 87.
94 Fanon, *Black Skin, White Masks*, 87.
95 Wilderson cites David Eltis, whose research shows the limits of economic explanations for slavery. See Eltis, 'Europeans and the Rise and Fall of African Slavery in the Americas: An Interpretation', *The American Historical Review* 98, no. 5 (1993): 1399–423.
96 Wilderson, *Red, White & Black*, 20.
97 Wilderson, *Red, White & Black*, 337; Fanon, *Black Skin, White Masks*, 71.
98 Sexton, 'The *Vel* of Slavery', 7.

99 Federici, *Caliban and the Witch*, 103.
100 Tuana, 'Viscous Porosity', 189–90. Tuana's notion of a dynamic unity or fundamental connectivity is echoed in a wide variety of attempts to develop new, scientifically aware forms of materialism. In particular, see Stacy Alaimo and Susan Hekman (eds), *Material Feminisms* (Bloomington: Indiana University Press, 2008); Diana Coole and Samantha Frost (eds), *New Materialisms: Ontology, Agency and Politics* (Durham, NC: Duke University Press, 2010); Jane Bennett, *Vibrant Matter* (Durham, NC: Duke University Press, 2010); and William E. Connolly, *The Fragility of Things: Self-Organizing Processes, Neoliberal Fantasies, and Democratic Activism* (Durham, NC: Duke University Press, 2013). As will become clear over the course of the rest of this book, I am persuaded by Adrian Johnston's transcendental materialist account of these dynamics. For the purposes of my argument, Johnston's linking of materialism, German Idealism and psychoanalysis is particularly useful for drawing connections between Hegel, political theology and apocalypticism. While I find Johnston's philosophy ideal for this task, it is unfortunate that contemporary materialist philosophy and theory often seems rigidly divided, particularly between vitalist or process approaches on the one hand and accounts indebted to German Idealism on the other. There is not a great deal of interaction between the two camps, though Johnston offers some critiques in the concluding chapter of *Adventures in Transcendental Materialism*. While these divisions are important, they often serve to obscure important connections between the two groups.
101 This interactionism thus avoids the critiques of those like Bruno Latour who argue against a globality that is a purposeful or static totality. See *Facing Gaia: Eight Lectures on the New Climatic Regime*, trans. Catherine Porter (Cambridge: Polity, 2017), 130–41.
102 Tuana, 'Viscous Porosity', 188 (italics in original). Tuana's approach thus echoes Latour's call to '*rematerialize our belonging to the world*' (*Facing Gaia*, 219).
103 Malm and Hornborg, 'Geology of Mankind?', 66.
104 While Donna Haraway has introduced the term 'Chthulucene' to capture the 'dynamic ongoing sym-chthonic forces and powers of which people are a part', I think Moore's Capitalocene already includes this sense of dynamic ongoingness ('Anthropocene, Capitalocene, Plantationocene, Chthulucene: Making Kin', *Environmental Humanities* 6 (2015): 159–65). Though perhaps, as Haraway argues, more than one name is necessary.
105 Malm and Hornborg, 'Geology of Mankind?', 63.
106 Anna Lowenhaupt Tsing, *The Mushroom at the End of the World: On the Possibility of Life in Capitalist Ruins* (Princeton, NJ: Princeton University Press, 2015), 22.

107 Tuana's account of hurricane Katrina in 'Viscous Porosity' is an example attending to this materiality of ideology. On the question of the reality of race, see also Michael Omi and Howard Winant, *Racial Formation in the United States*, 3rd edn (New York: Routledge, 2015), 110.
108 Tuana, 'Viscous Porosity', 189.
109 This notion of the world thinking itself is an effort to bypass Anthony Paul Smith's criticism of 'World's' dominance of environmental thought. For Smith, 'What the World provides philosophy is an abstract field where God and Nature become things that are subsumed within a transcendent form philosophical and/or theological thinking. The philosopher is always above the World as transcendental ego and the theological is always in the World, but not of it' (*A Non-Philosophical Theory of Nature: Ecologies of Thought* (New York: Palgrave Macmillan, 2013), 176). In the notion of world presented in this section, the subject is neither above the world, nor apart from it. The subject is the world thinking itself, though not exhaustively.
110 Angelica Nuzzo, 'Anthropology, *Geist*, and the Soul-Body Relation: The Systematic Beginning of Hegel's *Philosophy of Spirit*', in *Essays on Hegel's Philosophy of Subjective Spirit*, ed. David S. Stern (London: Bloomsbury, 2013), 1.
111 Nuzzo, 'Anthropology, *Geist*, and the Soul-Body Relation', 1.
112 Johnston's transcendental materialism can be interpreted as an example of such a rereading. Similarly, Nuzzo argues that Hegel is developing a philosophical perspective that transforms the opposition between idealism and materialism ('Anthropology, *Geist*, and the Soul-Body Relation', 13–14).
113 Heidegger is also noteworthy because Catherine Malabou explores the themes of plasticity, novelty and alterity through a reading of his work. While her argument in *The Heidegger Change: On the Fantastic in Philosophy*, trans. Peter Skafish (Albany: State University of New York Press, 2011) touches on many of the themes of apocalyptic political theology, discussing her detailed engagement with Heidegger's concepts of *Wandeln*, *Wandlungen* and *Verwandlungen* would require a level of attention that this current argument does not allow.
114 Martin Heidegger, *Being and Time*, trans. John Macquarrie and Edward Robinson (London: Blackwell, 1962), 92–5. For more on Heidegger's conception of the world, see Chapter 4 of Gaston's *The Concept of the World from Kant to Derrida*.
115 Martin Heidegger, *The Fundamental Concepts of Metaphysics: World, Finitude, Solitude*, trans. William McNeill and Nicholas Walker (Bloomington: Indiana University Press, 1995), 185.

116 Philip Tonner, 'Are Animals Poor in the World? A Critique of Heidegger's Anthropocentrism', in *Anthropocentrism: Humans, Animals, Environments*, ed. Rob Boddice (Leiden: Brill, 2011), 204.
117 Haslanger, *Resisting Reality*, 213.
118 This notion of the violence of the law clearly draws on Walter Benjamin's analysis of lawmaking and law-preserving violence in his 'Critique of Violence' in *Reflections: Essays, Aphorisms, Autobiographical Writings*, ed. Peter Demetz (New York: Schocken Books, 1978), 284–9.
119 Slavoj Žižek, *Violence: Six Sideway Reflections* (London: Profile, 2008), 8.
120 Rob Nixon, *Slow Violence and the Environmentalism of the Poor* (Cambridge, MA: Harvard University Press, 2011), 2.
121 On the invisibility of this violence, see Linda Martín Alcoff's summary of standpoint epistemology in her 'Epistemologies of Ignorance: Three Types' in *Race and Epistemologies of Ignorance*, ed. Shannon Sullivan and Nancy Tuana (Albany: State University of New York Press, 2007), 39–57. Though Alcoff does not employ the language of slow or objective violence, she describes the dynamics that enable people to not see systemic forms of injustice.
122 Federici makes this point in her 'Wages against Housework' in *Revolution at Point Zero: Housework, Reproduction and Feminist Struggle* (Oakland, CA: PM Press, 2012), 15–22. For an appreciative yet critical assessment of Federici's proposed solution, wages for housework, and the possibility of universal basic income as a means of updating those demands, see Chapter 3 of Kathi Weeks's *The Problem with Work: Feminism, Marxism, Antiwork Politics and Postwork Imaginaries* (Durham, NC: Duke University Press, 2011), 113–50.
123 Wilderson, *Red, White & Black*, 5.
124 As is clear from the above discussion of Wilderson, he argues that there is a unique antagonism between Blackness and the world that calls for the destruction of the world. In using his concept of antagonism, I am not suggesting a general analogy between worker, woman and slave, only suggesting that in a world constituted by nature, capital, gender and race that each of these divisions entails an unresolvable antagonism that exceeds any resolvable conflict. Put another way, each of these divisions denotes an antagonism, but that does not mean that they are all antagonisms in the same way.
125 Barber, 'World-Making and Grammatical Impasse', 181.
126 Walter Benjamin, 'Some Reflections on Kafka', in *Illuminations: Essays and Reflections*, ed. Hannah Arendt, trans. Harry Cohn (New York: Schocken Books, 1968), 144.
127 Wilderson, *Red, White & Black*, 2.
128 Fredric Jameson never actually writes this succinct version and there is some confusion about the saying's origins. In *The Seeds of Time*, he observes that

'[i]t seems to be easier for us today to imagine the thoroughgoing deterioration of the earth and of nature than the breakdown of late capitalism' (*The Seeds of Time* (New York: Columbia University Press, 1994), xii). He then references the same idea in a later essay, arguing that, '[s]omeone once said that it is easier to imagine the end of the world than to imagine the end of capitalism. We can now revise that and witness the attempt to imagine capitalism by way of imagining the end of the world' ('The Future City', *New Left Review* 21 (2003): 76). It is not clear if Jameson is in fact referring to his own earlier essay or noting a similar point made by someone else.

129 'Pericapitalist' is a term that Tsing uses to describe 'life processes' outside the direct control of capitalism, such as 'photosynthesis and animal digestion'. I am arguing that it is necessary to go beyond Tsing to recognize the way that even these processes exist or occur in a world structured by capital (Tsing, *Mushroom at the End of the World*, 62–3).

130 Deborah Danowski and Eduardo Viveiros de Castro, *The Ends of the World*, trans. Rodrigo Nunes (Cambridge: Polity, 2017), 122.

131 Eduardo Viveiros de Castro, *Cannibal Metaphysics*, trans. Peter Skafish (Minneapolis: University of Minnesota Press, 2014).

132 Malm, *Fossil Capital*, 39–40.

133 Latour makes this argument in chapter six of *Facing Gaia*. His argument includes a genealogy of apocalyptic thinking that is similar to the one offered in the next chapter but draws connections between apocalypticism and Gnosticism in order to critique the way religious ideas have shaped the 'ecological crisis' (pp. 194–210).

134 Roland Boer, 'Review, Jacob Taubes, Occidental Eschatology', *The Bible and Critical Theory* 8, no. 2 (2012): 99. In developing an immanent apocalyptic political theology, I have endeavoured to both eliminate this imprecision as well as respond to Boer's criticism of apocalypticism. The nature of this immanent apocalypticism will become clearer in Chapter 4.

135 Roland Boer, *Political Myth: On the Use and Abuse of Biblical Themes* (Durham, NC: Duke University Press, 2009), 18.

136 Boer, *Political Myth*, 19.

137 Boer, *Political Myth*, 19.

138 Boer, *Political Myth*, 19.

139 Boer, *Political Myth*, 20.

140 John J. Collins, *The Apocalyptic Imagination: An Introduction to Jewish Apocalyptic Literature*, 2nd edn (Grand Rapid, MI: William B. Eerdmans, 1998), 2. As Collins notes, it is possible to differentiate between apocalyptic as a noun, 'literary genre, apocalypticism as a social ideology, and apocalyptic eschatology as a set of ideas and motifs that may also be found in other literary genres and

social settings' (p. 2). These distinctions are further complicated within Collins's understanding of apocalypse as literary genre by the presence of different forms of apocalypse, such as 'other worldly journeys' and '"historical" apocalypses' (p. 7).
141 Collins, *Apocalyptic Imagination*, 13.
142 Malcolm Bull, *Seeing Things Hidden: Apocalypse, Vision, and Totality* (London: Verso, 1999), 48.
143 Collins, *Apocalyptic Imagination*, 13.
144 Bull, *Seeing Things Hidden*, 71.
145 Bull, *Seeing Things Hidden*, 61–2.
146 Bull, *Seeing Things Hidden*, 83.
147 See Christopher Rowland, *The Open Heaven: A Study of Apocalyptic in Judaism and Early Christianity* (London: SPCK, 1985).

2 Implicit Political Theology: Reading Hegel's Philosophy of Religion

1 Hegel's philosophy has been rejected for being generally dangerous and prone to totalitarianism. Karl Popper's infamous reading continues to be one of the most well-known dismissals. See his *The Open Society and Its Enemies*, 2nd edn (London: Routledge & Kegan Paul, 1952). Other critiques focus specifically on Hegel's treatment of gender or race. See, for example, Carla Lonzi, 'Let's Spit on Hegel', in *Feminist Interpretations of G.W.F. Hegel*, ed. Patricia Jagentowicz (University Park: Pennsylvania State University Press, 1996), 275–97; Robert Bernasconi, 'Hegel at the Court of Ashanti', in *Hegel After Derrida*, ed. Stuart Barnett (London: Routledge, 1998), 41–63; and Tsenay Serequeberhan, 'The Idea of Colonialism in Hegel's Philosophy of Right', *International Philosophical Quarter* 29, no. 3 (1989): 301–18. Despite Hegel's problematic positions, however, engagement with his wider philosophy continues to be a resource for those interested and critiquing and overcoming these divisions. See, for example, the collection edited by Kimberly Hutchings and Tuija Pulkkinen, *Hegel's Philosophy and Feminist Thought: Beyond Antigone* (New York: Palgrave Macmillan, 2010); Susan Buck-Morss, *Hegel, Haiti, and Universal History* (Pittsburgh, PA: University of Pittsburgh Press, 2009); Nick Nesbitt, 'Troping Toussaint, Reading Revolution', *Research in African Literatures* 35, no. 2 (2004): 18–33. These critical engagements do not necessarily take the form of redeeming Hegel's positions. They can also be creative appropriations of concepts in order to develop Hegelian ideas beyond the limits of Hegel's own work.

2 There is a significant body of literature that considers the relationship between Hegel, Joachim and Gnostic traditions. See, in particular, Cyril O'Regan, *The Heterodox Hegel* (Albany: State University of New York Press, 1994); Glenn Alexander Magee, *Hegel and the Hermetic Tradition* (Ithaca, NY: Cornell University Press, 2001); Henri de Lubac, *La Postérité spirituelle de Joachim de Flore: de Joachim à nos jours* (Paris: Cerf, 2014); Karl Löwith, *Meaning in History: The Theological Implications of the Philosophy of History* (Chicago, IL: Phoenix Books, 1949); Clark Butler, 'Hegel, Altizer and Christian Atheism', *Encounter* 41 (1980): 103–28; and Clark Butler, 'Hegelian Panentheism as Joachimite Christianity', in *New Perspectives on Hegel's Philosophy of Religion*, ed. David Kolb (Albany: State University of New York Press, 1992), 131–42.

3 Norman Cohn, *The Pursuit of the Millennium* (London: Secker & Warburg, 1957). Cohn is particularly concerned with millenarian forms of apocalypticism. Millenarianism, millennialism and chiliasm are sometimes used interchangeably as they all emphasize the 1,000-year reign of Christ. Bernard McGinn argues that the sociological study of millennialism, including Cohn's work, has emphasized the collective, immanent and earthy nature of the phenomenon, so the term chiliasm is better used to refer to the belief in the 1,000-year reign of Christ rather than the social features that often accompany that belief. McGinn is also critical of Cohn's sociological analysis, arguing that it is crude and reductive. While he notes that the later edition of Cohn's book addresses some of these concerns, it is the earlier edition that has most influenced the genealogy tradition and that I am citing here. See Bernard McGinn, *Visions of the End: Apocalyptic Traditions in the Middle Ages* (New York: Columbia University Press, 1979), 17n.56, 28–30.

4 Cohn, *Pursuit of the Millennium*, 22–32.

5 Yonina Talmon, 'Pursuit of the Millennium: The Relation between Religious and Social Change', *European Journal of Sociology/Archives Européennes De Sociologie* 3, no. 1 (1962): 137. Talmon specifies that this uneven relation occurs both in societies where population growth or industrialization frustrate traditional ways of life and in societies where industrialization or encounters with new societies introduce new expectations that cannot be fulfilled.

6 Thom Brooks explains this alienation in terms of stakeholder theory. 'The alienated are not merely disinterested like political agnostics but disengaged, and they lack the belief their alienation can or should be overcome. So the political disconnection someone may believe exists between him or her and others will seem fixed and either beyond his or her ability to fix or to care about changing' ('Ethical Citizenship and the Stakeholder Society', in *Ethical Citizenship: British Idealism and the Politics of Recognition*, ed. Thom Brooks (New York: Palgrave Macmillan, 2014), 131).

7 Cohn, *Pursuit of the Millennium*, 307.

8 McGinn, *Visions of the End*, 126–30.
9 Cohn, *Pursuit of the Millennium*, 109.
10 Marjorie Reeves and Warwick Gould, *Joachim of Fiore and the Myth of the Eternal Evangel in the 19th Century* (Oxford: Clarendon Press, 1987), 12.
11 Indeed, Cohn's work emerged out of a seminar on apocalypticism at the University of Manchester. Other works associated with the group include E. J. Hobsbawm, *Primitive Rebels: Studies in Archaic Forms of Social Movement in the 19th and 20th Centuries*, Norton Library (New York: Norton, 1965) and Peter Worsley, *The Trumpet Shall Sound: A Study of 'Cargo' Cults in Melanesia*, 2nd edn (London: MacGibbon & Kee, 1968). Worsley's book focuses on a different apocalyptic tradition, cargo cults, but it is notable that he identifies similar social conditions at the emergence of the apocalyptic groups.
12 Reeves and Gould, *Joachim of Fiore*, 2–3.
13 Cf. Talmon, 'Pursuit of the Millennium', 127. 'Cohn's study is extremely erudite and exhaustive. He over-stresses the analogy with modern totalitarian movements, yet this provides mainly a point of orientation and a general frame of reference and does not affect too much the study of medieval movements which stand in their own right.' Later in the essay she draws attention to his egregious attempt 'to equate communism and Nazism and treat them as one and the same for the purpose of comparison with millenarianism' (p. 145).
14 Indeed, Svenungsson's nuanced analysis of these historical connections is one of the great strengths of her book. On this point, see my 'Divining History: Prophetism, Messianism and the Development of the Spirit', *Jewish Culture and History* 19, no. 1 (2018): 111–13.
15 Daniel Bell, *End of Ideology: On the Exhaustion of Political Ideas in the Fifties* (Glencoe: Free Press, 1960), 285.
16 Norman Cohn, *The Pursuit of the Millennium: Revolutionary Millenarians and Mystical Anarchists of the Middle Ages* (London: Pimlico, 1993), 288.
17 Cohn, *Pursuit of the Millennium* (1957), 109.
18 Löwith, *Meaning in History*, 1.
19 Löwith, *Meaning in History*, 1.
20 Löwith, *Meaning in History*, 54.
21 Löwith, *Meaning in History*, 57.
22 Löwith, *Meaning in History*, 57–9.
23 Löwith, *Meaning in History*, 151.
24 Löwith, *Meaning in History*, 154.
25 Löwith, *Meaning in History*, 158.
26 Löwith himself was aware of the connections between their works. In a conversation with Hans Jonas, he reportedly said of *Occidental Eschatology* 'it's a very good book. And that's no accident – half of it's by you, and the other

half's by me'. Hans Jonas, *Memoirs*, ed. Christian Wiese, trans. Krishna Winston (Waltham, MA: Brandeis University Press, 2008), 168.

27 Ferdinand Christian Baur, *Die christliche Gnosis oder die christliche Religionsphilosophie in ihrer geschichtlichen Entwicklung.* (Darmstadt: Wissenschaftliche Buchgesellschaft, 1967). See also Laurence W. Dickey *Hegel: Religion, Economics, and the Politics of Spirit, 1770–1807* (Cambridge: Cambridge University Press, 1987) and Cyril O'Regan, *Heterodox Hegel* and Magee, *Hegel and the Hermetic Tradition*.

28 Taubes discusses the Hebrew origins of apocalypticism in Daniel before moving on to New Testament texts. When Löwith goes back to the biblical text, he focuses exclusively on the New Testament. Taubes, and Bloch too, therefore see something Jewish in the Christian apocalyptic tradition.

29 Svenungsson, *Divining History*, 37.

30 It is important to express again the point made by Löwith – Taubes, here, is expressing a valid reading of Joachim's prophecies that nonetheless break with Joachim's intentions.

31 Taubes presents, in a much abbreviated form, the same break between Old and Young Hegelians that Löwith discusses in *From Hegel to Nietzsche: The Revolution in Nineteenth Century Thought*, trans. David E. Green (Garden City, NY: Anchor Books, 1967). They concur on the nature of the relation between this division and Hegel himself: the careful balances Hegel strikes between individual/society and religion/philosophy are thrown off kilter by his successors. Löwith's book returns to these divisions continuously in describing the philosophical shifts that follow Hegel. Taubes describes this same unbalancing as the consequence of Marx and Kierkegaard's decision to follow one side or the other of these Hegelian oppositions. It should be noted that the depiction of Kierkegaard as an inwardly focused philosopher unconcerned with political issues has been challenged by recent work. For example, see the collection of essays edited by Jon Stewart, *Kierkegaard's Influence on Social-Political Thought* (Surrey: Ashgate, 2011) and Mark Dooley's *The Politics of Exodus: Søren Kierkegaard's Ethics of Responsibility* (New York: Fordham University Press, 2001). Michael O'Neill Burns's *Kierkegaard and the Matter of Philosophy: A Fractured Dialectic* (London: Rowman & Littlefield, 2015) is particularly significant in exploring Kierkegaard's political significance through a materialist approach similar to the reading of Hegel I am offering here.

32 Stephen Houlgate, *An Introduction to Hegel's Philosophy: Freedom, Truth and History*, 2nd edn (Oxford: Blackwell, 2005), 244.

33 In particular, see Angelica Nuzzo's work on the absolute, spirit, truth and method and Hegel. Nuzzo argues that absolute knowledge, a concept much derided by critics of Hegel, is a concept concerned with determining this

necessity. The truth of absolute knowing is not total knowledge of the world but a complete knowledge of knowing (and unknowing). She makes this argument in her essay '"... As If Truth Were a Coin!" Lessing and Hegel's Developmental Theory of Truth', *Hegel Studien* 44 (2009): 131–55. See also her 'Dialectic as Logic of Transformative Processes', in *Hegel: New Directions*, ed. Katerina Deligiorgi (Chesham: Acumen, 2006), 85–104; 'The End of Hegel's Logic: Absolute Idea as Absolute Method', in *Hegel's Theory of the Subject*, ed. David Carlson (Basingstoke: Palgrave Macmillan, 2005), 187–205; 'The Truth of *Absolutes Wissen* in Hegel's *Phenomenology of Spirit*', in *Hegel's Phenomenology of Spirit: New Critical Essays*, ed. Alfred Denker and Michael G. Vater (Amherst: Humanity, 2003), 265–93. This emphasis on Hegel's philosophy as primarily concerned with the shape of thought itself is key to the set of rereadings that have come to be known as 'non-metaphysical' interpretations of Hegel. Concepts like absolute spirit are no longer interpreted metaphysically, but rather articulate Hegel's concept of a socially embedded form of rationality. See in particular Robert B. Pippin, *Hegel's Idealism: The Satisfactions of Self-Consciousness* (Cambridge: Cambridge University Press, 1989) and Terry Pinkard, *Hegel's Phenomenology: The Sociality of Reason* (Cambridge: Cambridge University Press, 1994). For an overview of this approach, see Simon Lumsden, 'The Rise of the Non-Metaphysical Hegel', *Philosophy Compass* 3, no. 1 (2008): 51–65.

34 Pinkard, *Hegel's Phenomenology*, 255. H. S. Harris makes the same point, writing, 'The chapter on "Spirit" began with the immediate identification of the finite consciousness, with an absolute Law that it does not create, generate or legislate for itself but which is, on the contrary, *given* to it in the natural bonds of its organic morality ... In the true infinite community of Reason which eventually takes the place of that finite community, the Lawgiver is recognized as the immanent might of Reason itself ... the adequate embodiment of Reason is an actually infinite community of finite spirits' (*Hegel's Ladder II: The Odyssey of Spirit* (Indianapolis, IN: Hackett, 1997), 523).

35 Quentin Lauer, *Hegel's Concept of God* (Albany: State University of New York Press, 1982), 34.

36 Hodgson uses representation across his work on Hegel's philosophy of religion, including his translations of the *Lectures on the Philosophy of Religion*. Pinkard uses representation or representational thinking in his forthcoming new translation *Phenomenology of Spirit*. Thomas A. Lewis argues for representation instead of 'picture-thinking' in his work on Hegel, religion and politics. See his *Religion, Modernity, and Politics in Hegel* (Oxford: Oxford University Press, 2011), 156–8.

37 My emphasis.

38 It is this broad sense of political theology that has been the focus of recent work on Hegel, politics and religion. Lewis's *Religion, Modernity, and Politics in Hegel* is the most important recent analysis of the political significance of religion as representation. These themes are also taken up in the collection edited by Angelica Nuzzo, *Hegel on Religion and Politics* (Albany: State University of New York Press, 2013) as well as the volume co-edited by Slavoj Žižek and Creston Davis, *Hegel & the Infinite: Religion, Politics, and Dialectic* (New York: Columbia University Press, 2011). This more recent work builds off the legacy of earlier research on religion and politics in Hegel, such as Dickey's *Hegel: Religion, Economics, and the Politics of Spirit, 1770–1807* and Walter Jaeschke's essay 'Christianity and Secularity in Hegel's Concept of the State', *Journal of Religion* 61, no. 2 (1981): 127–45.

39 Malcolm Clark, *Logic and System: A Study of the Translation from 'Vorstellung' to Thought in the Philosophy of Hegel.* (The Hague: Martinus Nijhoff, 1971) and Kathleen Dow Magnus, *Hegel and the Symbolic Mediation of Spirit* (Albany: State University of New York Press, 2001). For additional context on Hegel's understanding of representation in relation to his philosophical contemporaries see Louis Dupré, 'Religion as Representation', in *The Legacy of Hegel: Proceedings of the Marquette Hegel Symposium 1970*, ed. J. J. O'Malley et al. (The Hague: Martinus Nijhoff, 1973), 137–43.

40 Clark, *Logic and System*, xi.

41 Magnus deals with a number of Derrida's texts, but most significantly, for the task of this present work, Jacques Derrida, 'The Pit and the Pyramid: Introduction to Hegel's Semiology', in *Margins of Philosophy*, trans. Alan Bass (Chicago, IL: University of Chicago Press, 1982); Jacques Derrida, 'From Restricted to General Economy: A Hegelianism without Reserve', in *Writing and Difference*, trans. Alan Bass (Chicago, IL: University of Chicago Press, 1978). Though she does not discuss Derrida's work on messianism, her refutation of Derrida's critique also bears on the differences between his messianism and Malabou's plasticity. See Jacques Derrida, *Specters of Marx: The State of the Debt, the Work of Mourning and the New International*, trans. Peggy Kamuf (London: Routledge, 2006). I address Malabou's critique of Derrida and develop a plastic apocalypticism in Chapter 4.

42 Magnus, *Hegel and the Symbolic Mediation of Spirit*, 9.

43 Magnus, *Hegel and the Symbolic Mediation of Spirit*, 181. My emphasis.

44 Clark, *Logic and System*, 38.

45 Magnus, *Hegel and the Symbolic Mediation of Spirit*, 34.

46 Clark, *Logic and System*, 128.

47 Clark, *Logic and System*, 40.

48 Magnus, *Hegel and the Symbolic Mediation of Spirit*, 33.

49 Magnus, *Hegel and the Symbolic Mediation of Spirit*, 33.
50 Magnus, *Hegel and the Symbolic Mediation of Spirit*, 213.
51 Magnus, *Hegel and the Symbolic Mediation of Spirit*, 31.
52 Lewis, *Religion, Modernity, and Politics in Hegel*, 2.
53 Lewis, *Religion, Modernity, and Politics in Hegel*, 116.
54 This section of the *Philosophy of Right* is particularly pertinent as it highlights the major tension in Hegel's assessment of religion – the same features of religion that make it necessary also make it dangerous. Only a few lines later, Hegel comments on the subjectivity of religion and cautions that this may lead to a negative attitude which 'may give rise to the religious *fanaticism* which, like fanaticism in politics, discards all political institutions and legal order as barriers cramping the inner life of the heart and incompatible with its infinity . . . But since even then decision must somehow be made for everyday life and practice, the same doctrine which we had before [subjectivity of the will which knows itself to be absolute] turns up again here, namely that subjective ideas, i.e. opinion and capricious inclination, are to do the deciding' (*PR* §270: 245/418–9).
55 Thomas A. Lewis, 'Beyond the Totalitarian: Ethics and the Philosophy of Religion in Recent Hegel Scholarship', *Religion Compass* 2, no. 4 (2008): 571.
56 George Di Giovanni, 'Faith without Religion, Religion without Faith: Kant and Hegel on Religion', *Journal of the History of Philosophy* 41, no. 3 (2003): 367. For Di Giovanni, this matrix is composed of those actions and self-understandings that require the total commitment of one's being.
57 In this regard, Hegel anticipates many of the themes of contemporary religious studies. Lewis develops and expands this insight in his *Why Philosophy Matters for the Study of Religion & Vice Versa* (Oxford: Oxford University Press, 2015).
58 Lewis, *Religion, Modernity, and Politics in Hegel*, 156.
59 John W Burbidge, 'Hegel's Open Future', in *Hegel and the Tradition: Essays in Honour of H.S. Harris*, ed. Michael Baur and John Edward Russon (Toronto: University of Toronto Press, 1997), 185. See also, Magnus, *Hegel and the Symbolic Mediation of Spirit*, 182, 208.
60 Lewis, *Religion, Modernity, and Politics in Hegel*, 78.
61 Lewis, *Religion, Modernity, and Politics in Hegel*, 96.
62 Lewis, *Religion, Modernity, and Politics in Hegel*, 97.
63 Thomas A. Lewis, 'Religion and Demythologization in Hegel's Phenomenology of Spirit', in *Hegel's Phenomenology of Spirit: A Critical Guide*, ed. Dean Moyar and Michael Quante (Cambridge: Cambridge University Press, 2008), 194–5.
64 Donald Phillip Verene, *Hegel's Absolute: An Introduction to Reading the Phenomenology of Spirit* (Albany: State University of New York Press, 2007), 91–2.

65 Karl Friedrich Göschel, *Aphorismen über Nichtwissen und absolutes Wissen im Verhältnisse zur christlichen Glaubenserkenntniss: ein Beytrag zum Verständnisse der Philosophie unserer Zeit* (Berlin: E. Franklin, 1829). In addition to this review, Hegel makes a complimentary reference to the work in the first paragraph on revealed religion in the *Encyclopaedia*: 'God is God only so far as he knows himself: his self-knowledge is, further, a self-consciousness in man and man's knowledge *of* God, which proceeds to man's self-knowledge *in* God. – See the profound elucidation of these propositions in the work from which they are taken: *Aphorisms on Knowing and Not-knowing*, &c., by C.F.G' (*E3*, §564: 298/374).
66 My emphasis.
67 G. W. F. Hegel, *Hegel: The Letters*, trans. Clark Butler and Christiane Seiler (Bloomington: Indiana University Press, 1984), 538.
68 Lewis makes much the same point, though his focus is on the transformation of ideas in relationship to religious communities (*Religion, Modernity, and Politics in Hegel*, 14).
69 Magnus, *Hegel and the Symbolic Mediation of Spirit*, 209.

3 Spiritual Disinvestment: Taubes, Hegel and Apocalypticism

1 The relationship between Schmitt and Taubes is a matter of some debate. From Taubes's own work, including his letters, it is clear that Schmitt is an important figure, but there is still the question of how much Schmitt's work influenced Taubes's thinking. Jamie Martin argues that while they consider many similar themes, Schmitt only features in Taubes's later writing. Earlier in his career, Taubes carefully avoids interaction with Schmitt. Martin worries that focus on their later correspondence has distracted from a more careful consideration of Taubes and his own distinctive intellectual context ('Liberalism and History after the Second World War: The Case of Jacob Taubes', *Modern Intellectual History* 14, no. 1 (2017): 133). Martin's position is an outlier, though. While their relationship is not as simple as direct influence, Taubes's political theology is in many ways written against Schmitt's. Their intellectual relationship thus precedes their personal encounter. See, for example, Marin Terpstra and Theo de Wit's '"No Spiritual Investment in the World as It Is": Jacob Taubes's Negative Political Theology', in *Flight of the Gods: Philosophical Perspectives on Negative Theology*, ed. Ilse N. Bulhof and Laurens ten Kate (New York: Fordham University Press, 2000), 327.
2 There is relatively little secondary literature on Taubes. In addition to the material discussed below, see the brief biographical sketch included in Martin Treml's

'Reinventing the Canonical: The Radical Thinking of Jacob Taubes', in *'Escape to Life': German Intellectuals in New York: A Compendium on Exile*, ed. Eckhart Goebel and Sigrid Weigel (Berlin: Walter de Gruyter, 2012), 460–5.

3 Aleida Assmann, Jan Assmann and Wolf-Daniel Hartwich, 'Introduction to the German Edition', in *From Cult to Culture: Fragments Towards a Critique of Historical Reason*, by Jacob Taubes, ed. Charlotte Elisheva Fonrobert and Amir Engel (Stanford, CA: Stanford University Press, 2010), xxi. For a systematic overview of Bloch, see Wayne Hudson, *The Marxist Philosophy of Ernst Bloch* (London: Macmillan, 1982). Hudson's study does not treat religious issues with as much depth as one might expect given the nature of Bloch's philosophy. For these issues see Roland Boer's work, especially *Criticism of Heaven: On Marxism and Theology* (Chicago, IL: Haymarket Books, 2009), 1–55, and *Political Myth*.

4 Anson Rabinbach, 'Between Enlightenment and Apocalypse: Benjamin, Bloch and Modern German Jewish Messianism', *New German Critique* 34 (1985): 78. As will be seen shortly, one difference between Taubes and these others is that Taubes sees his work as resolutely modern. He offers an immanent critique of modernity for modernity's sake, rather than developing a position in opposition to modernity. His position is not as firmly opposed to modernity as Benjamin, for example. Thus, Rabinbach's description of this period of thought as 'radical, uncompromising, and comprised of an esoteric intellectualism that is as uncomfortable with the Enlightenment as it is enamoured of apocalyptic visions' (p. 80), is less applicable to Taubes than Benjamin and Bloch. As the title suggests, Rabinbach's essay deals mostly with Benjamin, Bloch and, to a lesser extent, Luckás, as instrumental figures in the development of a messianism that broke with the more predominant options of assimilationist Judaism or Zionism. Much of his description captures themes congruent with Taubes's contribution to this distinctive version of twentieth-century Jewish thought, even though Taubes is not explicitly mentioned.

5 Bloch thus occupies a space in between Taubes and the rest of this tradition, sharing Taubes's deep exploration of the theological and religious traditions while also attending to art. For example, Bloch discusses musical theory in *The Spirit of Utopia*, trans. Anthony A. Nassar (Stanford, CA: Stanford University Press, 2000) and theorizes folklore in *Heritage of Our Times*, trans. Neville Plaice and Stephen Plaice (Cambridge: Polity Press, 1991). While it might seem pertinent to include Benjamin in my broader discussion of apocalyptic political theology, he differs from Taubes and Bloch in that Hegel plays a different role in his philosophy (on this role, see Susan Buck-Morss, *The Dialectics of Seeing: Walter Benjamin and the Arcades Project* (Cambridge, MA: MIT Press, 1989)). Most importantly, Hegel does not occupy the same place in Benjamin's conception of political theology and he does not emphasize Gnostic and apocalyptic tendencies within Hegel's work.

6 Rabinbach, 'Between Enlightenment and Apocalypse', 101.
7 Mohler was a right-wing thinker with whom Taubes corresponded. The letter was circulated amongst Mohler's acquaintances and eventually read by Schmitt, who seconded Taubes's appraisal of theologians. 'Taubes is right: today everything is theology, with the exception of what theologians talk about' (*CS*, 26). The circulation of the letter ultimately led to a meeting between Taubes, the left-wing Jew, and Schmitt, the Catholic defender of National Socialism. The details of this exchange are found in *To Carl Schmitt: Letters and Reflections*, trans. Keith Tribe (New York: Columbia University Press, 2013).
8 In *Occidental Eschatology*, Taubes relies solely on Baur, *Die christliche Gnosis oder die christliche Religionsphilosophie in ihrer geschichtlichen Entwicklung* (Darmstadt: Wissenschaftliche Buchgesellschaft, 1967), in other writings he cites Herbet Grundman, Hans Jonas and Eric Voeglin. See, in particular, the essays contained in Jacob Taubes, *From Cult to Culture: Fragments Towards a Critique of Historical Reason*, ed. Charlotte Elisheva Fonrobert and Amir Engel (Stanford, CA: Stanford University Press, 2010).
9 Jacob Taubes, 'Theodicy and Theology: A Philosophical Analysis of Karl Barth's Dialectical Theology (1954)', in *From Cult to Culture: Fragments Towards a Critique of Historical Reason*, ed. Charlotte Elisheva Fonrobert and Amir Engel (Stanford, CA: Stanford University Press, 2010), 177.
10 Taubes, 'Theodicy and Theology', 177.
11 Taubes, 'Theodicy and Theology', 178, my emphasis.
12 Taubes, 'Theodicy and Theology', 188.
13 Vattimo claims that global society is on the verge of the 'Age of the Spirit' understood as a cosmopolitan community that emerges out of Christianity but breaks with its hierarchical structures and outdated metaphysics: 'To understand modernity as secularization, namely as the inner and "logical" development of the Judeo-Christian revelation, and to grasp the dissolution of metaphysics as the manifestation of Being as event, as its philosophical outcome, means to read the signs of the times, in the spirit of Joachim of Fiore' (Gianni Vattimo, *After Christianity* (New York: Columbia University Press, 2002), 36). In one of his more well-known statements on religion, Žižek writes, 'My claim is not merely that I am a materialist through and through, and that the subversive kernel of Christianity is accessible also to a materialist approach; my thesis is much stronger: this kernel is accessible only to a materialist approach – and vice-versa: to become a true dialectical materialist, one should go through the Christian experience' (*The Puppet and the Dwarf: The Perverse Core of Christianity* (Cambridge, MA: MIT Press, 2003), 6.) Žižek's statement is more dramatically phrased, but the underlying Hegelian logic is the same as Taubes's – it is only by arriving at the materialist consequences of religious thought that

religious truth can be adequately comprehended. Žižek's frequent theological provocations could thus also be understood in the light of Hegel's two-way relation between concept and representation.

14 Jacob Taubes, 'The Dogmatic Myth of Gnosticism (1971)', in *From Cult to Culture: Fragments Towards a Critique of Historical Reason*, ed. Charlotte Elisheva Fonrobert and Amir Engel (Stanford, CA: Stanford University Press, 2010), 62, emphasis mine. Taubes also defends allegorical readings in *The Political Theology of Paul* where he argues that Paul uses allegorical readings of Hebrew scriptures (pp. 44–6).

15 Taubes, 'Dogmatic Myth of Gnosticism (1971)', 62. In a more practical vein, in *The Political Theology of Paul* he suggests the creation of chairs in Old Testament, New Testament and Church History within departments of philosophy in order to combat the isolation of the departments (p. 4).

16 Anthony Paul Smith and Daniel Whistler use this notion of 'contamination' to define their understanding of contemporary continental philosophy of religion: 'The task here is simply that of finding a way to perform a philosophical operation upon theological material, while retaining something properly philosophical. Here philosophy turns outwards, both as a critical operation on theology and *as a liberation of aspects of religion from their own theological contamination*' ('What Is Continental Philosophy of Religion Now?', 2). They also hold out the possibility of 'an aggressive alternative: a complementary philosophical contamination of theology. Experimentation here risks a disintegration of the philosophical body, in order to disturb theology's ideological and orthodox identity (that is, to contaminate it). What is at stake in both cases is a practice of philosophy which avoids dissolving into theology or becoming a tool of theological thought' (p. 2). Equally, it is the case that theology should not become merely a tool of philosophical thought. Rather, political theology in the Taubesian vein is an example of Smith and Whistler's proposed 'experimenting on and with theological and religious material' (p. 4).

17 Agata Bielik-Robson, 'Modernity: The Jewish Perspective', *New Blackfriars* 94, no. 1050 (2013): 189.

18 Bielik-Robson, 'Modernity', 189–90. David Kolb makes a similar claim, though focusing on Hegel's understanding of civil society as a distinctly modern phenomenon. For Kolb, Hegel critiques civil society in the name of the freedom which only a reformed civil society can sustain. See Kolb, *The Critique of Pure Modernity: Hegel, Heidegger, and After* (Chicago: University of Chicago Press, 1988).

19 Bielik-Robson, 'Modernity', 191.

20 Taubes, 'Dogmatic Myth of Gnosticism (1971)', 67.

21 Mike Grimshaw, 'Introduction: "A Very Rare Thing"', in *To Carl Schmitt: Letters and Reflections*, by Jacob Taubes, trans. Keith Tribe (New York: Columbia University Press, 2013), xvii.
22 Grimshaw, 'Introduction', xxiv.
23 Jacob Taubes, 'On the Nature of the Theological Method: Some Reflections on the Methodological Principles of Tillich's Theology (1954)', in *From Cult to Culture: Fragments towards a Critique of Historical Reason*, ed. Charlotte Elisheva Fonrobert and Amir Engel (Stanford, CA: Stanford University Press, 2010), 205.
24 Tina Beattie, 'Nothing Really Matters: a Bohemian Rhapsody for a Dead Queen', in *Theology after Lacan: The Passion for the Real*, ed. Marcus Pound, Clayton Crockett and Creston Davis (Eugene, OR: Cascade Books, 2014), 34.
25 Jacob Taubes, 'Culture and Ideology (1969)', in *From Cult to Culture: Fragments towards a Critique of Historical Reason*, ed. Charlotte Elisheva Fonrobert and Amir Engel (Stanford, CA: Stanford University Press, 2010), 275.
26 Taubes, 'Culture and Ideology (1969)', 265.
27 Karl Marx, 'Manifesto of the Communist Party', in *Karl Marx, Frederick Engels: Collected Works, Vol. 6, Marx and Engels: 1845-1848*, trans. Jack Cohen et. al. (New York: International Publishers, 2005), 176.
28 Taubes, 'Theodicy and Theology', 178.
29 Taubes, 'Culture and Ideology (1969)', 264.
30 Jean Hyppolite makes this point in his discussion of the relationship between Hegel and Marx. 'Hegel retains the notion of alienation even within his conception of the Absolute. It is only in appearance that the Absolute transcends contradiction, that is, the movement of alienation. There is no synthesis for the Absolute apart from the presence of a permanent internal antithesis. Indeed, it is natural to think that Absolute Knowledge still contains alienation, along with a movement to transcend it . . . The Spirit is the identity of Logos and Nature, though the opposition between these two moments is always present within it, even if continuously transcended. In Language, the expression of this notion of the Absolute is the Hegelian Aufhebung. For Marx, on the other hand, there is in history a definitive synthesis that excludes the permanence of the antithesis.' *Studies on Marx and Hegel*, trans. John O'Neill (New York: Basic Books, 1969), 86.
31 Adrian Johnston, 'Points of Forced Freedom: Eleven (More) Theses on Materialism', *Speculations IV* (2013): 94.
32 Adrian Johnston, *Žižek's Ontology: A Transcendental Materialist Theory of Subjectivity* (Evanston, IL: Northwestern University Press, 2008), xxiii.
33 This series of refutations focusing on the relationship between actuality and idea also reiterates, in a different form, Magnus's insight from Chapter 2 concerning the persistence of sensuousness in the symbolic.

34 Jacob Taubes, 'Theology and Political Theory (1955)', in *From Cult to Culture: Fragments towards a Critique of Historical Reason*, ed. Charlotte Elisheva Fonrobert and Amir Engel (Stanford, CA: Stanford University Press, 2010), 230. Taubes is not the only Jewish Messianic thinker to struggle with this tension. Rabinbach includes it as one of the defining characteristics of this form of thought. Rabinbach, 'Between Enlightenment and Apocalypse', 86.

35 Bielik-Robson, 'Modernity', 192.

36 Bielik-Robson, 'Modernity', 193. While I ultimately disagree with Bielik-Robson, we are agreed on the nature of the world; the combination of Schmitt's analysis of *nomos* and my account of nature, capital, gender and race is a more fully described version of this naturalized, hierarchical, spatialized and ideologically stabilized form of power.

37 Svenungsson, *Divining History*, 22–3.

38 Bielik-Robson, 'Modernity', 193.

39 Bielik-Robson, 'Modernity', 196.

40 Bielik-Robson, 'Modernity', 197. Rabinbach, whom Bielik-Robson cites throughout, is again useful on this point: 'the cataclysmic element is explicit and consequently makes redemption independent of either any immanent historical "forces" or personal experience of liberation' (Rabinbach, 'Between Enlightenment and Apocalypse', 86).

41 The question of the redemption of the world is a constant problem for Christian theodicy and animating force for Gnosticism. On the philosophical issues it presents, see Quentin Meillassoux, 'The Spectral Dilemma', *Collapse* IV (2008): 261–76. Malabou offers a reading of Meillassoux's argument for the necessity of contingency in *Before Tomorrow: Epigenesis and Rationality* (Cambridge: Polity, 2016), 353–60. She focuses on Meillassoux's mathematical rather than apocalyptic notion of contingency, which she finds ultimately unable to provide the possibility of genuine alterity.

42 Rabinbach identifies a similar relation to nature in Bloch, describing it in quite Hegelian terms: 'History for Bloch is predicated on a future oriented knowledge that transcends the empirical order of things, that does not take flight in false images or fall prey to naturalism, but is directed beyond the existing world toward a yet unrealized "messianic goal"' (Rabinbach, 'Between Enlightenment and Apocalypse', 100).

43 Bielik-Robson, 'Modernity', 198.

44 'Between Enlightenment and Apocalypse', 85.

45 Rabinbach, 'Between Enlightenment and Apocalypse', 86. This linking of messianism and apocalypticism is at odds with more recent political theology. As seen in the first chapter, and as will become even more important in the next, the opposition between messianism and apocalypticism is often couched in terms of the former's rejection of the latter's violence.

46 Rabinbach, 'Between Enlightenment and Apocalypse', 87.
47 Rabinbach, 'Between Enlightenment and Apocalypse', 87. Rabinbach thus confirms Bielik-Robson's claim that Taubes offers a 'polemical alternative' to Karl Löwith's thesis on secularization in his *Meaning in History* (Bielik-Robson, 'Modernity', 191).
48 This ambiguity is also addressed in his discussion of connections between National Socialism and German mystic and pagan traditions (*HT*, 48–62).
49 On the complexity of Marx's critique of religion, see Alberto Toscano, 'Beyond Abstraction: Marx and the Critique of the Critique of Religion', *Historical Materialism* 18 (2010): 3–29.
50 Bielik-Robson, 'Modernity', 191.
51 See Hudson, *Marxist Philosophy of Ernst Bloch*, 31–49. As Hudson makes clear, Bloch's connection to both Marxist theory and Communist politics was never simple. He inevitably advocated positions that were at odds with main-line positions. This perpetual heterodoxy is also highlighted in Rabinbach, 'Between Enlightenment and Apocalypse'.
52 Grimshaw, 'Introduction', xvii.
53 Grimshaw, 'Introduction', xi.
54 Marx, 'Manifesto of the Communist Party', 489.
55 Grimshaw, 'Introduction', xxxi. Grimshaw's point mirrors Žižek's claims about objective and subjective violence. Liberalism's denunciation of subjective, interpersonal violence is dependent upon an objective level of violence that maintains the societal norms which in turn provide the baseline for measuring subjective violence. See Slavoj Žižek, *Violence* (London: Profile, 2008), 9–15.
56 Karin de Boer, '"Democracy Out of Joint?" The Financial Crisis in Light of Hegel's Philosophy of Right', *Hegel Bulletin* 33, no. 2 (2012): 37. While I am using de Boer's work to describe an anti-liberal tendency within Hegel, that does not mean that de Boer argues for an anti-liberal position or that Hegel's philosophy is thoroughly anti-liberal. De Boer is not concerned with rejecting liberalism but with offering a critical assessment of its limitations. Her concern is that a liberal democracy that privileges individual rights above all else is incapable of meeting contemporary crises. The internal tensions of liberalism have thus generated a tragic political situation. In addition to 'Democracy Out of Joint?', see her 'Hegel Today: Towards a Tragic Conception of Intercultural Conflicts', *Cosmos and History: The Journal of Natural and Social Philosophy* 3, nos 2–3 (2007): 117–31 and 'A Greek Tragedy? A Hegelian Perspective on Greece's Sovereign Debt Crisis', *Cosmos and History: The Journal of Natural and Social Philosophy* 9, no. 1 (2013): 358–75. On Hegel's own complex relationship to liberalism, see Part 2 of Dominic Losurdo's *Hegel and the Freedom of the Moderns* (Durham, NC: Duke University Press, 2004). As Losurdo shows, it is not that Hegel is

straightforwardly anti-liberal but that there are anti-liberal aspects to Hegel's philosophy.

57 In Hegel's remarks on this paragraph, he explores this point further: 'the individual is a genus, but it has its immanent universal actuality in the next genus. – Hence the individual fulfils his actual and living vocation for universality only when he becomes a member of a corporation, a community, etc.' (*PR*, §308r: 295/477).

58 Robert B. Pippin, *Hegel's Practical Philosophy: Rational Agency as Ethical Life* (Cambridge: Cambridge University Press, 2008), 4.

59 Pippin, *Hegel's Practical Philosophy*, 23.

60 de Boer, 'Democracy Out of Joint?', 39.

61 As Bielik-Robson writes, 'modernity can be regarded as the most religious of all epochs, precisely in its consciously historiosophic emphasis on the messianic transformation of our earthly conditions, aiming at achieving a better, more meaningful, freer life here and now. In its attempt to achieve this goal, *modernitas* walks a thin line between messianism and nihilism, which, for Taubes, is not necessarily a bad thing' (Bielik-Robson, 'Modernity', 192).

62 This returns to Brooks's idea of stakeholders, discussed in Chapter 2. Those who identify as members of a society 'believe that any problems are best resolved within the system rather than without . . . the essential concern is whether persons identify themselves as having a stake in the political community or not. Some may believe they do not have a shared stake and can "opt out" in a position we might call political exceptionalism, which is rooted in alienation.' Thom Brooks, *Punishment* (London: Routledge, 2012), 145.

63 Wolf-Daniel Hartwich, Aleida Assmann and Jan Assmann, 'Afterword', in *The Political Theology of Paul*, by Jacob Taubes, trans. Dana Hollander (Stanford, CA: Stanford University Press, 2004), 121.

64 Johnston's most sustained development of these ideas is in *Žižek's Ontology*. He further explores these ideas in *Adventures in Transcendental Materialism: Dialogues with Contemporary Thinkers*. In this latter text he also differentiates transcendental materialism from vitalist materialisms represented in much of New Materialism and feminist materialisms. For a more condensed explanation of the key themes of Johnston's materialism, see 'Points of Forced Freedom', 8.

65 Adrian Johnston and Catherine Malabou, *Self and Emotional Life: Philosophy, Psychoanalysis, and Neuroscience* (New York: Columbia University Press, 2013).

66 Karl Marx, *Marx & Engels: Collected Works, Vol. 3, Karl Marx and Frederick Engels: 1843–1844*, trans. Jack Cohen et al., 229–346 (New York: International Publishers, 2005), 296–7.

67 Johnston, *Žižek's Ontology*, 275.

68 Indeed, Hegel's understanding of nature, specifically the view that emerges in the transition between the *Philosophy of Nature* and the *Philosophy of Mind* in the *Encyclopaedia* is central to Johnston's philosophical project.
69 Bielik-Robson, 'Modernity', 191.
70 Taubes, 'Nachman Krochmal and Modern Historicism (1963)', in *From Cult to Culture: Fragments towards a Critique of Historical Reason*, ed. Charlotte Elisheva Fonrobert and Amir Engel (Stanford, CA: Stanford University Press, 2010), 30.
71 Johnston, *Žižek's Ontology*, 235.
72 This understanding of the relationship between religion and philosophy is an overarching argument of Magnus's work *Hegel and the Symbolic Mediation of Spirit*. See, in particular, the section on spirit's self-determination (235–7).
73 See, in particular, his 'Conflicted Matter: Jacques Lacan and the Challenge of Secularising Materialism', *Pli: The Warwick Journal of Philosophy* 19 (2008): 166–88.
74 Taubes, 'Nachman Krochmal and Modern Historicism (1963)', 30.
75 Boer, *Criticism of Heaven*, 451.

4 Plastic Apocalypticism

1 Agata Bielik-Robson, 'Modernity: The Jewish Perspective', *New Blackfriars* 94, no. 1050 (2013): 191.
2 In recent years, Malabou has gradually turned from the development of the concept of plasticity in this sense to the concept of 'neuroplasticity'. See her *What Should We Do with Our Brain?*, trans. Sebastian Rand (New York: Fordham University Press, 2008), and *The New Wounded: From Neurosis to Brain Damage*, trans. Steven Miller (New York: Fordham University Press, 2012). While the two explorations of plasticity are clearly related, and the connection between biology, freedom and the subject is pertinent to the ontology of the world developed in the first chapter, I am focusing on her engagement with Hegel so as to draw out the resonance between her work and Taubes. For the connection between her two explorations of plasticity, including the link to transcendental materialism, see her collaboration with Adrian Johnston in *Self and Emotional Life: Philosophy, Psychoanalysis, and Neuroscience* (New York: Columbia University Press, 2013).
3 While differing on the implications of Hegel's understanding of possibility and contingency, the basic outlines provided by Houlgate and Burbidge are two of the most significant explanations of the relevant passages of the *Science of Logic*. Stephen Houlgate, 'Necessity and Contingency in Hegel's Science of Logic', *The*

Owl of Minerva 27, no. 1 (1995): 37–49, and John W. Burbidge, *Hegel on Logic and Religion* (Albany: State University of New York Press, 1992). Both make reference to Dieter Henrich's classic essay 'Hegels Theorie über den Zufall' in his *Hegel im Kontext* (Frankfurt: Suhrkamp, 1971). I return to this discussion later in the chapter.

4 Collins, *Apocalyptic Imagination*, 13.
5 Aleida Assmann, Jan Assmann and Wolf-Daniel Hartwich, 'Introduction to the German Edition', in *From Cult to Culture: Fragments Towards a Critique of Historical Reason*, by Jacob Taubes, ed. Charlotte Elisheva Fonrobert and Amir Engel (Stanford, CA: Stanford University Press, 2010), xxii.
6 Taubes, 'On the Nature of the Theological Method: Some Reflections on the Methodological Principles of Tillich's Theology (1954)', In *From Cult to Culture: Fragments towards a Critique of Historical Reason*, ed. Charlotte Elisheva Fonrobert and Amir Engel (Stanford, CA: Stanford University Press, 2010), 208.
7 Taubes, 'On the Nature of the Theological Method (1954)', 210. Drawing a connection between Hegel and Tillich is not surprising given the latter's engagement with German Idealism. The nature of religion and theological method, however, is a point of particular confluence. See Merold Westphal, 'Hegel, Tillich, and the Secular', *Journal of Religion* 52, no. 3 (1972): 223–39.
8 Taubes, 'On the Nature of the Theological Method (1954)', 210.
9 Taubes, 'On the Nature of the Theological Method (1954)', 210–11.
10 Jacob Taubes, 'Notes on Surrealism (1966)', in *From Cult to Culture: Fragments towards a Critique of Historical Reason*, ed. Charlotte Elisheva Fonrobert and Amir Engel (Stanford, CA: Stanford University Press, 2010), 120.
11 Taubes, 'Notes on Surrealism (1966)', 107.
12 Taubes, 'On the Nature of the Theological Method (1954)', 208.
13 My emphasis.
14 It is important to note that Hegel is talking about pure, abstract being and nothing. As he explains later in the section, any determination which would enable one to distinguish between the two would shift the conversation to determinate being and determinate nothing (*SL*, 92/5:95).
15 Malcolm Bull, Seeing Things Hidden: *Apocalypse, Vision, and Totality* (London: Verso, 1999), 104.
16 Bull, *Seeing Things Hidden*, 109.
17 Stephen Houlgate, *An Introduction to Hegel's Philosophy: Freedom, Truth and History*, 2nd edn (Oxford: Blackwell, 2005), 25.
18 Bielik-Robson, 'Modernity', 193.
19 Malabou makes a similar point in *The Ontology of the Accident*: 'Destructive plasticity enables the appearance or formation of alterity where the other is

absolutely lacking. Plasticity is the form of alterity where the other is absolutely lacking. Plasticity is the form of alterity when no transcendence, flight or escape is left. The only other that exists in this circumstance is being other to the self' (p. 11).
20 Karl Löwith, Meaning in History: *The Theological Implications of the Philosophy of History* (Chicago: Phoenix Books, 1949), 54–9.
21 Non-contemporaneity is a translation of the German *Ungleichzeitigkeit*, which is also sometimes translated as non-synchronicity. Both translations are acceptable, but I will use non-contemporaneity throughout for the sake of consistency.
22 John Russon develops a reading of Hegelian 'non-synchronous temporalities' that is in some ways similar to this treatment. Russon does not discuss Bloch, but he is developing an open reading of Hegel in which '[t]he past and the future are not "out there" as existent, alien realities that we somehow have to get to. The past and the future are always of the subject, of spirit. What we have seen from looking at spirit is that history is that identity *as* accomplishment, and what we have seen from looking at the thing and the body is that the future is precisely what those identities *make possible*' ('Temporality and the Future of Philosophy in Hegel's Phenomenology', *International Philosophical Quarterly* 48, no. 1 (2008): 67). Russon even cites Malabou as offering a similar reading of temporality in Hegel. Russon, however, emphasizes the non-synchronous temporality as a division that occurs within the subject – it is the difference between the temporalities of the subject as living body and the subject as living spirit (p. 66). Bloch's non-contemporaneity denotes an intersubjective phenomenon and while there is a sense of difference between humanity as it is and humanity as it could be, this difference does not map on to a body/spirit division.
23 Bloch also uses the opportunity to draw the contrast between the On-high and From-below: 'The more the situation of the peasants and ordinary urban citizens worsened, and the more visibly on the other hand mercantile capital and territorial princedom succeeded and the purely feudal empire, founded on economic modes of the past, disintegrated, the more powerfully the prophecy of a new, an "evangelical" age necessarily struck home; in the case of Münzer as peasant – proletarian – petit-bourgeois battle-cry against increased exploitation, in the case of Luther, of course, as the ideology of the princes against central power and the Church' (*HT*, 118).
24 Adrian Johnston, *Žižek's Ontology: A Transcendental Materialist Theory of Subjectivity* (Evanston: Northwestern University Press, 2008), 61.
25 See also Bloch's discussion of transcending without the 'transcendent-hypostasizing' in his earlier sections on the development of biblical hermeneutics (*AC*, 39).

26 Ben Anderson, '"Transcending without Transcendence" Utopianism and an Ethos of Hope', *Antipode* 38, no. 4 (2006): 700.
27 See Markus Gabriel's *Transcendental Ontology: Essays in German Idealism* (London: Continuum, 2011) and Žižek's work in *The Parallax View* (Cambridge, MA: MIT Press, 2006) and *Less Than Nothing: Hegel and the Shadow of Dialectical Materialism* (London: Verso, 2012). They also have collaborated on *Mythology, Madness, and Laughter: Subjectivity in German Idealism* (London: Continuum, 2009). Quentin Meillassoux explores contingency in relation to his concept of divine inexistence. He develops a philosophical defence of contingency in *After Finitude: An Essay on the Necessity of Contingency*, trans. Ray Brassier (London: Continuum, 2010), and uses his understanding of contingency to defend the notion of an inexistent God in 'The Spectral Dilemma'. Extracts detailing this 'divinology' are available as an appendix to Graham Harman, *Quentin Meillassoux: Philosophy in the Making* (Edinburgh: Edinburgh University Press, 2011). There is a striking parallel between Bloch's claim that '[t]he idea of the Creator-of the-world as well as of its Lord, had to retreat continually before that of the Spirit of the Goal, who has no fixed abode. – All the more so, the more the Promised Land beyond the desert was still conceived of in terms of Egypt. The more the Canaan here-and-now was disappointing, in accordance with a God who is himself not yet what he is: who is only in the future of his promise-to-be – if he should keep his word – and in no other way' (*AC*, 81) and Meillassoux's contention that only an inexistent God is congruent with a demand for justice. Further, the language of divine inexistence recalls language prevalent in Gnostic traditions. Similar ideas connecting Meillassoux and Žižek are developed in Michael O'Neill Burns, 'The Hope of Speculative Materialism', in *After the Postsecular and the Postmodern: New Essays in Continental Philosophy of Religion*, ed. Anthony Paul Smith and Daniel Whistler (Newcastle upon Tyne: Cambridge Scholars, 2010), 316–34.
28 Houlgate, 'Necessity and Contingency in Hegel's Science of Logic', 38.
29 Houlgate, 'Necessity and Contingency in Hegel's Science of Logic', 39.
30 Houlgate, 'Necessity and Contingency in Hegel's Science of Logic', 41.
31 Houlgate, 'Necessity and Contingency in Hegel's Science of Logic', 42.
32 Houlgate, 'Necessity and Contingency in Hegel's Science of Logic', 43.
33 Houlgate, 'Necessity and Contingency in Hegel's Science of Logic', 44.
34 Houlgate, 'Necessity and Contingency in Hegel's Science of Logic', 45.
35 Houlgate, 'Necessity and Contingency in Hegel's Science of Logic', 47.
36 Houlgate, 'Necessity and Contingency in Hegel's Science of Logic', 48.
37 Houlgate, 'Necessity and Contingency in Hegel's Science of Logic', 49.
38 Houlgate, 'Necessity and Contingency in Hegel's Science of Logic', 49.

39 John W. Burbidge, *Hegel's Systematic Contingency* (Basingstoke: Palgrave Macmillan, 2007), 23. In his review of Malabou's *The Future of Hegel*, William Dudley argues that one of the missed opportunities of the book is engagement with the Anglo-American work done on themes of openness and contingency in Hegel's philosophy. He specifically mentions Kolb and Burbidge, both of whom will feature in this section. I am indebted to Dudley's review for drawing attention to these connections. See William Dudley, 'The Future of Hegel: Plasticity, Temporality and Dialectic (Review)', *Notre Dame Philosophical Review* (2006), http://ndpr.nd.edu/news/25128-the-future-of-hegel-plasticity-temporality-and-dialectic/.
40 Burbidge, *Hegel's Systematic Contingency*, 12.
41 Burbidge, *Hegel's Systematic Contingency*, 9.
42 Translation modified from Miller's.
43 Burbidge, *Hegel's Systematic Contingency*, 64.
44 Burbidge, *Hegel's Systematic Contingency*, 62.
45 Burbidge, *Hegel's Systematic Contingency*, 6.
46 John W. Burbidge, 'Hegel's Open Future', In *Hegel and the Tradition: Essays in Honour of H.S. Harris*, ed. Michael Baur and John Edward Russon. Toronto: University of Toronto Press, 1997, 182.
47 Žižek, *Less Than Nothing*, 464.
48 Žižek, *Less Than Nothing*, 467.
49 Žižek, *Less Than Nothing*, 467.
50 Žižek, *Less Than Nothing*, 468.
51 Gabriel, *Transcendental Ontology*, 102–3. Gabriel's argument is not that Hegel is right, but that Hegel claims being has a necessary form. This point is part of his larger argument for Schelling's superior philosophy of contingency. 'If I claim that the necessity of 2 + 2 = 4 could be otherwise, and even that any logical necessity could be otherwise, I am not saying that it is arbitrary to believe that 2 + 2 = 4 rather than 2 + 2 = 5. I am only claiming that the possibility of revision is built into every belief system. And even if mathematics were the attempt to map an eternal realm of laws (whatever that might mean), it would have to map it, and that is to say it would have to consist of claims. Claims are finite, because they are determinate, and determinacy entails higher-order contingency, as I hope to make plausible in this chapter against Hegel's claim to a closure of the indeterminacy of determining' (p. 103).
52 Houlgate, *Freedom, Truth and History*, 24.
53 Žižek, *Less Than Nothing*, 464.
54 Žižek, *Less Than Nothing*, 464.
55 As Hudson explains, 'concrete utopia and the new metaphysics are synonymous: transcending without Transcendence. There is no mythological

"Transcendence" and no need for other-worldly assumptions, because the world itself contains immanent reference to a possible perfection towards which it is driving, and a forward driving *transcendere* pervades the process forms' (Wayne Hudson, *The Marxist Philosophy of Ernst Bloch* (London: Macmillan, 1982), 99).

56 Burbidge, *Hegel's Systematic Contingency*, 48.
57 Others continue to argue for eschatology or messianism. Graham Ward, for example, reaches a similar conclusion, but finds the latter term appropriate: 'Governed by a messianic reason, Hegel is committed politically to a condition approaching Lenin's notion of the permanent revolution. Absolute spirit working in and as the human spirit continually transforms the cultural given' ('Hegel's Messianic Reasoning and Its Politics' in *Politics to Come: Power, Modernity and the Messianic*, ed. Arthur Bradley and Paul Fletcher (London: Continuum, 2010), 91).
58 Clayton Crockett, *Radical Political Theology: Religion and Politics After Liberalism* (New York: Columbia University Press, 2011), 106.
59 Clayton Crockett and Catherine Malabou, 'Plasticity and the Future of Philosophy and Theology', *Political Theology* 11, no. 1 (2010): 30.

5 Pessimism and Hope in Apocalyptic Living

1 Carl Schmitt, *The Crisis of Parliamentary Democracy*, trans. Ellen Kennedy (Cambridge, MA: MIT Press, 1988), 50.
2 Schmitt, *Crisis of European Democracy*, 71.
3 Jayne Svenungsson, *Divining History: Prophetism, Messianism and the Development of the Spirit*, trans. Stephen Donovan, (Oxford: Berghahn Books, 2016), 176.
4 Saidiya V. Hartman makes this point in regard to reparations for slavery. Regarded by many as an extreme and unattainable attempt to make amends for American history, Hartman identifies the political problem at its core. For her, 'reparations seem like a very limited reform: a liberal scheme based upon certain notions of commensurability that reinscribe the power of the law and of the state to make right a certain situation, when, clearly, it cannot' (Saidiya V. Hartman and Frank B. Wilderson III, 'The Position of the Unthought', *Qui Parle: Critical Humanities and Social Sciences* 13, no. 2 (2003): 198).
5 Judith Butler, *Gender Trouble: Feminism and the Subversion of Identity* (New York: Routledge, 1999). She defines the matrix as 'that grid of cultural intelligibility through which bodies, genders, and desires are naturalized' (194n.6).

6 Daniel Colucciello Barber, 'World-Making and Grammatical Impasse', *Qui Parle: Critical Humanities and Social Sciences* 25, nos 1–2 (2016): 181–2.
7 Svenungsson, *Divining History*, 178.
8 Lee Edelman, *No Future: Queer Theory and the Death Drive* (Durham, NC: Duke University Press, 2004), 4.
9 China Miéville, 'The Dusty Hat', in *Three Moments of an Explosion: Stories* (London: Macmillan, 2015), 243. While Miéville uses serf rather than slave, his visceral choice of imagery should be read in the light of Wilderson's concern that 'the image of the Slave as an enabling vehicle that [animates] the evolving discourses of . . . emancipation' (Frank B. Wilderson III, *Red, White & Black: Cinema and the Structure of U.S. Antagonisms*, (Durham, NC: Duke University Press, 2010), 19). Wilderson argues that even the emancipation of the slave is appropriated to fund the discourses of other struggles. The concrete liberation of the slave, the end of race, must therefore be at the centre of any invocation of the image of the slave.
10 Thomas More, *Utopia* (London: Verso, 2016), 72–3.
11 Rebecca Solnit, *Hope in the Dark: Untold Histories, Wild Possibilities* (Edinburgh: Canongate Books, 2016), 20.
12 Solnit, *Hope in the Dark*, 20.
13 Solnit, *Hope in the Dark*, xii.
14 It is worth noting that the sources of this pessimism – queer theory and Afro-Pessimism – both come from positions that Solnit argues have benefited from progress. As she argues, 'In the past half century, the state of the world has declined dramatically, measured by material terms and by the brutality of wars and ecological onslaughts. But we have also added a huge number of intangibles, of rights, ideas, concepts, words to describe and to realize what was once invisible or unimaginable' (*Hope in the Dark*, 13). She cites marriage equality as evidence of the improvement of society (p. xiv).
15 To be clear, this reading of Edelman and Wilderson is not an effort to uncover theological determinations of their positions (an all too common practice when theology of any kind engages with other disciplines). Nor am I arguing that Edelman and Wilderson offer the same pessimism. The argument is simply that both oppose the future of the world in a way that can inform an apocalyptic disposition.
16 James Bliss, 'Hope Against Hope: Queer Negativity, Black Feminist Theorizing, and Reproduction without Futurity', *Mosaic: A Journal for the Interdisciplinary Study of Literature* 48, no. 1 (2015): 86.
17 On the park and bus station, see José Esteban Muñoz, *Cruising Utopia: The Then and There of Queer Futurity* (New York: New York University Press, 2009).

18 Edelman, *No Future*, 75. It is worth recalling Federici's argument that fears of witches and other persecutions of women focused on reproduction. Infanticide, abortion, contraception and the incantations of witches were diabolical in their disruption of the reproduction of the future.
19 Edelman, *No Future*, 4.
20 Edelman, *No Future*, 17.
21 Edelman, *No Future*, 25.
22 Non-reproductivity has long been a theme in condemnations of homosexuality as deviant. Of course, suspicion of the childless is not only limited to homosexuality. For example, there was widespread controversy over Andrea Leadsom's suggestion that the future UK Prime Minister, Theresa May, lacked a real stake in the future because she does not have children. See Sam Coates and Rachel Sylvester, 'Being a Mother Gives Me an Edge on May – Leadsom', *The Times*, 9 July 2016, and Ashley Cowburn, 'Andrea Leadsom Attacked by Tory MPs over "Vile" and "Insulting" Comments on Theresa May's Childlessness', *The Independent*, 10 July 2016.
23 Edelman, *No Future*, 30.
24 Nina Power, 'Non-Reproductive Futurism: Rancière's Rational Equality against Edelman's Body Apolitic', *Borderlands* 8, no. 2 (2009): 15.
25 Power, 'Non-Reproductive Futurism', 2.
26 Muñoz, *Cruising Utopia*, 1.
27 Muñoz, *Cruising Utopia*, 13.
28 Muñoz, *Cruising Utopia*, 83.
29 Muñoz, *Cruising Utopia*, 91.
30 Muñoz, *Cruising Utopia*, 175.
31 Edelman, *No Future*, 48, 101.
32 Edelman, *No Future*, 30.
33 Muñoz, *Cruising Utopia*, 7.
34 On the queer hope enabled by non-reproductive futurity, see Bliss, 'Hope Against Hope'.
35 Kara Keeling describes something similar in her exploration of the poetry of the future. She writes of an impossible possibility that 'is a felt presence of the unknowable, the content of which exceeds its expression and therefore points toward a different epistemological, if not ontological and empirical, regime' (p. 567). See 'Looking for M—: Queer Temporality, Black Political Possibility, and Poetry from the Future', *GLQ: A Journal of Lesbian and Gay Studies* 15, no. 4 (2009): 578.
36 Keeling, 'Looking for M – ', 578.
37 Wilderson, *Red, White & Black*, 9, 10, 20, 49–50. On the specific limitations of Marxism for thinking about the position of the slave, see Wilderson's 'Gramsci's

Black Marx: Whither the Slave in Civil Society?', *Social Identities* 9, no. 2 (2003): 225–40.
38 Wilderson, *Red, White & Black*, 9.
39 Wilderson, *Red, White & Black*, 49.
40 Howard Caygill discusses this approach in his philosophical investigation of resistance and the work needed to cultivate the ability to exist in a state of resistance. Though he has greater hope in a constructive response to the world than apocalypticism, his notion that resistant subjective 'do not enjoy the freedom of possibility, but only a bare capacity to resist enmity and chance' and are in some 'sense already dead' describes the form of subjectivity shared by apocalyptic dispositions (*On Resistance: A Philosophy of Defiance* (London: Bloomsbury, 2013), 98). Barber also discusses this same idea by analysing the difference between tiredness and exhaustion in Deleuze. 'With tiredness . . . possibility persists. Such possibility is evidently marked by failure . . . With exhaustion, or the failure to possibility, things are quite different. This is because exhaustion challenges the very existence of possibility . . . The failure indexed by exhaustion is the failure to inhabit a frame in which possibility would even exist' ('World-Making and Grammatical Impasse', 205n.25).
41 Wilderson, *Red, White & Black*, 338.
42 Wilderson, *Red, White & Black*, 66.
43 Hartman and Wilderson, 'The Position of the Unthought', 187.
44 Hartman and Wilderson, 'The Position of the Unthought', 187.
45 Fanon's famous meditation on violence traces the absolute necessity for violence, but also the ways that 'unsuccessful' violence can reinforce colonial power and 'successful' violence haunts those who forge a new society in the wake of colonial rule. Violence is tragic in its necessity. See Frantz Fanon, *The Wretched of the Earth*, trans. Richard Philcox (New York: Grove, 2014), 1–51. On the post-revolutionary legacy of violence, see Caygill, *On Resistance*, 103.
46 George Yancy makes precisely this point in his discussion of teaching white students about race. Even the best students, after deep introspection, reassume the sense of autonomy and agency needed to fix the problem of agency. They 'presume that when it comes to the complexity and depth of their own racism, they possess the capacity for absolute epistemic clarity and that the self is transparent' ('Looking at Whiteness: Tarrying with the Embedded and Opaque White Racist Self', in *Look, a White! Philosophical Essays on Whiteness* (Philadelphia, PA: Temple University Press, 2012), 168).
47 Solnit, *Hope in the Dark*, 11.
48 Solnit, *Hope in the Dark*, 22.
49 Lauren Berlant, 'Cruel Optimism: On Marx, Loss and the Senses', *New Formations: A Journal of Culture/Theory/Politics* 63 (2007): 33.

50 Franco Berardi, *Heroes: Mass Murder and Suicide* (London: Verso, 2015), 225.
51 Bliss, 'Hope Against Hope', 94.
52 It is inevitable in this discussion to cite Adorno's much-quoted line, 'Wrong life cannot be lived rightly.' (*Minima Moralia: Reflections from Damaged Life*, trans. E. F. N. Jephcott (London: Verso, 2005), 39).
53 I explore the political implications of Kierkegaard's reading of Abraham in relation to Hegel in 'Hegel and *Fear and Trembling*', in *Facing Abraham: Seven Readings of Kierkegaard's Fear and Trembling*, ed. Frederiek Depoortere (Leuven: Peeters, 2017), 31–50.
54 In Kierkegaard's telling of his story, the knight is male, so I am preserving his gendered language.
55 Søren Kierkegaard, *Fear and Trembling: Repetition*, trans. Howard V. Kong and Edna H. Kong (Princeton, NJ: Princeton University Press, 1983), 43.
56 Kierkegaard, *Fear and Trembling*, 46.
57 For this notion of the expressible within the world, see Barber, 'World-Making and Grammatical Impasse'.
58 Kierkegaard, *Fear and Trembling*, 39.
59 Kierkegaard, *Fear and Trembling*, 38.
60 E. J. Hobsbawm, *Primitive Rebels: Studies in Archaic Forms of Social Movement in the 19th and 20th Centuries* (New York: W. W. Norton, 1965), 2. He describes those who make up millennial sects as 'a pre-political people who have not yet found, or only begun to find, a specific language in which to express their aspirations about the world'.
61 Alberto Toscano, *Fanaticism: On the Uses of an Idea* (London: Verso, 2010), 48.
62 Toscano, *Fanaticism*, 49.
63 Jimmy Carter, 'Address to the Nation on Energy and National Goals: "The Malaise Speech"', *The American Presidency Project*, 15 July 1979. Available at: http://www.presidency.ucsb.edu/ws/?pid=32596 (accessed 15 December 2017).
64 Carter, 'Address to the Nation'.

Bibliography

Adorno, Theodor. *Minima Moralia: Reflections from Damaged Life*, translated by E. F. N. Jephcott. London: Verso, 2005.

Agrama, Hussein Ali. *Questioning Secularism: Islam, Sovereignty, and the Rule of Law in Modern Egypt*. Chicago, IL: University of Chicago Press, 2012.

Alaimo, Stacy, and Susan Hekman (eds). *Material Feminisms*. Bloomington: Indiana University Press, 2008.

Alcoff, Linda Martín. 'Epistemologies of Ignorance: Three Types'. In *Race and Epistemologies of Ignorance*, edited by Shannon Sullivan and Nancy Tuana, 39–57. Albany: State University of New York Press, 2007.

Anderson, Ben. ' "Transcending without Transcendence": Utopianism and an Ethos of Hope'. *Antipode* 38, no. 4 (2006): 691–710.

Assmann, Aleida, Jan Assmann, and Wolf-Daniel Hartwich. 'Introduction to the German Edition'. In *From Cult to Culture: Fragments toward a Critique of Historical Reason*, by Jacob Taubes, edited by Charlotte Elisheva Fonrobert and Amir Engel, xviii–l. Stanford, CA: Stanford University Press, 2010.

Balakrishnan, Gopal. *The Enemy: An Intellectual Portrait of Carl Schmitt*. London: Verso, 2000.

Barber, Daniel Colucciello. 'World-Making and Grammatical Impasse'. *Qui Parle: Critical Humanities and Social Sciences* 25, nos 1–2 (2016): 179–206.

Baur, Ferdinand Christian. *Die christliche Gnosis oder die christliche Religionsphilosophie in ihrer geschichtlichen Entwicklung*. Darmstadt: Wissenschaftliche Buchgesellschaft, 1967.

Beattie, Tina. 'Nothing Really Matters: A Bohemian Rhapsody for a Dead Queen'. In *Theology after Lacan: The Passion for the Real*, edited by Marcus Pound, Clayton Crockett and Creston Davis, 34–57. Eugene, OR: Cascade, 2014.

Bell, Daniel. *The End of Ideology: On the Exhaustion of Political Ideas in the Fifties*. Glencoe, IL: Free Press, 1960.

Benjamin, Walter. 'Some Reflections on Kafka'. In *Illuminations: Essays and Reflections*, edited by Hannah Arendt and translated by Harry Cohn, 141–5. New York: Schocken Books, 1968.

Benjamin, Walter. 'Critique of Violence'. In *Reflections: Essays, Aphorisms, Autobiographical Writings*, edited by Peter Demetz, 277–300. New York: Schocken Books, 1978.

Berardi, Franco. *Heroes: Mass Murder and Suicide*. London: Verso, 2015.

Berger, Peter L. 'The Desecularization of the World: A Global Overview'. In *The Desecularization of the World: Resurgent Religion and World Politics*, edited by Peter L. Berger, 1–18. Grand Rapids, MI: William B. Eerdmans, 1999.

Berlant, Lauren. 'Cruel Optimism: On Marx, Loss and the Senses'. *New Formations: A Journal of Culture/Theory/Politics* 63 (2007): 33–51.

Bernasconi, Robert. 'Hegel at the Court of Ashanti'. In *Hegel after Derrida*, edited by Stuart Barnett, 41–63. London: Routledge, 1998.

Bielik-Robson, Agata. 'Modernity: The Jewish Perspective'. *New Blackfriars* 94, no. 1050 (2013): 188–207.

Bliss, James. 'Hope Against Hope: Queer Negativity, Black Feminist Theorizing, and Reproduction without Futurity'. *Mosaic: A Journal for the Interdisciplinary Study of Literature* 48, no. 1 (2015): 83–98.

Bloch, Ernst. *Heritage of Our Times*, translated by Neville Plaice and Stephen Plaice. Cambridge: Polity, 1991.

Bloch, Ernst. *The Principle of Hope*, vol. 1, translated by Neville Plaice, Stephen Plaice and Paul Knight. Cambridge, MA: MIT Press, 1995.

Bloch, Ernst. *The Spirit of Utopia*, translated by Anthony A. Nassar. Stanford, CA: Stanford University Press, 2000.

Bloch, Ernst. *Atheism in Christianity: The Religion of the Exodus and the Kingdom*, translated by J. T. Swann, 2nd edn. London: Verso, 2009.

Blond, Phillip. 'Introduction: Theology before Philosophy'. In *Post-Secular Philosophy: Between Philosophy and Theology*, edited by Phillip Blond, 1–66. London: Routledge, 1998.

Boer, Roland. *Criticism of Heaven: On Marxism and Theology*. Chicago, IL: Haymarket Books, 2009.

Boer, Roland. *Political Myth: On the Use and Abuse of Biblical Themes*. Durham, NC: Duke University Press, 2009.

Boer, Roland. 'Review, Jacob Taubes, Occidental Eschatology'. *The Bible & Critical Theory* 8, no. 2 (2012): 99–100.

Bredekamp, Horst. 'From Walter Benjamin to Carl Schmitt, via Thomas Hobbes'. Critical Inquiry 25, no. 2 (1999): 247–66.

Brooks, Thom. *Punishment*. London: Routledge, 2012.

Brooks, Thom. 'Ethical Citizenship and the Stakeholder Society'. In *Ethical Citizenship: British Idealism and the Politics of Recognition*, edited by Thom Brooks, 125–38. New York: Palgrave Macmillan, 2014.

Buck-Morss, Susan. *The Dialectics of Seeing: Walter Benjamin and the Arcades Project*. Cambridge, MA: MIT Press, 1989.

Buck-Morss, Susan. *Hegel, Haiti, and Universal History*. Pittsburgh, PA: University of Pittsburgh Press, 2009.

Bull, Malcolm. *Seeing Things Hidden: Apocalypse, Vision, and Totality*. London: Verso, 1999.

Burbidge, John W. *Hegel on Logic and Religion: The Reasonableness of Christianity*. Albany: State University of New York Press, 1992.

Burbidge, John W. 'Hegel's Open Future'. In *Hegel and the Tradition: Essays in Honour of H.S. Harris*, edited by Michael Baur and John Edward Russon. Toronto: University of Toronto Press, 1997.

Burbidge, John W. *Hegel's Systematic Contingency*. Basingstoke: Palgrave Macmillan, 2007.

Burns, Michael O'Neill. 'The Hope of Speculative Materialism'. In *After the Postsecular and the Postmodern: New Essays in Continental Philosophy of Religion*, edited by Anthony Paul Smith and Daniel Whistler, 316–34. Newcastle upon Tyne: Cambridge Scholars, 2010.

Burns, Michael O'Neill. *Kierkegaard and the Matter of Philosophy: A Fractured Dialectic*. London: Rowman & Littlefield, 2015.

Butler, Clark. 'Hegel, Altizer and Christian Atheism'. *Encounter* 41 (1980): 103–28.

Butler, Clark. 'Hegelian Panentheism as Joachimite Christianity'. In *New Perspectives on Hegel's Philosophy of Religion*, edited by David Kolb, 131–42. Albany: State University of New York Press, 1992.

Butler, Judith. *Gender Trouble: Feminism and the Subversion of Identity*. New York: Routledge, 1999.

Cacciari, Massimo. *The Withholding Power: An Essay on Political Theology*. London: Bloomsbury, 2018.

Caldwell, Peter C. 'Controversies over Carl Schmitt: A Review of Recent Literature'. *The Journal of Modern History* 77, no. 2 (2005): 357–87.

Carter, Jimmy. 'Address to the Nation on Energy and National Goals: "The Malaise Speech"'. *The American Presidency Project*. 15 July 1979. Available at: http://www.presidency.ucsb.edu/ws/?pid=32596 [accessed 15 December 2017].

Cavanaugh, William T. *Theopolitical Imagination*. London: T & T Clark, 2002.

Caygill, Howard. *On Resistance: A Philosophy of Defiance*. London: Bloomsbury, 2013.

Chakrabarty, Dipesh. 'The Climate of History: Four Theses'. *Critical Inquiry* 35, no. 2 (2009): 197–222.

Chakrabarty, Dipesh. 'Climate and Capital: On Conjoined Histories'. *Critical Inquiry* 41, no. 1 (2014): 1–23.

Clark, Malcolm. *Logic and System: A Study of the Translation from 'Vorstellung' to Thought in the Philosophy of Hegel*. The Hague: Martinus Nijhoff, 1971.

Coates, Sam, and Rachel Sylvester. 'Being a Mother Gives Me an Edge on May – Leadsom'. *The Times*, 9 July 2016. Available at: https://www.thetimes.co.uk/article/being-a-mother-gives-me-edge-on-may-leadsom-0t7bbm29x [accessed 14 July 2017].

Cohn, Norman. *The Pursuit of the Millennium*. London: Secker & Warburg, 1957.

Cohn, Norman. *The Pursuit of the Millennium: Revolutionary Millenarians and Mystical Anarchists of the Middle Ages*. London: Pimlico, 1993.

Collins, John J. *The Apocalyptic Imagination: An Introduction to Jewish Apocalyptic Literature*, 2nd edn. Grand Rapids, MI: William B. Eerdmans, 1998.

Connolly, William E. *The Fragility of Things: Self-Organizing Processes, Neoliberal Fantasies, and Democratic Activism*. Durham, NC: Duke University Press, 2013.

Coole, Diana, and Samantha Frost (eds). *New Materialisms: Ontology, Agency and Politics*. Durham, NC: Duke University Press, 2010.

Cover, Robert. 'Nomos and Narrative'. In *Narrative, Violence, and the Law: The Essays of Robert Cover*, edited by Martha Minow, Michael Ryan and Austin Sarat, 95–172. Ann Arbor: University of Michigan Press, 1993.

Cowburn, Ashley. 'Andrea Leadsom Attacked by Tory MPs over "Vile" and "Insulting" Comments on Theresa May's Childlessness'. *The Independent*, 10 July 2016. Available at: http:/www.independent.co.uk/news/uk/politics/andrea-leadsom-theresa-may-vile-insulting-children-conservative-leadership-tory-a7128311.html [accessed 14 July 2017].

Crockett, Clayton. *Radical Political Theology: Religion and Politics after Liberalism*. New York: Columbia University Press, 2011.

Crockett, Clayton, and Catherine Malabou. 'Plasticity and the Future of Philosophy and Theology'. *Political Theology* 11, no. 1 (2010): 15–34.

Danowski, Deborah, and Eduardo Viveiros de Castro. *The Ends of the World*, translated by Rodrigo Nunes. Cambridge: Polity, 2017.

de Boer, Karin. 'Hegel Today: Towards a Tragic Conception of Intercultural Conflicts'. *Cosmos and History: The Journal of Natural and Social Philosophy* 3, nos 2–3 (2007): 117–31.

de Boer, Karin. 'Democracy Out of Joint? The Financial Crisis in Light of Hegel's Philosophy of Right'. *Hegel Bulletin* 33, no. 2 (2012): 36–53.

de Boer, Karin. 'A Greek Tragedy? A Hegelian Perspective on Greece's Sovereign Debt Crisis'. *Cosmos and History: The Journal of Natural and Social Philosophy* 9, no. 1 (2013): 358–75.

de Castro, Eduardo Viveiros. *Cannibal Metaphysics*, translated by Peter Skafish. Minneapolis: University of Minnesota Press, 2014.

Deleuze, Gilles, and Felix Guattari. *A Thousand Plateaus: Capitalism and Schizophrenia*, translated by Brian Massumi. London: Bloomsbury, 2013.

de Lubac, Henri. *La Postérité spirituelle de Joachim de Flore: de Joachim à nos jours*. Paris: Cerf, 2014.

Derrida, Jacques. 'From Restricted to General Economy: A Hegelianism without Reserve'. In *Writing and Difference*, translated by Alan Bass. Chicago, IL: University of Chicago Press, 1978.

Derrida, Jacques. 'The Pit and the Pyramid: Introduction to Hegel's Semiology'. In *Margins of Philosophy*, translated by Alan Bass. Chicago, IL: University of Chicago Press, 1982.

Derrida, Jacques. *Specters of Marx: The State of the Debt, the Work of Mourning and the New International*, translated by Peggy Kamuf. London: Routledge, 2006.

de Vries, Hent, and Lawrence E. Sullivan (eds). *Political Theologies: Public Religions in a Post-Secular World*. New York: Fordham University Press, 2006.

Dickey, Laurence W. *Hegel: Religion, Economics, and the Politics of Spirit, 1770–1807*. Cambridge: Cambridge University Press, 1987.

Di Giovanni, George. 'Faith without Religion, Religion without Faith: Kant and Hegel on Religion'. *Journal of the History of Philosophy* 41, no. 3 (2003): 365–83.

Dooley, Mark. *The Politics of Exodus: Søren Kierkegaard's Ethics of Responsibility*. New York: Fordham University Press, 2001.

Dudley, William. 'The Future of Hegel: Plasticity, Temporality and Dialectic' (Review). *Notre Dame Philosophical Review* (2006). Available at: http://ndpr.nd.edu/news/25128-the-future-of-hegel-plasticity-temporality-and-dialectic/ [accessed 13 February 2013].

Dupré, Louis. 'Religion as Representation'. In *The Legacy of Hegel: Proceedings of the Marquette Hegel Symposium 1970*, edited by J. J. O'Malley, K. W. Algozin, H. P. Kainz and L. C. Rice, 137–43. The Hague: Martinus Nijhoff, 1973.

Edelman, Lee. *No Future: Queer Theory and the Death Drive*. Durham, NC: Duke University Press, 2004.

Eltis, David. 'Europeans and the Rise and Fall of African Slavery in the Americas: An Interpretation'. *The American Historical Review* 98, no. 5 (1993): 1399–423.

Fanon, Frantz. *Black Skin, White Masks*, translated by Charles Lam Markmann. London: Pluto, 1986.

Fanon, Frantz. *The Wretched of the Earth*, translated by Richard Philcox. New York: Grove, 2004.

Federici, Silvia. *Caliban and the Witch: Women, the Body and Primitive Accumulation*. Brooklyn: Autonomedia, 2004.

Federici, Silvia. 'Wages Against Housework'. In *Revolution at Point Zero: Housework, Reproduction and Feminist Struggle*, 15–22. Oakland, CA: PM Press, 2012.

Fraser, Nancy. 'Expropriation and Exploitation in Racialized Capitalism: A Reply to Michael Dawson'. *Critical Historical Studies* 3, no. 1 (2016): 163–78.

Gabriel, Markus. *Transcendental Ontology: Essays in German Idealism*. London: Continuum, 2011.
Gabriel, Markus. *Fields of Sense: A New Realist Ontology*. Edinburgh: Edinburgh University Press, 2015.
Gabriel, Markus. *Why the World Does Not Exist*, translated by Gregory Moss. Cambridge: Polity, 2015.
Gabriel, Markus, and Slavoj Žižek. *Mythology, Madness, and Laughter: Subjectivity in German Idealism*. London: Continuum, 2009.
Gaston, Sean. *The Concept of the World from Kant to Derrida*. London: Rowman & Littlefield, 2013.
Goodchild, Philip. 'Debt, Epistemology and Ecotheology'. *Journal for the Study of Religion, Nature and Culture* 9, no. 2 (2004): 151–77.
Göschel, Karl Friedrich. *Aphorismen über Nichtwissen und absolutes Wissen im Verhältnisse zur christlichen Glaubenserkenntniss: ein Beytrag zum Verständnisse der Philosophie unserer Zeit*. Berlin: E. Franklin, 1829.
Gray, John. *Black Mass: Apocalyptic Religion and the Death of Utopia*. London: Penguin, 2008.
Grimshaw, Mike. 'Introduction: "A Very Rare Thing"'. In *To Carl Schmitt: Letters and Reflections*, by Jacob Taubes, translated by Keith Tribe, ix–xliii. New York: Columbia University Press, 2013.
Haraway, Donna. 'Anthropocene, Capitalocene, Plantationocene, Chthulucene: Making Kin'. *Environmental Humanities* 6 (2015): 159–65.
Harman, Graham. *Quentin Meillassoux: Philosophy in the Making*. Edinburgh: Edinburgh University Press, 2011.
Harris, H. S. *Hegel's Ladder II: The Odyssey of Spirit*. Indianapolis, IN: Hackett, 1997.
Hartman, Saidiya V., and Frank B. Wilderson III. 'The Position of the Unthought'. *Qui Parle: Critical Humanities and Social Sciences* 13, no. 2 (2003): 183–201.
Hartwich, Wolf-Daniel, Aleida Assmann, and Jan Assmann. 'Afterword'. In *The Political Theology of Paul*, by Jacob Taubes, translated by Dana Hollander, 115–42. Stanford, CA: Stanford University Press, 2004.
Haslanger, Sally. *Resisting Reality: Social Construction and Social Critique*. Oxford: Oxford University Press, 2012.
Hegel, G. W. F. *Gesammelte Werke*. Hamburg: Felix Meiner Verlag, 1968.
Hegel, G. W. F. *Science of Logic*, translated by A. V. Miller. London; New York: George Allen & Unwin; Humanities Press, 1969.
Hegel, G. W. F. *Werke*, edited by Eva Moldenhauer and Karl Markus Michel, 20 vols. Frankfurt: Suhrkamp, 1969.

Hegel, G. W. F. *Hegel's Philosophy of Nature: Part Two of the Encyclopaedia of the Philosophical Sciences (1830) with Zusätze*, translated by A. V. Miller. Oxford: Clarendon Press, 1970.
Hegel, G. W. F. *Phenomenology of Spirit*, translated by A. V. Miller. Oxford: Oxford University Press, 1979.
Hegel, G. W. F. *Hegel: The Letters*, translated by Clark Butler and Christiane Seiler. Bloomington: Indiana University Press, 1984.
Hegel, G. W. F. 'Review of C.F. Göschel's *Aphorisms: Parts One and Two*', translated by Clark Butler. *Clio: A Journal of Literature, History, and the Philosophy of History* 17, no. 4 (1988): 369–93.
Hegel, G. W. F. 'Review of C.F. Göschel's *Aphorisms: Part Three*', translated by Clark Butler. *Clio: A Journal of Literature, History, and the Philosophy of History* 18, no. 4 (1989): 379–85.
Hegel, G. W. F. *Hegel's Philosophy of Mind: Part Three of the Encyclopaedia of the Philosophical Sciences (1830) with Zusätze*, translated by W. Wallace and A. V. Miller. Oxford: Clarendon Press, 1990.
Hegel, G. W. F. *The Encyclopaedia Logic: Part I of the Encyclopaedia of Philosophical Sciences with the Zusätze*, translated by T. F. Geraets, W. A. Suchting and H. S. Harris. Indianapolis, IN: Hackett, 1991.
Hegel, G. W. F. *Early Theological Writings*, translated by T. M. Knox and Richard Kroner. Philadelphia: University of Pennsylvania Press, 1996.
Hegel, G. W. F. *Lectures on the Philosophy of Religion*, translated by R. F. Brown, P. C. Hodgson and J. M. Stewart, edited by P. C. Hodgson. 3 vols. Oxford: Oxford University Press, 2007.
Hegel, G. W. F. *Outlines of the Philosophy of Right*, translated by T. M. Knox and Stephen Houlgate. Oxford: Oxford University Press, 2008.
Heidegger, Martin. *Being and Time*, translated by John Macquarrie and Edward Robinson. London: Blackwell, 1962.
Heidegger, Martin. *The Fundamental Concepts of Metaphysics: World, Finitude, Solitude*, translated by William McNeill and Nicholas Walker. Bloomington: Indiana University Press, 1995.
Hell, Julia. '*Katechon*: Carl Schmitt's Imperial Theology and the Ruins of the Future'. *The Germanic Review: Literature, Culture, Theory* 84, no. 4 (2009): 283–326.
Henrich, Dieter. *Hegel im Kontext*. Frankfurt: Suhrkamp, 1971.
Hobsbawm, E. J. *Primitive Rebels: Studies in Archaic Forms of Social Movement in the 19th and 20th Centuries*. New York: W. W. Norton, 1965.
Houlgate, Stephen. 'Necessity and Contingency in Hegel's Science of Logic'. *The Owl of Minerva* 27, no. 1 (1995): 37–49.

Houlgate, Stephen. *An Introduction to Hegel's Philosophy: Freedom, Truth and History*, 2nd edn. Oxford: Blackwell, 2005.

Hudson, Wayne. *The Marxist Philosophy of Ernst Bloch*. London: Macmillan, 1982.

Hutchings, Kimberly, and Tuija Pulkkinen (eds). *Hegel's Philosophy and Feminist Thought: Beyond Antigone*. New York: Palgrave Macmillan, 2010.

Hyppolite, Jean. *Studies on Marx and Hegel*, translated by John O'Neill. New York: Basic Books, 1969.

Jaeschke, Walter. 'Christianity and Secularity in Hegel's Concept of the State'. *Journal of Religion* 61, no. 2 (1981): 127–45.

Jameson, Fredric. *The Seeds of Time*. New York: Columbia University Press, 1994.

Jameson, Fredric. 'The Future City'. *New Left Review* 21 (2003): 65–79.

Johnston, Adrian. 'Conflicted Matter: Jacques Lacan and the Challenge of Secularising Materialism'. *Pli: The Warwick Journal of Philosophy* 19 (2008): 166–88.

Johnston, Adrian. *Žižek's Ontology: A Transcendental Materialist Theory of Subjectivity*. Evanston, IL: Northwestern University Press, 2008.

Johnston, Adrian. 'Points of Forced Freedom: Eleven (More) Theses on Materialism'. *Speculations IV* (2013): 91–8.

Johnston, Adrian. *Adventures in Transcendental Materialism: Dialogues with Contemporary Thinkers*. Edinburgh: Edinburgh University Press, 2014.

Johnston, Adrian, and Catherine Malabou. *Self and Emotional Life: Philosophy, Psychoanalysis, and Neuroscience*. New York: Columbia University Press, 2013.

Jonas, Hans. *Memoirs*, edited by Christian Wiese, translated by Krishna Winston. Waltham, MA: Brandeis University Press, 2008.

Keeling, Kara. 'Looking for M—: Queer Temporality, Black Political Possibility, and Poetry from the Future'. *GLQ: A Journal of Lesbian and Gay Studies* 15, no. 4 (2009): 565–82.

Kierkegaard, Søren. *Fear and Trembling: Repetition*, translated by Howard V. Hong and Edna H. Hong. Princeton, NJ: Princeton University Press, 1983.

Kirwan, Michael. *Political Theology: A New Introduction*. Minneapolis, MN: Fortress, 2008.

Kolb, David. *The Critique of Pure Modernity: Hegel, Heidegger, and After*. Chicago, IL: University of Chicago Press, 1988.

Kotsko, Adam. 'The Problem of Evil and the Problem of Legitimacy: On the Root and Future of Political Theology'. *Crisis & Critique* 2, no. 1 (2015): 285–99.

Kotsko, Adam. *The Prince of This World*. Stanford, CA: Stanford University Press, 2016.

Latour, Bruno. *Facing Gaia: Eight Lectures on the New Climatic Regime*, translated by Catherine Porter. Cambridge: Polity, 2017.

Lauer, Quentin. *Hegel's Concept of God*. Albany: State University of New York Press, 1982.

Lazier, Benjamin. 'On the Origins of "Political Theology": Judaism and Heresy between the World Wars'. *New German Critique* 35, no. 3 (2008): 143–64.

Lewis, Thomas A. 'Beyond the Totalitarian: Ethics and the Philosophy of Religion in Recent Hegel Scholarship'. *Religion Compass* 2, no. 4 (2008): 556–74.

Lewis, Thomas A. 'Religion and Demythologization in Hegel's Phenomenology of Spirit'. In *Hegel's Phenomenology of Spirit: A Critical Guide*, edited by Dean Moyar and Michael Quante, 192–209. Cambridge: Cambridge University Press, 2008.

Lewis, Thomas A. *Religion, Modernity, and Politics in Hegel*. Oxford: Oxford University Press, 2011.

Lewis, Thomas A. *Why Philosophy Matters for the Study of Religion & Vice Versa*. Oxford: Oxford University Press, 2015.

Lilla, Mark. *The Reckless Mind: Intellectuals in Politics*. New York: New York Review of Books, 2016.

Lilla, Mark. *The Stillborn God: Religion, Politics, and the Modern West*. New York: Vintage Books, 2008.

Lloyd, Vincent. 'Introduction'. In *Race and Political Theology*, edited by Vincent Lloyd, 1–21. Stanford, CA: Stanford University Press, 2012.

Lonzi, Carla. 'Let's Spit on Hegel'. In *Feminist Interpretations of G.W.F. Hegel*, edited by Patricia Jagentowicz Mills, 275–97. University Park: The Pennsylvania State University Press, 1996.

Losurdo, Dominico. *Hegel and the Freedom of the Moderns*. Durham, NC: Duke University Press, 2004.

Löwith, Karl. *Meaning in History: The Theological Implications of the Philosophy of History*. Chicago, IL: Phoenix Books, 1949.

Löwith, Karl. *From Hegel to Nietzsche: The Revolution in Nineteenth Century Thought*, translated by David E. Green. Garden City, NY: Anchor Books, 1967.

Lumsden, Simon. 'The Rise of the Non-Metaphysical Hegel'. *Philosophy Compass* 3, no. 1 (2008): 51–65.

Lynch, Thomas. 'Hegel and *Fear and Trembling*'. In *Facing Abraham: Seven Readings of Kierkegaard's Fear and Trembling*, edited by Frederiek Depoortere, 31–50. Leuven: Peeters, 2017.

Lynch, Thomas. 'Transcendental Materialism as a Theoretical Orientation to the Study of Religion'. *Method & Theory in the Study of Religion* 29, no. 2 (2017): 133–54.

Lynch, Thomas. 'Divining History: Prophetism, Messianism and the Development of the Spirit'. *Jewish Culture and History* 19, no. 1 (2018): 111–13.

Magee, Glenn Alexander. *Hegel and the Hermetic Tradition*. Ithaca, NY: Cornell University Press, 2001.

Magnus, Kathleen Dow. *Hegel and the Symbolic Mediation of Spirit*. Albany: State University of New York Press, 2001.

Malabou, Catherine. *The Future of Hegel: Plasticity, Temporality and Dialectic*, translated by Lisabeth During. London: Routledge, 2005.

Malabou, Catherine. *What Should We Do with Our Brain?*, translated by Sebastian Rand. New York: Fordham University Press, 2008.

Malabou, Catherine. *Plasticity at the Dusk of Writing: Dialectic, Destruction, Deconstruction*, translated by Carolyn Shread. New York: Columbia University Press, 2010.

Malabou, Catherine. *The Heidegger Change: On the Fantastic in Philosophy*, translated by Peter Skafish. Albany: State University of New York Press, 2011.

Malabou, Catherine. *The New Wounded: From Neurosis to Brain Damage*, translated by Steven Miller. New York: Fordham University Press, 2012.

Malabou, Catherine. *The Ontology of the Accident: An Essay on Destructive Plasticity*, translated by Carolyn Shread. Cambridge: Polity, 2012.

Malabou, Catherine. *Before Tomorrow: Epigenesis and Rationality*. Cambridge: Polity, 2016.

Malm, Andreas. *Fossil Capital: The Rise of Steam Power and the Roots of Global Warming*. London: Verso, 2016.

Malm, Andreas. 'Who Lit This Fire? Approaching the History of the Fossil Economy'. *Critical Historical Studies* 3, no. 2 (2016): 215–48.

Malm, Andreas, and Alf Hornborg. 'The Geology of Mankind? A Critique of the Anthropocene Narrative'. *The Anthropocene Review* 1, no. 1 (2014): 62–9.

Martin, Jamie. 'Liberalism and History after the Second World War: The Case of Jacob Taubes'. *Modern Intellectual History* 14, no. 1 (2017): 131–52.

Marx, Karl. 'Economic and Philosophic Manuscripts of 1844'. In *Marx & Engels: Collected Works, Vol. 3, Karl Marx and Frederick Engels: 1843-1844*, translated by Jack Cohen et al., 229–346. New York: International Publishers, 2005.

Marx, Karl. 'Manifesto of the Communist Party'. In *Marx & Engels: Collected Works, Vol. 6, Karl Marx and Frederick Engels: 1845–1848*, translated by Jack Cohen et al., 175–87. New York: International Publishers, 2005.

McGinn, Bernard. *Visions of the End: Apocalyptic Traditions in the Middle Ages*. New York: Columbia University Press, 1979.

Mehring, Reinhard. *Carl Schmitt: A Biography*, translated by Daniel Steer. Cambridge: Polity, 2014.

Meiehenrich, Jens, and Oliver Simons (eds). *The Oxford Handbook of Carl Schmitt*. Oxford: Oxford University Press, 2016.

Meillassoux, Quentin. 'The Spectral Dilemma'. *Collapse* IV (2008): 261–76.

Meillassoux, Quentin. *After Finitude: An Essay on the Necessity of Contingency*, translated by Ray Brassier. London: Continuum, 2010.

Mies, Maria. *Patriarchy and Accumulation on a World Scale: Women in the International Division of Labour*. London: Zed Books, 2014.

Miéville, China. 'The Dusty Hat'. In *Three Moments of an Explosion: Stories*, 223–47. London: Macmillan, 2015.

Mills, Charles W. *The Racial Contract*. Ithaca, NY: Cornell University Press, 1997.

Moore, Jason W. 'The End of Cheap Nature, or, How I Learned to Stop Worrying about "The" Environment and Love the Crisis of Capitalism'. In *Structures of the World Political Economy and the Future Global Conflict and Cooperation*, edited by Christian Suter and Christopher Chase-Dunn, 285–314. Berlin: LIT, 2014.

More, Thomas. *Utopia*. London: Verso, 2016.

Mouffe, Chantal (ed.). *The Challenge of Carl Schmitt*. London: Verso, 1999.

Muñoz, José Esteban. *Cruising Utopia: The Then and There of Queer Futurity*. New York: New York University Press, 2009.

Neocleous, Mark. 'Friend or Enemy? Reading Schmitt Politically'. *Radical Philosophy* 79 (1996): 13–23.

Nesbitt, Nick. 'Troping Toussaint, Reading Revolution'. *Research in African Literatures* 35, no. 2 (2004): 18–33.

Nixon, Rob. *Slow Violence and the Environmentalism of the Poor*. Cambridge, MA: Harvard University Press, 2011.

Nuzzo, Angelica. 'The Truth of *Absolutes Wissen* in Hegel's *Phenomenology of Spirit*'. In *Hegel's Phenomenology of Spirit: New Critical Essays*, edited by Alfred Denker and Michael G. Vater, 265–93. Amherst, NY: Humanity Books, 2003.

Nuzzo, Angelica. 'The End of Hegel's Logic: Absolute Idea as Absolute Method'. In *Hegel's Theory of the Subject*, edited by David Carlson, 187–205. Basingstoke: Palgrave Macmillan, 2005.

Nuzzo, Angelica. 'Dialectic as Logic of Transformative Processes'. In *Hegel: New Directions*, edited by Katerina Deligiorgi, 85–104. Chesham: Acumen, 2006.

Nuzzo, Angelica. '"… As If Truth Were a Coin!" Lessing and Hegel's Developmental Theory of Truth'. *Hegel-Studien* 44 (2009): 131–55.

Nuzzo, Angelica. 'Anthropology, *Geist*, and the Soul-Body Relation: The Systematic Beginning of Hegel's *Philosophy of Spirit*'. In *Essays on Hegel's Philosophy of Subjective Spirit*, edited by David S. Stern, 1–17. London: Bloomsbury, 2013.

Nuzzo, Angelica (ed.). *Hegel on Religion and Politics*. Albany: State University of New York Press, 2013.

Omi, Michael, and Howard Winant. *Racial Formation in the United States*, 3rd edn. New York: Routledge, 2015.

O'Regan, Cyril. *The Heterodox Hegel*. Albany: State University of New York Press, 1994.

Pinkard, Terry. *Hegel's Phenomenology: The Sociality of Reason*. Cambridge: Cambridge University Press, 1994.

Pippin, Robert B. *Hegel's Idealism: The Satisfactions of Self-Consciousness*. Cambridge: Cambridge University Press, 1989.

Pippin, Robert B. *Hegel's Practical Philosophy: Rational Agency as Ethical Life*. Cambridge: Cambridge University Press, 2008.

Plumwood, Val. *Feminism and the Mastery of Nature*. London: Routledge, 1993.

Popper, Karl R. *The Open Society and Its Enemies*, 2nd edn. London: Routledge & Kegan Paul, 1952.

Power, Nina. 'Non-Reproductive Futurism: Rancière's Rational Equality against Edelman's Body Apolitic'. *Borderlands* 8, no. 2 (2009): 1–16. Available at: http://www.borderlands.net.au/vol8no2_2009/power_futurism.pdf.

Rabinbach, Anson. 'Between Enlightenment and Apocalypse: Benjamin, Bloch and Modern German Jewish Messianism'. *New German Critique* 34 (1985): 78–124.

Reeves, Marjorie, and Warwick Gould. *Joachim of Fiore and the Myth of the Eternal Evangel in the Nineteenth Century*. Oxford: Clarendon Press, 1987.

Rowland, Christopher. *The Open Heaven: A Study of Apocalyptic in Judaism and Early Christianity*. London: SPCK, 1985.

Russon, John. 'Temporality and the Future of Philosophy in Hegel's Phenomenology'. *International Philosophical Quarterly* 48, no. 1 (2008): 59–68.

Schmitt, Carl. *The Crisis of Parliamentary Democracy*, translated by Ellen Kennedy. Cambridge, MA: MIT Press, 1988.

Schmitt, Carl. *The Nomos of the Earth in the International Law of the Jus Publicum Europaeum*, translated by G. L. Ulmen. New York: Telos, 2003.

Schmitt, Carl. *Political Theology: Four Chapters on the Concept of Sovereignty*, translated by George Schwab. Chicago, IL: University of Chicago Press, 2006.

Schmitt, Carl. *The Concept of the Political*, translated by George Schwab. Chicago: University of Chicago Press, 2007.

Schmitt, Carl. *Theory of the Partisan: Intermediate Commentary on the Concept of the Political*, translated by G. L. Ulmen. New York: Telos, 2007.

Scott, Peter, and William T. Cavanaugh (eds). *The Blackwell Companion to Political Theology*. Oxford: Blackwell, 2004.

Serequeberhan, Tsenay. 'The Idea of Colonialism in Hegel's Philosophy of Right'. *International Philosophical Quarter* 29, no. 3 (1989): 301–18.

Sexton, Jared. 'The Social Life of Social Death: On Afro-Pessimism and Black Optimism'. *Intensions* 5 (2011): 1–47.

Sexton, Jared. 'The *Vel* of Slavery: Tracking the Figure of the Unsovereign'. *Critical Sociology* 42, nos 4–5 (2014): 1–15.

Shanks, Andrew. *Hegel's Political Theology*. Cambridge: Cambridge University Press, 1991.

Sheth, Falguni A. *Toward a Political Philosophy of Race*. Albany: State University of New York Press, 2009.

Smith, Anthony Paul. *A Non-Philosophical Theory of Nature: Ecologies of Thought*. New York: Palgrave Macmillan, 2013.

Smith, Anthony Paul, and Daniel Whistler. 'What Is Continental Philosophy of Religion Now?' In *After the Postsecular and the Postmodern: New Essays in Continental Philosophy of Religion*, edited by Anthony Paul Smith and Daniel Whistler, 1–25. Newcastle upon Tyne: Cambridge Scholars, 2010.

Smith, Ted A. *Weird John Brown: Divine Violence and the Limits of Ethics*. Stanford, CA: Stanford University Press, 2015.

Solnit, Rebecca. *Hope in the Dark: Untold Histories, Wild Possibilities*. Edinburgh: Canongate Books, 2016.

Steffen, Will, et al. 'The Anthropocene: Conceptual and Historical Perspectives'. *Philosophical Transactions of the Royal Society of London A: Mathematical, Physical and Engineering Sciences* 369, no. 1938 (2011): 842–67.

Stewart, Jon (ed.). *Kierkegaard's Influence on Social-Political Thought*. Surrey: Ashgate, 2011.

Svenungsson, Jayne. *Divining History: Prophetism, Messianism and the Development of the Spirit*, translated by Stephen Donovan. Oxford: Berghahn Books, 2016.

Talmon, Yonina. 'Pursuit of the Millennium: The Relation between Religious and Social Change'. *European Journal of Sociology / Archives Européennes De Sociologie* 3, no. 1 (1962): 125–48.

Taubes, Jacob. *The Political Theology of Paul*, translated by Dana Hollander. Stanford, CA: Stanford University Press, 2004.

Taubes, Jacob. *Occidental Eschatology*, translated by David Ratmoko. Stanford, CA: Stanford University Press, 2009.

Taubes, Jacob. 'Culture and Ideology (1969)'. In *From Cult to Culture: Fragments toward a Critique of Historical Reason*, edited by Charlotte Elisheva Fonrobert and Amir Engel, 248–67. Stanford, CA: Stanford University Press, 2010.

Taubes, Jacob. 'The Dogmatic Myth of Gnosticism (1971)'. In *From Cult to Culture: Fragments toward a Critique of Historical Reason*, edited by Charlotte Elisheva Fonrobert and Amir Engel, 61–75. Stanford, CA: Stanford University Press, 2010.

Taubes, Jacob. *From Cult to Culture: Fragments toward a Critique of Historical Reason*, edited by Charlotte Elisheva Fonrobert and Amir Engel. Stanford, CA: Stanford University Press, 2010.

Taubes, Jacob. 'Nachman Krochmal and Modern Historicism (1963)'. In *From Cult to Culture: Fragments toward a Critique of Historical Reason*, edited by Charlotte Elisheva Fonrobert and Amir Engel, 28–44. Stanford, CA: Stanford University Press, 2010.

Taubes, Jacob. 'Notes on Surrealism (1966)'. In *From Cult to Culture: Fragments toward a Critique of Historical Reason*, edited by Charlotte Elisheva Fonrobert and Amir Engel, 98–123. Stanford, CA: Stanford University Press, 2010.

Taubes, Jacob. 'On the Nature of the Theological Method: Some Reflections on the Methodological Principles of Tillich's Theology (1954)'. In *From Cult to Culture: Fragments toward a Critique of Historical Reason*, edited by Charlotte Elisheva Fonrobert and Amir Engel, 195–213. Stanford, CA: Stanford University Press, 2010.

Taubes, Jacob. 'Theodicy and Theology: A Philosophical Analysis of Karl Barth's Dialectical Theology (1954)'. In *From Cult to Culture: Fragments toward a Critique of Historical Reason*, edited by Charlotte Elisheva Fonrobert and Amir Engel, 177–94. Stanford, CA: Stanford University Press, 2010.

Taubes, Jacob. 'Theology and Political Theory (1955)'. In *From Cult to Culture: Fragments toward a Critique of Historical Reason*, edited by Charlotte Elisheva Fonrobert and Amir Engel, 222–32. Stanford, CA: Stanford University Press, 2010.

Taubes, Jacob. *To Carl Schmitt: Letters and Reflections*, translated by Keith Tribe. New York: Columbia University Press, 2013.

Terpstra, Marin, and Theo de Wit. '"No Spiritual Investment in the World as It Is": Jacob Taubes's Negative Political Theology'. In *Flight of the Gods: Philosophical Perspectives on Negative Theology*, edited by Ilse N. Bulhof and Laurens ten Kate, 319–53. New York: Fordham University Press, 2000.

Tonner, Philip. 'Are Animals Poor in the World? A Critique of Heidegger's Anthropocentrism'. In *Anthropocentrism: Humans, Animals, Environments*, edited by Rob Boddice, 203–21. Leiden: Brill, 2011.

Toscano, Alberto. 'Beyond Abstraction: Marx and the Critique of the Critique of Religion', *Historical Materialism* 18 (2010): 3–29.
Toscano, Alberto. *Fanaticism: On the Uses of an Idea*. London: Verso, 2010.
Treml, Martin. 'Reinventing the Canonical: The Radical Thinking of Jacob Taubes'. In *'Escape to Life': German Intellectuals in New York: A Compendium on Exile after 1933*, edited by Eckhart Goebel and Sigrid Weigel, 457–78. Berlin: Walter de Gruyter, 2012.
Tsing, Anna Lowenhaupt. *The Mushroom at the End of the World: On the Possibility of Life in Capitalist Ruins*. Princeton, NJ: Princeton University Press, 2015.
Tuana, Nancy. 'Viscous Porosity: Witnessing Katrina'. In *Material Feminisms*, edited by Stacy Alaimo and Susan Hekman, 188–213. Bloomington: Indiana University Press, 2008.
Vattimo, Gianni. *After Christianity*. New York: Columbia University Press, 2002.
Verene, Donald Phillip. *Hegel's Absolute: An Introduction to Reading the Phenomenology of Spirit*. Albany: State University of New York Press, 2007.
Ward, Graham. 'Hegel's Messianic Reasoning and Its Politics'. In *Politics to Come: Power, Modernity and the Messianic*, edited by Arthur Bradley and Paul Fletcher, 78–97. London: Continuum, 2010.
Warren, Karen J. 'Ecological Feminist Philosophies: An Overview of the Issues'. In *Ecological Feminist Philosophies*, edited by Karen J. Warren, ix–xvi. Bloomington: Indiana University Press, 1996.
Weeks, Kathi. *The Problem with Work: Feminism, Marxism, Antiwork Politics and Postwork Imaginaries*. Durham, NC: Duke University Press, 2011.
Westphal, Merold. 'Hegel, Tillich, and the Secular'. *The Journal of Religion* 52, no. 3 (1972): 223–39.
Wilderson III, Frank B. 'Gramsci's Black Marx: Whither the Slave in Civil Society?' *Social Identities* 9, no. 2 (2003): 225–40.
Wilderson III, Frank B. *Red, White & Black: Cinema and the Structure of U.S. Antagonisms*. Durham, NC: Duke University Press, 2010.
Wilderson III, Frank B. 'Afro-pessimism & the End of Redemption'. *The Occupied Times*, 30 March 2016. Available at: https://theoccupiedtimes.org/?p=14236 [accessed 7 July 2017].
Worsley, Peter. *The Trumpet Shall Sound: A Study of 'Cargo' Cults in Melanesia*, 2nd edn. London: MacGibbon & Kee, 1968.
Yancy, George. 'Looking at Whiteness: Tarrying with the Embedded and Opaque White Racist Self'. In *Look, a White! Philosophical Essays on Whiteness*, 152–75. Philadelphia, PA: Temple University Press, 2012.

Žižek, Slavoj. *The Puppet and the Dwarf: The Perverse Core of Christianity*. Cambridge, MA: MIT Press, 2003.
Žižek, Slavoj. *The Parallax View*. Cambridge, MA: MIT Press, 2006.
Žižek, Slavoj. *Violence*. London: Profile, 2008.
Žižek, Slavoj. *Less Than Nothing: Hegel and the Shadow of Dialectical Materialism*. London: Verso, 2012.
Žižek, Slavoj, Clayton Crockett, and Creston Davis (eds). *Hegel & the Infinite: Religion, Politics, and Dialectic*. New York: Columbia University Press, 2011.

Index

Adorno, Theodor 180 n. 52
Afro-pessimism 24, 131
Agrama, Hussein Ali 144 n. 7
alienation 40, 90, 104, 106
alterity 104, 106, 110–12
Anderson, Ben 113
antagonism 20, 28–32, 34, 35, 90, 128, 129, 136, 141
Anthropocene 18–20, 138
anti-liberalism 11–12, 86–9
apocalypticism 2–3, 10, 12, 28, 30, 31–2, 32–5, 35–6, 63, 67–8, 73, 82, 83–4, 90, 103, 112, 118, 120–1, 124, 131, 135, 137–40, 141
  annihilation 79–81, 95, 101, 102–3, 122, 134, 138
  destruction 28, 36, 78, 101, 103
  externality 12, 32–3, 34, 78, 80, 146 n. 26
  genealogy of 37–48, 154 n. 133
  immanent 73, 78, 80–1, 84, 85, 93, 99, 110, 137
  plastic apocalypticism 102, 130
  as revelation 33–5, 35, 77, 78–80, 81, 95, 101, 103, 112
  transcendence, *see* externality
appropriation 14, 15, 17, 129
Augustine 39, 45

Barber, Daniel Coluccielo 30, 179 n. 40, 180 n. 57
Beattie, Tina 73
Bell, Daniel 42
Benjamin, Walter 10, 30, 66, 154 n. 118, 164 n. 4, 164 n. 5
  and Schmitt 144 n. 6
Berlant, Laura 136
Bielik-Robson, Agata 69, 78–81, 93, 103
Bifo (Franco Berardi) 136
Blackness 23–4, 134, 135, 151 n. 88, 154 n. 124

Bloch, Ernst 45, 47–8, 63, 66, 82–5, 88–90, 95, 101, 102, 104, 111–13, 123–4, 133, 136, 164 n. 4, 164 n. 5, 168 n. 42, 173 n. 23
Boer, Roland 32–3, 94, 101
Brooks, Thom 90
Bull, Malcolm 33–4, 36, 80
Burbidge, John 58, 118–23
Burns, Michael O'Neill 159 n. 31, 174 n. 27
Butler, Clark 61
Butler, Judith 129

capital 17–18, 19–20, 21–2, 25, 27, 28–9, 35, 129, 136
capitalism 19, 23, 24–5, 29, 30–1, 87, 90, 134, 140
Carter, Jimmy 141
Caygill, Howard 179 n. 40
Césaire, Aimé 25
Chakrabarty, Dipesh 19–20
Clark, Malcolm 54–6, 58
climate change 1, 19–20, 26, 29
Cohn, Norman 39–43, 48, 90
Collins, John J. 33
colonialism 20, 23, 25, 90
contingency 131
  in Hegel 57, 100–1, 114–25
  of the world 15–16, 27, 31

de Boer, Karin 88–9
de Castro, Eduardo Vivieros 31
Derrida, Jacques 55, 57, 106–7, 111
disinvestment 79, 81, 83, 91, 133, 134, 136–7, 139

ecofeminism 22, 150 n. 79
Edelman, Lee 131–3
eschatology 32–3, 46–7, 73, 90, 101, 109, 110, 176 n. 57

Fanon, Franz 24, 135, 179 n. 45
Federici, Silvia 20–2
freedom 41, 47, 75, 81, 83, 88, 93, 109–10, 112–13, 116–17, 120, 128, 133
Fraser, Nancy 24
future 68, 80–1, 83, 100–1, 110, 111, 121, 123, 132–4, 141

Gabriel, Markus 121–2, 147 n. 32, 174 n. 27
gender 17–18, 20–2, 27, 28–9, 129, 136
Gimshaw, Mike 71, 86, 87
Göschel, C. F. 60–2, 94
Gould, Warwick 41–2
Gray, John 10–13, 36, 37, 42–3

Haraway, Donna 152 n. 104
Hartman, Saidiya V. 135, 176 n. 4
Haslanger, Sally 27, 31, 74, 92, 146–7 n. 30
Hegel, G. W. F. 26, 37–8, 41, 43, 45, 46, 67, 71, 83, 85, 88, 92, 99
  actuality 51, 59, 74–7, 101, 109, 114–16, 118, 125
  Encyclopaedia 49–50, 52, 76, 77, 107, 163 n. 65
  fanaticism 162 n. 54
  implicit political theology 3, 9, 37–8, 39, 53–4, 62–3, 81
  the infinite 108–9
  Lectures on the Philosophy of Religion 52–3
  nature 74, 75–7, 83, 93
  necessity 100–1, 114–18, 118, 121, 122, 124
  Phenomenology of Spirit 50–1, 55, 59, 71–2, 76–7, 94, 98, 105, 107, 109, 119, 121
  philosophy of history 44, 100, 110
  Philosophy of Right 40, 53, 57–8, 88, 162 n. 54
  plasticity 98–9
  Rabble 40, 90
  religion 49–53, 57–8, 59, 60, 71–2, 94, 104, 119–20
  representation, *see under* representation
  review of Göschel 60–2
  Science of Logic 99, 101, 107–9, 114–16
  spirit 50, 51, 56–7
Heidegger, Martin 27, 67

history 40–8, 63, 68, 74, 78–81, 84, 118, 128–9
Hobsbawm, E. J. 140, 180 n. 60
Hodgson, Peter 51
the Holocaust 24
hope 24, 28, 30, 32, 41, 83, 86, 90, 95, 123, 131–2, 134, 136–7, 138, 139, 141
  in the end 14, 86, 130, 136, 141
Hornborg, Alf 19–20, 26
Houlgate, Stephen 109, 114–18, 121, 122, 122–3
Hyppolite, Jean 167 n. 30

immanence 61, 70, 75, 99, 104–6, 106–7, 109–10, 112–13, 120, 137

Jameson, Frederic 30
Joachim of Fiore 10, 38–43, 45, 47–8, 67, 105
Johnston, Adrian 75–6, 91–4, 112–13, 152 n. 100

katechon 15–16, 28, 86, 129–30, 141
Kierkegaard, Søren 47, 71, 77, 138–40
  and politics 159 n. 31
Kirwan, Michael 9
Kotsko, Adam 144 n. 7, 150 n. 85

Latour, Bruno 31, 152 n. 101, 152 n. 102
law 14, 28, 128–9, 147–8 n. 37
Lewis, Thomas A. 54, 57–8, 161 n. 38
liberalism 11–12, 81, 87–8, 90, 128, 176 n. 4
Lilla, Mark 10–13, 36, 37, 42–3
Lloyd, Vincent 9
Losurdo, Dominic 169–70 n. 56
Löwith, Karl 43–6, 48, 110

Magnus, Kathleen 54–8
Malabou, Catherine 30, 57
  on Derrida 106–7
  The Future of Hegel 99–101, 102, 107, 111
  on Heidegger 153 n. 113
  materialism 91–2, 125
  The Ontology of the Accident 99, 103, 125, 133–4, 137
  plasticity, *see under* plasticity

Plasticity at the Dusk of Writing 100, 102, 103, 106, 110
Malm, Andreas 19–20, 26, 31
Marx, Karl 10, 39, 42, 43, 45–7, 48, 71, 73–5, 82, 85, 87, 92, 100, 110, 167 n. 30
Marxism 24, 41, 45, 123
materialism 15, 17, 25–6, 27, 31–2, 35–6, 70, 81, 84, 90, 103, 113, 125
  transcendental 74–6, 91–3, 112–13, 152 n. 100
Meillassoux, Quentin 174 n. 27
messianism 12–13, 32–3, 38–9, 66–7, 70, 80–1, 83, 100, 106–7, 110, 112, 125, 168 n. 45, 176 n. 57
Miéville, China 130
millennialism 38–9, 140, 157 n. 3
Mills, Charles W. 148 n. 53
Mohler, Armin 67, 70
Moore, Jason 19–20, 21
  Capitalocene 19, 26, 31
  cheap nature 19
Muñoz, José Esteban 133
Müntzer, Thomas 39, 47, 48, 83

National Socialism 15, 39, 42, 43, 67, 143–4 n. 6, 169 n. 48
nature 17–23, 26, 27, 28–9, 30–1, 74–7, 83, 92–3, 105, 113, 115–16, 136, 140
negativity 56–7, 65, 75–7, 79–80, 102, 108, 111, 116, 127, 130–5, 137, 138
newness, *see* novelty
nihilism 67, 84, 90, 95, 133
Nixon, Rob 28
nomos (*see* Schmitt)
novelty 95, 106, 110, 120, 125, 137
Nuzzo, Angelica 26, 159–60 n. 33

optimism 11, 84, 117, 123, 131, 136

passivity 79, 83, 85, 104, 110, 131
patriarchy 22, 129, 140
Patterson, Orlando 23
Paul, Saint 39, 46, 83, 85, 91, 131
pessimism 131, 135, 136–7, 139–40, 141
Pinkard, Terry 50–1, 160 n. 33
Pippin, Rotbert 88, 160 n. 33
plasticity
  destructive 137
  explosive 29, 99, 101, 102, 124–5, 135

Malabou 29, 99–103, 106, 107, 110–11, 112, 123, 137
political theology 38–9, 62, 82–3, 86, 102
  apocalyptic 12, 31, 35–6, 78, 80, 83, 85, 99, 110–11, 112, 115–16, 141
  definition of 7–13, 36
  as methodology 10
  the political 12–13, 86
  possibility 30–2, 83, 121, 122, 128, 133–5, 136–7
  Hegel 100, 101, 114–16
primitive accumulation 20, 21

quietism, *see* passivity

Rabinbach, Anson 66, 80–1, 102, 164 n. 4
race 17–18, 23–5, 26, 27, 28–9, 129, 136
  and the devil 23
Reeves, Marjoree 41–2
representation (*Vorstellung*) 38, 51–3, 53–8, 72, 73, 85, 104, 119
  return to 59–63, 67, 94–5
reproduction 21, 132–3, 178 n. 22
Rowland, Christopher 34

Schmitt, Carl 7–9, 10, 12–13, 25, 39, 67, 70, 74, 91
  critique of liberalism 11–12, 17, 128
  enemy 16
  nomos 14–17, 147 n. 65
secular 11, 66, 72, 81
  asecularity 11, 144 n. 7
  desecularization 11, 63, 67, 84, 146 n. 23
  post-secularism 11, 146 n. 22
  secularization 39, 45, 48, 70, 106
Shanks, Andrew 9–10, 11
slavery 22, 23–5, 150 n. 84, 177 n. 9
Smith, Anthony Paul 146 n. 22, 153 n. 109, 166 n. 16
Solnit, Rebecca 131, 136, 177 n. 14
sovereignty 15
Svenungsson, Jayne 12–13, 32, 36, 37, 42, 43, 47, 79

Taubes, Jacobs 9, 32, 45, 92–5, 104–6, 125, 131, 139, 164 n. 4
  apocalypticism 67, 71, 73, 78–81, 82, 86, 92–5, 102, 123
  and Bloch 47–8, 63, 82–5, 88–90, 123

disinvestment, *see under* disinvestment
Hegel 46–7, 63, 67–8, 74–8, 105
modernity 69–70, 77–8, 87, 95
Occidental Eschatology 32, 46–7, 67, 73, 77, 78–9, 86, 89, 92, 94, 102
political theology 67–8, 70, 71, 74, 86, 94
The Political Theology of Paul 66, 79, 82–3, 86, 131
and Schmitt 67, 70, 74, 86–8, 91, 94, 143 n. 6, 163 n. 1
Tillich, Paul 105–6
Toscano, Alberto 140
transcendence 78, 80, 92, 95, 103–4, 105, 106–7, 109–10, 112–13, 120, 124
trauma 32, 35, 36, 79, 125, 137, 138
Tsing, Anna 26, 155 n. 129
Tuana, Nancy 25–7, 31, 74, 92, 146–7 n. 30

utopia 80, 82, 84, 85, 89, 133, 140
concrete utopia 84, 89, 95, 123–4
Moore, Thomas 16, 130

Vattimo, Gianni 69, 165 n. 13
violence 11–12, 28–9, 132, 135, 137–8, 179 n. 40
gratuitous 24, 134

invisibility of 28, 29, 35, 80, 130, 154 n. 121
and liberalism 128–9, 169 n. 55
objective 28, 29
of the world 28, 29, 80, 130, 138
slow 28, 29, 138

Whistler, Daniel 166 n. 16
Wilderson III, Frank B. 23–5, 29, 90, 131, 134–6, 151 n. 88, 154 n. 124
witches 22, 23
world 129–30, 134–6, 139
constitution of 14, 17–18, 23, 25, 27–9, 30, 31–2, 35–6, 74–5, 80, 81, 136
and earth 14, 15
end of 30, 78–81, 83–4, 103, 116, 118, 125
inescapability of 20, 28, 30, 80, 139
redemption of 12, 32, 79, 80, 137, 139, 168 n. 41
rejection of 128

Yancy, George 179 n. 46

Žižek, Slavoj 28, 69, 91, 121–2, 165–6 n. 13, 174 n. 27

Lightning Source UK Ltd.
Milton Keynes UK
UKHW020622250320
360829UK00003B/231